Fifth edition

Corporate Fundraising and Partnerships

Edited by
Valerie Morton

In association with:

dsc
direct**o**ry of social change

**SUSTAINABLE
PHILANTHROPY
WITH
PLYMOUTH
UNIVERSITY**

Institute of
Fundraising

Published by the Directory of Social Change (Registered Charity no. 800517 in England and Wales)

Head office: Resource for London, 352 Holloway Rd, London N7 6PA

Northern office: Suite 103, 1 Old Hall Street, Liverpool L3 9HG

Tel: 020 7697 4200

Visit www.dsc.org.uk to find out more about our books, subscription funding websites and training events. You can also sign up for e-newsletters so that you're always the first to hear about what's new.

The publisher welcomes suggestions and comments that will help to inform and improve future versions of this and all of our titles. Please give us your feedback by emailing publications@dsc.org.uk.

It should be understood that this publication is intended for guidance only and is not a substitute for professional advice. No responsibility for loss occasioned as a result of any person acting or refraining from acting can be accepted by the authors or publisher.

First edition published 1999 by the Charities Aid Foundation
Second edition published 2002 by the Directory of Social Change
Reprinted 2006 and 2007
Third edition 2007
Reprinted 2010
Fourth edition 2012
Reprinted 2015 and 2016
Published digitally 2016
Fifth edition in both print and digital formats published 2017

ISBN 978 1 78482 028 2 (print edition)
ISBN 978 1 78482 029 9 (digital edition)

British Library Cataloguing in Publication Data
A catalogue record for this book is available from the British Library

Cover and text design by Kate Griffith
Typeset by Marlinzo Services, Frome
Print edition printed and bound in Great Britain by CPI Group, Croydon

Contents

About the Fundraising Series

Despite paid fundraisers having existed in some form since the middle ages, fundraising as we know it today is still an emerging profession. The Institute of Fundraising has only been in existence for just over 30 years, and it is only relatively recently that academics have begun to pay attention to the science behind giving to others.

A vitally important element of any profession is its body of knowledge – it's what enables members of a profession to grow, learn and reflect. Immersing oneself in that knowledge is, arguably, what makes one a professional fundraiser.

This series is an important part of bringing together fundraising's body of knowledge. It combines the best of the practical knowledge of experienced fundraisers with, increasingly, the expanding body of academic knowledge around giving and asking.

The series seeks to address the full range of fundraising activities and techniques. Each volume addresses a key element in the spectrum of fundraising techniques. As fundraising techniques evolve and develop, new titles in the series are added and old ones revised. Each title seeks to explore a fundraising activity within its historical, ethical and theoretical context, and relate it to current fundraising practice as well as guide future strategy. The series offers something for anyone who is aspiring to be a professional, whatever the size or type of their organisation, or stage of their career.

The University of Plymouth Hartsook Centre for Sustainable Philanthropy is proud to partner with the Directory of Social Change in the series' production. Furthermore, the series would not be possible without the input of many dedicated professionals involved in its writing and production: we thank everyone who has contributed to its development.

Adrian Sargeant PhD, Professor of Fundraising and Director
Claire Routley PhD, Research Fellow
Hartsook Centre for Sustainable Philanthropy, University of Plymouth

About the Directory of Social Change

The Directory of Social Change (DSC) has a vision of an independent voluntary sector at the heart of social change. We believe that the activities of independent charities, voluntary organisations and community groups are fundamental to achieve social change. We exist to support these organisations in achieving their goals.

We do this by:

• providing practical tools that organisations and activists need, including online and printed publications, training courses and conferences on a huge range of topics;

• acting as a 'concerned citizen' in public policy debates, often on behalf of smaller charities, voluntary organisations and community groups;

• leading campaigns and stimulating debate on key policy issues that affect those groups;

• carrying out research and providing information to influence policy-makers, as well as offering bespoke research for the voluntary sector.

DSC is the leading provider of information and training for the voluntary sector and publishes an extensive range of guides and handbooks covering subjects such as fundraising, management, communication, finance and law. Our subscription-based websites contain a wealth of information on funding from grant-making charities, companies and government sources. We run more than 300 training courses each year, including bespoke in-house training provided at the client's location. DSC conferences and fairs, which take place throughout the year, also provide training on a wide range of topics and offer a welcome opportunity for networking.

For details of all our activities, and to order publications and book courses, go to www.dsc.org.uk, call 020 7697 4200 or email cs@dsc.org.uk.

About the authors

Rachel Billsberry-Grass

Rachel is a freelance consultant who provides fundraising and marketing support for a wide range of organisations through her consultancy, Causeworks. Working in the voluntary sector since 1991, she initially specialised in corporate fundraising and has been responsible for winning and leading successful partnerships across the corporate fundraising portfolio with companies including Deutsche Bank, Tesco, Transco and Regus.

She began freelancing in 2001, delivering strategic planning, training and mentoring as well as operational fundraising. She also offers interim senior management and has led fundraising departments at charities including Age Concern England, Breast Cancer Care, Muscular Dystrophy UK and St Wilfrid's Hospice.

Serena Castiglione

Serena has 20 years of experience in sales management, marketing and professional relations in the commercial and charity sectors. She started her career in the pharmaceutical industry, where she led business development teams at global companies such as Abbott Laboratories (now Abbvie) and Novartis Pharmaceuticals. In 2013 she moved to the charity sector, where she specialised in corporate partnerships. She used her broad commercial experience to win some of the largest corporate partnerships at CLIC Sargent and Age UK and subsequently led the corporate engagement team at Breast Cancer Now. She is Head of New Markets at the International HIV/AIDS Alliance, leading on strategy for corporate, philanthropic and individual-giving fundraising.

Natalie Chevin

Natalie is the Head of Corporate and Major Gifts at Haven House Children's Hospice. Having joined the charity in 2014, Natalie works with her team to deliver the organisation's flagship events and her team delivers in excess of £1.2 million gross per year for the charity. This makes up a large proportion of the £3.9 million Haven House needs to generate each year to support the children and families it works with.

Natalie has worked on successful corporate partnerships with companies such as the Bank of England, Euromoney, the Financial Ombudsman

Service and Mizuho. Prior to working with Haven House, Natalie spent seven years working at the Langdon Foundation.

Beth Courtier

Beth has spent over 15 years of her career with BT managing the company's charity programme and its volunteering and education activities. She has led corporate partnerships with many charities, including BBC Children in Need, British Red Cross, Cancer Research UK, Comic Relief, Disasters Emergency Committee, the NSPCC and Unicef and has developed programmes such as community webkits and BT's online giving platform.

Beth has picked up global awards across specialisms, demonstrating the quantifiable benefits of corporate partnerships which transcend geography and disciplines. She is also a former trustee of Childreach International, an NSPCC Honorary Member of Council and a member of the Institute of Fundraising.

James Deacon

James is Head of Corporate Responsibility for Ricoh UK Ltd, having worked for Ricoh since 2001 and in his current role since 2007. He specialises in selecting and implementing sustainability and community investment programmes that provide opportunities for employee involvement and engagement in conjunction with delivering strong social outcomes.

James is a keen fundraiser and a volunteer. Notable achievements include serving as a school governor since 2009, piloting a scheme to help primary school pupils with their reading, and cycling from London to Barcelona with 30 other Ricoh cyclists in 2015, collectively raising £150,000 for the Institute of Liver Studies at King's College Hospital NHS Foundation Trust.

Paul Glazier

Paul is Head of Corporate New Business at Macmillan Cancer Support and has over 10 years' experience working in corporate fundraising. He previously worked at Cancer Research UK and Breakthrough Breast Cancer (now called Breast Cancer Now).

During this time, Paul has developed sector-leading partnerships with some of the largest companies in the UK through innovation, commercial understanding and a passion for improving the lives of people affected by cancer.

Lynda Harwood

Lynda is National Corporate Partnerships Account Manager at Guide Dogs and has over 15 years' experience in the charity sector specialising in inclusion, sight loss and education. Lynda has worked with and dedicated her time to several charities, including Chest Heart & Stroke Scotland, Deafblind Scotland, Make a Wish and RNIB and has been a fundraiser since 2012. Lynda specialises in strategic national corporate partnerships as well as managing the development and integration of a number of key fundraising products and campaigns.

In 2014, Lynda was awarded the Erasmus EuroMedia Award Seal of Approval for her short film to promote awareness and fundraising for Guide Dogs' Children's Services. Lynda is an advocate for access to education for all and has spoken at the European Parliament, the Houses of Parliament and the Scottish Parliament regarding education and support for children and young people with sight loss.

Rei Kanemura

Rei is a Researcher at nfpSynergy, a specialist non-profit research agency. At nfpSynergy she works on syndicated tracking research in the general public for charities across a range of sectors from animal welfare to health and disability. She also leads nfpSynergy's research with children, young people and parents.

Chris Knight

Chris has over 20 years' experience advising on legal and governance issues, the vast majority of that in the charity sector. He is Head of Charities and Education at Hewitsons LLP, which advises on every aspect of law, regulation and governance for the charity sector.

Chris's particular interests lie in converting complex legal and regulatory issues into practical solutions for charities on the ground. He writes and speaks widely on charity issues and has served as a trustee, volunteer or legal sounding board for many charities.

Mark Line

Mark is a freelance corporate sustainability consultant with over 30 years' experience. He has supported major multinational corporations across most industry sectors, working with corporations including ArcelorMittal, Bacardi Limited, Guardian News and Media, and Toyota Motor North America. For nearly a decade, he signed off Unilever's global environmental disclosures.

Mark was a co-founder of the sustainability agency Two Tomorrows and played a leading role in developing the international team that joined DNV GL in 2012.

Valerie Morton

Valerie's career in the voluntary sector has spanned four decades and has included holding senior positions in charities such as Help the Aged, RNIB and YMCA. She now combines providing consultancy support to charities with training, advising and commentating on best practice.

Valerie's passion for the opportunities created by corporate–charity partnerships began at the NSPCC, where she secured and managed the first-ever UK £1 million adoption with Asda and launched the then newly created payroll giving scheme. Valerie has held numerous voluntary positions including membership of the Institute of Fundraising's Standards Committee and its Policy Advisory Board and is honoured to have been awarded the position of Fellow of the Institute. She is a trustee of the RNIB Retirement Benefit Scheme and of a small grant-making trust in Newcastle.

Cian Murphy

Cian is Head of Data Analysis at nfpSynergy, a specialist non-profit research agency. He has previously worked on the Fundraising Insights Team at the British Red Cross, and has led on quantitative research projects with many of the UK's largest fundraising charities while at nfpSynergy.

Cian now works across the agency's syndicated and bespoke tracking research to develop its quantitative research offering, focusing in particular on segmentations, driver analysis and other advanced data analysis. He is also responsible for statistics training and has helped many nfpSynergy staff members to achieve qualifications from the Royal Statistical Society.

Andrew Peel

Andrew is an award-winning fundraiser and consultant with 25 years' experience in the UK charity sector. Having led fundraising teams at Help the Aged, the British Red Cross and Sightsavers, he set up Peel Consulting in 2007 and has now worked with more than 70 charities including the British Heart Foundation, Diabetes UK, Guide Dogs, Saltdean Lido, TB Alert and a wide range of hospitals and hospices.

Andrew specialises in corporate and trust fundraising, and in developing impactful proposals, applications, pitches and strategies for clients. He is also a trustee of two charities in Brighton. A full member of the Institute of Fundraising, Andrew received its Professional Fundraiser of the Year Award in 1997.

Sarah Pye

Sarah has worked at Haven House as a full-time Corporate Partnerships Manager since March 2016 and manages partnerships with the likes of the Bank of England, Insight Investment and Mizuho.

Sarah previously worked for children's and youth charities: Barnardo's in new business development, and The Prince's Trust in Yorkshire and at the Trust's London headquarters as project manager of the corporate employee-engagement challenge, Million Makers.

Preface

Welcome to this the fifth edition of what I am honoured to be able to describe as the UK's bestselling book on corporate fundraising. Followers of previous editions will have noticed the new title: *Corporate Fundraising and Partnerships*. Any long-established corporate fundraiser will say that, although raising money through working with companies has always been their key objective, the very nature of companies, their resources and their influences has meant that many of the benefits charities have gained have been other than directly financial. What we have seen in the course of the past 20 or so years is that these benefits are being formalised and considered strategically rather than being considered a 'nice-to-have' added extra. For this reason, we felt that simply repeating the title *Corporate Fundraising* was doing a disservice to the many people who are creating inspiring and multi-faceted relationships between charities and the corporate sector. The addition of the term 'Partnerships' not only demonstrates this still-growing development but also describes more accurately the relationship between the two sectors. No longer is it simply transactional; it is now a bringing together of two parties working together, creating ideas for mutual benefit. Several of the chapters expand upon this theme and set out some of the wide-ranging benefits that can be achieved in this way.

Reflecting on the development of the corporate–charity environment over the 20 or so years since the first edition of this book, it is interesting to note that – even in that early edition – the contributors heavily emphasised best practice, standards and responsibilities. Nowadays these principles are all part of our common vocabulary and the issue of standards in fundraising is now particularly front of mind with the birth of the Fundraising Regulator. Charities now are looking at how to embed fundraising standards in their day-to-day working, and some guidance on this is offered in 'A note on best practice' on page xvi.

The term 'corporate social responsibility' first made an entrance in the second edition (in 2002), but readers of this latest edition will note that the concept is now more commonly known as 'corporate responsibility' (and in some arenas 'corporate responsibility and sustainability'). 'Corporate responsibility' is the standard term used in this book. Despite changes in terminology, the elements of this fundamental principle remain the same but are now embedded in society through the UN Sustainable Development Goals, as explained in chapter 1. Other terminology choices in the book include:

• 'charities' and 'the charity sector', except when referring to the wider sector, where we alternatively refer to the not-for-profit sector, or when a different context is being reported on, such as referring to studies that use the term 'NGOs';

• 'companies' or 'corporates' – these terms are intended to include all forms of business entity, including public limited companies, companies limited by guarantee, limited liability partnerships, sole traders and, in some cases, employers.

Corporate fundraising managers in the process of developing their latest strategy will inevitably, during their research into the market place, be considering whether the Charity of the Year concept is reaching the end of its product life cycle. This has been a subject of discussion for some time now; however, it is clear that, although the name may be changing (such agreements often involve more than one charity and may not last for exactly one year), the concept of a company adopting one or more charities with which to work alongside for a period of time is alive and well. The principles of managing those relationships effectively have stood the test of time.

The innovative and effective case studies showcased in this book are a testament to the excellent work of those who operate in the corporate partnership arena. I hope these, and the wise words of the chapter authors, provide inspiration to a new generation working in this incredibly rewarding environment.

Valerie Morton

Acknowledgements

I would like to thank all the charities, companies and individuals who have given of their time and experience and provided case studies to enrich the value of this book to readers.

Andrew Peel, in addition to being a contributing author, has been a trusted advisor to me throughout the gestation of this book. His analysis, challenges and perceptive attention to detail have been invaluable and his good-humoured approach much appreciated.

This fifth edition of *Corporate Fundraising and Partnerships* (formerly *Corporate Fundraising*) has been completely revised and updated but I have retained some material from previous editions where I feel it still reflects current thinking and best practice. I would therefore like to recognise and thank in particular Alice Collins, Ian MacQuillin, Anne Shinkwin and the late Claire Wilson.

The first chapter of the first edition of this book (published in 1999) was written by Tony Elischer, who sadly passed away in 2016. Tony was a great advocate of corporate–charity partnerships and he and I worked together to develop the first training courses on the subject for the Institute of Fundraising. His passion and enthusiasm for fundraising have impacted so many of us over the years and I hope that this book is a fitting reflection of his inspiration.

The publisher and I would like to thank the following people and organisations for their contributions to the case studies:

• Chapter 2: Richard Turner, former Chief Fundraiser and Head of Operations at SolarAid (2011–2016).

• Chapter 4: Ollie Langham, Corporate Partnership Manager at St Elizabeth Hospice; Willis Towers Watson.

• Chapters 5 and 6: Lila Dowie, Senior Corporate Partnerships Manager, and Claire Ellis-Waghorn, Head of Fundraising at Demelza; Ben Swart, Head of New Business at the NSPCC.

• Chapter 7: Andrea Berriman, Corporate Partnerships Specialist; Marks & Spencer; WWF-UK.

• Chapter 8: Hannorah Lee, Head of Corporate and Community Partnerships at Age UK; Kate Lovesey, Senior Corporate Volunteering Manager at Macmillan Cancer Support; Nick Vassallo, New Partnerships Manager at Alzheimer's Society.

- Chapter 9: BMW Group UK.

- Chapter 11: Sandra Arellano, Communication Manager at BT; Jane Lamb, Senior Corporate Partnerships Manager, Comic Relief.

- Chapter 12: Serena Castiglione, Head of New Markets at the International HIV/AIDS Alliance and former Head of Corporate Engagement at Breast Cancer Now (2016–2017).

- Chapter 14: Jenni Anderson, Director of Fundraising at the Duke of Edinburgh's Award and former Director of Income Generation and Marketing at Haven House Children's Hospice (2013–2017).

- Chapter 15: Hannah Brewer, Corporate Partnerships Manager, The Prince's Trust; Fiona Wolstenholme, Corporate Partnership Manager, BBC Children in Need.

We would also like to thank the following people and organisations for their kind permission to reproduce their material:

- Harvard Business Publishing for adapting and reprinting 'Strategies for Diversification' by H. Igor Ansoff;

- Gavin Kennedy, Chairman of Negotiate Ltd and author of *Kennedy on Negotiation* and *Perfect Negotiation*, for the use of his LIMit model;

- the Gap Partnership for the use of its negotiation-moves planning table and its system for recording negotiation offers and counter-offers.

A note on best practice

Introduction

Charities are accountable, in some form or another, to a wide range of stakeholders, including donors and beneficiaries. From the perspective of an individual charity, following best practice ensures that donors' money gives the maximum possible outcome for beneficiaries and the cause. From a sector-wide perspective, following best practice is fundamental to maintaining reputation across the whole not-for-profit environment.

The issue of best practice can be broken down into two parts. The first is to ensure that fundraising is carried out using methodologies and processes which are known to offer the best return on investment. In the field of corporate fundraising this would include, as explained in chapters 2 and 4, taking a relationship-building approach or, as identified in chapter 10, negotiating a minimum guarantee when committing charity resources to a corporate partnership.

The second part relates to the standards all fundraisers must follow, which are set by the Fundraising Regulator to ensure that fundraising is respectful, open, honest and accountable to the public. These standards are set out in the Code of Fundraising Practice and include legal requirements. As public scrutiny of fundraising is ever present, corporate fundraising activities are likely to be in the spotlight as much as individual giving.

With the Code of Practice being front of mind in many charities from a governance perspective, it is important that charity leaders recognise that the Code is a set of standards, not a training manual on how to fundraise effectively. Therefore, following the standards set out in the Code does not guarantee the quality of the fundraising itself. This principle is mirrored in other industries – for example, in advertising, where the Committee of Advertising Practice sets the rules for advertising, which are regulated by the Advertising Standards Authority, but practitioners still need to receive training and qualifications in the field of marketing. A car MOT offers evidence that a vehicle is roadworthy but says nothing about the skill of the driver.

When budgets are tight, it is often the training and development budget that is cut. Charity leaders should appreciate, however, that investment in developing the knowledge and skills of their fundraisers is the foundation of best practice.

Embedding the Code of Fundraising Practice

Although some sections of the Code stand out as being relevant to corporate fundraisers (such as 'Corporate partners' and 'Fundraising through payroll giving'), any fundraiser involved in working with companies will, from time to time, need to have knowledge of other aspects of the Code (for example 'Payment of fundraisers', 'Raffles and lotteries' and 'Handling donations'). It is important, therefore, that charities have systems and processes in place to ensure corporate fundraisers understand the principles behind the Code, know the detail of its specific sections and have a good appreciation of its full content so that they are attuned to occasions where less obvious aspects become relevant.

The Code of Fundraising Practice is regularly updated to reflect changes in laws and issues which have been profiled through the Fundraising Regulator's complaints procedure, so embedding any changes in day-to-day fundraising is vital. Although it is tempting to concentrate on ensuring staff have knowledge of the details within the Code, there is a danger that this will simply lead to staff having a peak of knowledge at the start of the process with this knowledge naturally declining over time.

An effective four-stage approach involves:

• **Stage 1:** Gain top-level commitment (from trustees and directors) to follow best practice in all fundraising activities and agree a headline strategy which includes policy decisions arising from the Code; the investment that will be made (in terms of both time and money) to address any identified issues; and charity-wide implications and impacts, such as with regard to financial systems and HR. This stage should also involve ensuring that all trustees have an appropriate understanding of the principles of fundraising, that they appreciate their responsibilities with respect to fundraising and, if necessary, that they have access to a relevant development programme.

• **Stage 2:** Develop buy-in from fundraising staff to the concept and structure of the Code and understanding of the principle and practice of regulation. This can be achieved through specific stand-alone training sessions or in existing meetings, such as team meetings or away days. Most fundraisers are committed to working to high standards and may see the Code as something which reflects how they operate rather than being something they have to have read, understand and follow. This stage is crucial to avoid reading of the Code being seen as a burden. Staff need to be enthused by the benefits of following best practice and to recognise that this supports the status of fundraising as a profession.

• **Stage 3:** Ensure all fundraisers read the Code. Reading it in one session or over a short time frame will clearly be a challenge and is unlikely to result in much of the information being retained. However, it can be effective to incentivise the reading of the Code over a specific time frame by, for example, offering allocated reading times, group reading and time off to read at home, alongside a promotional campaign.

• **Stage 4:** Policies, procedures and infrastructure need to be developed and implemented to ensure that the momentum is maintained, that new starters are integrated into the systems and that control mechanisms are in place. This may include considering the roles of the induction process, appraisal systems and links with internal audit functions.

Best practice in corporate fundraising and partnerships

The chapters and case studies in this book reflect the key elements of best practice as set out in the Code at the time of publication. Although fundraisers working in this area need to have detailed knowledge of the elements of the Code that specifically relate to corporate fundraising and partnerships, it is important to have knowledge of other aspects which impact on fundraising generally and which could be relevant when working with companies. Examples include working with third parties, use of lotteries, collection of cash donation and working with volunteers.

Valerie Morton

Foreword

My charity is just not sexy – no brands will want to be associated with us.

My charity will never win a staff vote.

My colleagues think life would be so much easier without corporate partners to consider.

Many corporate fundraisers in their darkest days will have had one or all of those feelings – I know I have. One of the benefits of reading the new edition of *Corporate Fundraising and Partnerships* is that it makes you realise you are not alone. Although our organisations and the causes we fight for may be unique, the challenges we face as fundraisers are not. In this book, Valerie Morton has assembled a brilliant group of contributors to share their wisdom with you, and the result is a hugely useful guide to how others have met these challenges head on and overcome them.

I also know, from my own experience (most recently at Anthony Nolan and at Macmillan) and from reading this new edition, that building successful partnerships doesn't have to involve a revolutionary new approach. Instead, it is based on having a great understanding of the discipline and the processes required for success. Setting firm foundations for your work with a clear vision, the right team structure and a strong focus on the right opportunities will put you in a good place to make you ready to enter into a partnership. It doesn't matter whether your organisation is big or small, or whether you have a sexy brand or are relatively unknown – get the basics sorted and you are in the game along with everyone else.

This book is a great reminder of what the current best practice is and it offers priceless practical advice on the best methods and approaches to take at any given stage of a corporate partnership, from creating your corporate fundraising strategy and targeting new partners right through to how to negotiate effectively and manage the corporate account.

Corporate Fundraising and Partnerships offers wisdom and advice on the full spectrum of the subject, from a helpful history to the latest trends and techniques. More crucially, it will set you right for your future fundraising path by making you better prepared and more confident, with a greater prospect of achieving fantastic charity–corporate partnerships. Happy reading.

Alix Wooding, Director of Development, Southbank Centre

CHAPTER ONE

Corporate–charity partnerships: history, evolution and future

Valerie Morton and Mark Line

Introduction

In 1887, Lever Brothers ran what is believed to be one of the earliest recorded cause-related marketing campaigns in the UK. Archives from the Royal National Lifeboat Institution show an engraving of *Sunlight No. 1* lifeboat (see figure 1.1), which was donated by Lever Brothers in 1887. Llandudno Lifeboat Station reported that Lever Brothers 'ran a special competition to fund the new lifeboats'.[1]

Over a century later, in 2017, the most admired corporate–cause partnership, as voted for by companies and NGOs in the *C&E Corporate–NGO Partnerships Barometer* 2016 report,[2] involved GlaxoSmithKline (GSK) and Save the Children. It was described by GSK as a 'blueprint for a new way of working, transforming the traditional fundraising NGO/corporate model'.[3] The Lever Brothers example ultimately helped to save lives at sea whereas the GSK partnership is focused on preventing children from dying unnecessarily. This demonstrates that despite the many changes in society over that time period, and the advent of the term 'corporate social responsibility', a thread of common objectives remains.

This chapter provides the history and context of corporate involvement with the charity sector and considers what the future may hold.

The corporate perspective: the rise of corporate social responsibility

The beating corporate heart has clearly always been there. From Cadbury and the chocolate company's creation of cocoa as the healthy alternative to alcohol to the Joseph Rowntree Foundation and social housing, many businesses established themselves with sound principles which aimed to help employees, local people and their communities.

The move towards a more structured approach to responsible business practice was initially driven by environmental concerns. Throughout the 1980s, a series of high-profile accidents focused public attention on environmental protection and a wider responsibility towards communities impacted by hazardous operations globally. Events such as the explosions at the Bhopal chemical plant in 1984, the accident at the Chernobyl nuclear power plant in 1986 and the Exxon Valdez oil spill in 1989 polarised public opinion. They created a wave of green consumerism and a sharpened focus upon the responsibilities of multinational corporations. The interdependence of environmental and social issues was not yet understood at this time, and so companies' responses to pollution and social issues were disconnected and fragmented.

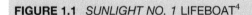

FIGURE 1.1 *SUNLIGHT NO. 1* LIFEBOAT[4]

By 2000, the early movers in the corporate world were concentrating on environmental issues that were under their direct control. The social conscience that had been common in companies in the Victorian era, in the likes of Boots, Colman's, Guinness and Unilever, had yet to re-emerge formally. The main social focus, if any, was on the health and safety of employees. Issues such as corruption and bribery were regarded as the responsibility of governments.

As the concept of corporate social responsibility matured, most companies that responded initially interpreted it as a local or community endeavour, involving activities such as investment in sporting facilities, a charitable donation to aid organisations in developing countries or support for staff volunteering. Contributions to good causes were largely ad hoc and far from entailing strategic, long-term collaborations with expectations of positive social outcomes. There were hardly any tools or practical guidance for companies, which retained a largely adversarial stance in their relationships with pressure groups and NGOs. The idea of a company and an NGO working in strategic partnership had yet to fully evolve.

With a backdrop of high-profile corporate failures, such as Enron and Parmalat, the 2000s witnessed a progressive acceptance that companies should recognise and respond to a wide spectrum of stakeholder concerns. In fact, fostering positive relationships started to strengthen many companies' wider right to do business. As a result, the breadth of new issues that previously had not been on the agenda in the boardroom started to increase.

National laws were generally not able to keep up with the globalisation of business, and, although many regulations were adopted on specific issues, these remained fragmented. Moreover, particularly in developing countries, governments failed to enforce their own legislation.

Since the 1990s, our understanding of how business interacts with society has matured considerably. Companies now know that they cannot thrive in a failing world and so many of the social, environmental and ethical factors which underpin their approach to what is now increasingly termed just corporate responsibility (as opposed to corporate *social* responsibility) have become integrated into their core business strategy. Many have started to regard their corporate responsibility programmes as part of a wider focus on sustainability, and the two terms are often used interchangeably and with similar meaning.

Recognised frameworks have evolved to support companies' corporate responsibility and sustainability efforts – the most widely adopted being the United Nations Global Compact, which started in 2000. Fifteen years later, business participation had grown from an initial 44 companies to more than 8,300 worldwide, embracing not only their own operations but also, increasingly, their whole supply chain.[5]

In 2015, the United Nations announced the Sustainable Development Goals. Officially known as 'Transforming Our World: The 2030 agenda for sustainable development', this is a set of 17 aspirational global goals with 169 targets between them. These goals were developed in collaboration with business and are set to be hugely influential on corporate responsibility and sustainability strategy.[6]

As companies become increasingly clear on their social and environmental priorities, there is a growing focus on their ability to demonstrate that their efforts are resulting in a real and positive impact – in other words, making a measurable difference. These developments will also set the scene for tomorrow's successful corporate–charity partnerships. There is a growing recognition that success means being able to demonstrate a contribution to systemic change rather than single high-profile initiatives.

With the core elements of corporate responsibility (staff, human rights, supply chain, environment and community) now being addressed more holistically, a key trend relates to the involvement of employees in company programmes. Businesses are using the skills and expertise of their people to maximise the effectiveness of corporate–charity partnerships and in many cases have a specific volunteering strategy as part of an overarching health and well-being or engagement strategy.

The development of corporate–charity partnerships

Since the 1980s there has been a major evolution both in the way that companies have embraced the concept of working with charities and in the increased number of businesses that are proactively engaged in working with charities to achieve mutually agreed objectives. Charities are responding by becoming more strategic to ensure they maximise the opportunities offered by this positive approach.

Charities' relationships with companies in the 1970s tended towards the great-and-the-good approach, where charitable support was often at the whim of the chair or CEO, and resulted in little involvement of the staff or connection to the business. In the 1980s it was common to give sponsorship in return for the company's logo on the charity's headed paper or in the pages of the annual report or a high-profile event programme. The 1980s also saw many new developments such as the arrival of the now widespread Charity of the Year (COTY) concept, which, as an example, formed part of the NSPCC's successful Centenary Appeal. Charities began to create business development boards to spearhead corporate involvement. The organisation Business in the Community was established in 1982 to champion 'corporate community involvement'. The tax-effective payroll giving scheme was launched in 1987 to encourage employees to donate to charity with the support of their employers. Then, at the turn of the decade, the first formal £1 million COTY partnership was achieved with a partnership between Asda and the NSPCC.[7]

During the 1990s, the emphasis moved to a more considered, businesslike approach, reflected in Business in the Community's shift to championing 'corporate community investment'. This era also heralded the term 'cause-related marketing'. Both fundraisers and companies started using the terms 'mutually beneficial' and 'win-win' to describe their corporate–charity partnerships.

A prime example is The Prince's Trust's £1 million Mercury Communications sponsorship, which was an initiative led from the marketing departments of Mercury and the trust's fundraising team.[8] Because of Mercury's major financial commitment, the partnership travelled throughout the company from the top down. This was a multi-stranded, multi-functional relationship that involved national and regional events, senior

4

management, employees, marketing, suppliers and customers and resulted in what is now the well-established Mercury Prize.

Moving to the new millennium, there was an increase in focus on what the charity agenda could bring to business. With companies creating robust corporate responsibility strategies, three- and five-year cause-led partnerships were being developed. For example, the Vodafone Foundation developed a three-year, three-tier corporate responsibility programme with Samaritans, Shelter and YouthNet that reflected a major breakthrough in genuine social investment over donation.[9]

In 2010, new driving factors for the corporate–charity partnership emerged and, crucially, companies and charities entered the corporate responsibility stakes from very different angles. The first edition of the *C&E Corporate–NGO Partnerships Barometer* report served to corroborate what was already accepted sector wisdom: businesses and charities want different things from partnerships. An overwhelming 94% of companies questioned said that it was corporate reputation first and an opportunity to find new ways of addressing challenges second that drove the corporate responsibility agenda. For charities, it was unreservedly financial support first: 95% put this as the primary driver, with the second being access to people and contacts.[10] The second edition of the report reiterated these findings, with 92% of companies stating that their main motivation for partnering was for reputation and credibility, while the same percentage of charities as in the previous report – 95% – cited access to funds.[11]

The fact that charities have often seen financial support as their main priority in a partnership is unsurprising. However, as the opportunities for charities to benefit from broader partnerships with the business sector have grown, there has been an increasing trend towards integrated partnerships. This trend is demonstrated by the GSK–Save the Children example and other partnerships, such as those between Boots and Macmillan Cancer Support, Specsavers and RNIB, and Marks & Spencer and Oxfam. As a result, the corporate fundraiser role within charities has come to be seen as concerning more than simply raising money. It has evolved into a brokerage role between the two organisations to achieve a wide range of objectives, with a clear focus on the impact that the partnership is having on specific issues. The GSK–Save the Children partnership, for example, is described as a 'multi-layered, shared value partnership [that] incorporates programme work, advocacy and campaigning, employee engagement, marketing initiatives and the research and development of child-friendly medicines'.[12]

The desire for corporate responsibility programmes to support companies' corporate reputations is not to be underestimated. The number of award schemes for businesses and their corporate responsibility programmes has increased over time. Third Sector's Business Charity Awards inaugural event in 2010 had 60 company entries. In 2011 the number doubled to more than 130 entries and included household names such as Tesco and Virgin, and smaller businesses such as Simplyhealth and Coventry Building Society, all keen to make their mark.[13] In 2017, there were 23 categories and winners ranged from BMW Group UK with Whizz-Kidz (in the Charity Partnership category) to the Rail Industry Suicide Stakeholder Group with Samaritans (in the Marketing Initiative of the Year category).

Trends and future opportunities

Despite all of these positive developments, trust in the four pillars of business, government, media and NGOs continues to diminish, suggesting a growing lack of confidence in the world order.[14] A driving force behind these concerns seems to be that the benefits of globalisation are not being shared by all. The perceived upside of being able to access affordable mass-market products is being supplanted by concerns about outsourcing of jobs to lower-cost markets and loss of low-skilled jobs to automation. Any forward-thinking company will be considering what these trends mean for its business strategy, and we should anticipate an even greater focus on what this means for 'responsible capitalism'. Many of the most progressive companies have responded early by setting out their case for how their business models create quantifiable, shared benefits for the communities in which they operate. This is likely to be the tip of the iceberg and there is a need for a fundamental shift in the quality of leadership across all domains, focused on this question of impact.

The wide range and nature of the 17 United Nations Sustainable Development Goals – from 'No Poverty' to 'Climate Action' to 'Good Health and Well-Being' – suggest that they will resonate with virtually every charitable organisation. Environmental and international development charities have led the way in addressing how these organisations can play their part in the achievement of the goals. The challenge in the coming years will be for other sectors to assess their roles and integrate the Sustainable Development Goals into their strategies.

Within larger, multinational companies, the goals should become key drivers of corporate responsibility strategies; however, there will still be some companies which prefer to adopt tick-box corporate responsibility programmes. Similarly, many smaller companies will continue to struggle to find the resources to adopt a more progressive approach. In both these examples, there is great potential for companies to be influenced by forward-thinking charities. The aim should be for charities to work more effectively with business to fulfil the potential of mutually beneficial partnerships.

What is sometimes described as an increasing commercialism of charities is particularly pertinent to corporate–charity partnerships, which by their very nature involve the use of marketing-led strategies. In future years, these will come under increasing scrutiny and there will be a growing importance for companies to demonstrate their connections to a charity's cause and a necessity for them to be completely transparent about their choice of charity partners, their objectives and return on investment.

Conclusion

The reasons why companies want to work with charities and why charities want to partner with companies is simple: mutual benefit. This is made easier by each side recognising the part the other plays.

Cross-sector partnerships are essential for meeting society's development needs and always have been, which is why there have been corporate–cause partnerships dating back to the late 1800s. Companies cannot claim to be the experts on matters that are outside their core business, and charities cannot operate in isolation from private sector influences. Companies need the support of charities to tackle issues; charities need businesses to provide resources and capabilities.

Given that corporate responsibility is unlikely to go away, it is encouraging to know that both companies and charities need each other in the pursuit of their various objectives and overall in driving social impact: a powerful partnership.

Notes

1   The original source of the image was from an undated web page entitled 'Sunlight No. 1 1887 to 1902' on the Llandudno Lifeboat website, www.llandudnolifeboat.org.uk, and was accessed on 12 December 2011; at the time of writing this website no longer exists.

2   *C&E Corporate–NGO Partnerships Barometer*, London, C&E Advisory Services, 2017.

3   'Save the Children Partnership' [web page], GSK, 2016, www.gsk.com/en-gb/ about-us/corporate-partnerships/save-the-children-partnership/#a-new-way-of-working, accessed 27 January 2017.

4   Illustration by H. C. Seppings Wright, 'Rescue of Fishermen by the Life-Boat *Sunlight No. 1* at Llandudno', *Illustrated London News*, 19 October 1889.

5   *Impact: Transforming business, changing the world* [PDF], DNV GL and United Nations Global Compact, 2015, www.unglobalcompact.org/docs/publications/ ImpactUNGlobalCompact2015.pdf, accessed 13 June 2017.

6   See *Transforming Our World: The 2030 agenda for sustainable development* [PDF], United Nations, 2015, https://sustainabledevelopment.un.org/post2015/ transformingourworld/publication, accessed 13 June 2017.

7   Set up and run by the author, Valerie Morton.

8   William Drew, 'Prince's Trust Gets the Buzz with Mercury', *Marketing*, 14 October 1993.

9   *Collaboration: Working together for a better future*, Newbury, The Vodafone UK Foundation, 2007, p. 6.

10   *C&E Corporate–NGO Partnerships Barometer*, London, C&E Advisory Services, 2010, p. 8.

11   *C&E Corporate–NGO Partnerships Barometer*, London, C&E Advisory Services, 2011, p. 12.
12   'Our Partners: GSK' [web page], Save the Children, 2016, www.savethechildren.org.uk/about-us/who-we-work-with/corporate-partnerships/our-partners/gsk, accessed 9 February 2017.
13   Stephen Cook, 'The Business Charity Awards 2011 Shortlist' [web page], *Third Sector*, 21 March 2011, www.thirdsector.co.uk/business-charity-awards-2011-shortlist/article/1061013, accessed 13 June 2017.
14   '2017 Edelman Trust Barometer Reveals Global Implosion of Trust' [press release], www.edelman.com/news/2017-edelman-trust-barometer-reveals-global-implosion, 15 January 2017.

CHAPTER TWO

Developing a strategic approach to corporate partnerships

Andrew Peel

Introduction

Against a backdrop of shrinking corporate donations budgets and a heightened awareness of corporate responsibility, this chapter examines the form and direction that corporate fundraising must now take. It outlines the wider role that it can play for your charity in terms of promoting its brand, core messages and services, and strategies that you can employ in order to build strong, sustainable corporate relationships in what is, for most, a challenging and uncertain climate.

The chapter emphasises that corporate fundraising is not a fast track to 'easy' or 'big' money, and that the path to what funding there is can be a difficult one to navigate. Corporate fundraising can be a slow and labour-intensive process, involving long periods of research and analysis, relationship-building and negotiation within the charity and the company, and many dead ends, pitfalls and frustrations along the way. However, as the examples and case studies in this chapter show, if your charity is prepared to invest time and resources in planning, structuring and managing corporate fundraising, and in understanding what companies want from working with you, the benefits for both parties and the communities you serve can be considerable.

From philanthropic support to strategic partnerships

The overarching purpose of a charity's corporate fundraising function might be said to be to initiate, develop and retain relationships with businesses that maximise net income for the charity and, where feasible and desirable, generate additional opportunities and benefits for both parties.

As this definition implies, there is more to corporate fundraising than simply attempting to secure a financial contribution. In fact, while some charities do manage to regularly land significant corporate donations, large no-strings cash gifts are few and far between. Companies are seldom the vast financial reservoirs that many perceive them to be, and those that are tend to feel more beholden to their shareholders than to their communities.

The latest, and possibly last, figures we have on cash gifts, are from *The Company Giving Almanac 2013*. This is because, as highlighted in chapter 3, companies in the UK do not (starting with the 2012/13 financial year) have a legal obligation to declare charitable donations. This means that it is no longer possible for researchers to make meaningful estimates of the annual levels of cash gifts from companies.

The almanac reports that the overall level of corporate giving in 2011 (including in-kind contributions) was startlingly low in the UK, accounting for around only 2% of charitable income,[1] despite more intense scrutiny from customers, staff, charities, pressure groups, the media, government and more socially conscious shareholders. (Note that NCVO reports higher overall corporate giving figures but includes contributions from non-UK companies and has a wider definition of in-kind giving. For further details, see 'Comparing financial data in the UK' on page 35.) The same source reveals that the value of support given to charities and communities by the most generous 418 UK companies in 2011 was only £603 million, which equates to 0.4% of their pre-tax profits. If gifts in kind and other forms of non-financial support are stripped out, cash donations represent only 0.3% of pre-tax profits – well below the 1% figure once deemed a respectable benchmark of corporate giving. In addition, the almanac reveals that significant giving is concentrated among a few large companies: 20% of companies donate 90% of the cash, the majority of which goes to educational causes, community or social welfare, and children and young people.[2]

Furthermore, many companies that traditionally provided financial support to charities have shifted their focus from philanthropy towards relationships of a more strategic nature: a move, in other words, from donations towards investment of resources, staff expertise and other assets. This change of emphasis has been driven by the need for companies to be seen to be behaving responsibly and for more tangible business benefits to come out of such projects. Consumers now expect a great deal more from businesses, including meaningful social and environmental impact.

This observation is underlined by a 2015 study which revealed that 91% of shoppers worldwide expect companies to do more than make a profit and that 90% would switch to brands that support a good cause, given similar price and quality. Furthermore, the research found that businesses that are not socially responsible run the risk of alienating their customer base, with 90% of those surveyed saying they would boycott companies found to be engaged in irresponsible business practices.[3]

Unfortunately, this shift in emphasis has increased the scale of the task facing charities that target the corporate sector. It presents such organisations with a considerable set of challenges. And yet, for the creative, astute and commercially minded fundraiser, this new climate means that there really is no limit to the ways in which a charity can engage with a company.

This assertion is borne out by a quick trawl through the annual Business Charity Awards, with the winning partnerships revealing the unprecedented depth and scope of many of today's best charity–corporate tie-ups. The 2016 winners, for example, included a partnership between Unilever's Lynx brand and the male-suicide-prevention charity Campaign Against Living Miserably, aimed at raising awareness of the issue of young male suicide, and a three-year partnership between retailer Halfords and the charity Re~Cycle, which has resulted in the public donating more than 20,000 unwanted bicycles to be refurbished and reused in Africa.[4]

Focus on value, not cash

Clearly, corporate–charity partnerships should no longer be viewed simply from a financial perspective but in terms of the wider value that can be gained by both parties and wider society. The aforementioned Halfords partnership with Re~Cycle, for example, looks set to have far-reaching social and societal outcomes – bicycles provide an invaluable resource for African schoolchildren, farmers, health workers and others not in a position to purchase a new one. In addition, Re~Cycle believes that, because bikes are generally shared, an estimated 120,000 people have benefitted from the donation of 20,000 bicycles.[5]

It is evident, then, that corporate fundraisers who think of themselves simply as 'raisers of corporate funds' are going to be destined for frustration and failure. Some might also argue that the very label 'corporate fundraiser', while remaining a useful generic term, has become something of a misnomer because of the need to think about the role in a broader, more strategic way.

The time has come to regard a corporate partner not as the proverbial cash cow to be milked as rapidly as possible but as a multi-dimensional resource that, if managed skilfully, can present a plethora of opportunities for both organisations. For your charity, as well as being a potential source of income, a company might represent a route to heightened awareness, a source of invaluable pro bono support or gifts in kind, or a new audience for challenge events. For the company, the charitable association might provide benefits such as positive PR, staff development opportunities, access to policymakers or improved sales.

However, research carried out for C&E's annual *Corporate–NGO Partnerships Barometer* reveals that companies' motivations to get involved in charity partnerships usually differ from NGOs': in 2017, 92% (compared to 91% in 2016) of businesses stated that the reputational benefits of associations with NGOs were their key driver, whereas 93% (compared to 92% in 2016) of NGOs stated that the financial returns were their leading reason for partnering. So the key challenge is: how can this difference be reconciled? The answer is that charities and corporates must work together to identify areas of mutual interest and use these drivers as the basis for initial discussions and joint working. Indeed, one area of mutual interest, as identified in the C&E report, is the opportunity to gain access to people and contacts.[6]

Put the customer first

To keep businesses engaged for longer, charities should aim to adopt a broader, more customer-orientated approach to corporate relationships and seek to open them up on a number of mutually beneficial fronts. This will lead to a more equal and sustainable partnership and may even help to generate some of the funding your charity might have originally anticipated.

The main implication of a more externally focused approach is that a big shift in mindset is usually required. The focal point becomes the *company's* objectives yet with an added awareness of your organisation's strategy, values, brand and offer.[7] This mindset puts you in a strong position to negotiate and balance your charity's needs with those of the company.

Of course, a well-written generic proposal will sometimes hit the mark if it lands on the right desk at the right time. However, such an approach will usually fail because your charity's proposition is likely to lack that crucial element of strategic insight required to align perfectly with the company's requirements.

As a stark indicator of the fruitlessness of cold and untargeted approaches, each year, HSBC receives around 10,000 unsolicited sponsorship proposals, of which no more than four (0.04%) are successful.[8] Every other major brand marketer will tell a similar story. The challenge when approaching companies, then, is to do whatever homework is necessary to make it into the top 0.04% rather than the bottom 99.96%. This means forensically examining the target company's needs, engaging its people in dialogue and then creating a tailored proposition. By adopting a more outward-facing and customer-led stance, your chances of success will be significantly increased.

This is an important principle. Look at any successful modern company, be it Amazon, Google, Specsavers or Tesco, and it is clear that they are where they are today because they have put the customer at the core of their planning. Amazon's chief executive, Jeff Bezos, is widely quoted as saying, 'We start with the customer and we work backwards.' We could do well to take a leaf out of his book.

Adopt an organisational approach

Another key principle is that corporate fundraising is unlikely to succeed in a vacuum. It requires a coordinated, organisational approach and, in particular, the support and buy-in of the senior management team and trustees. They must recognise that they have a pivotal role to play in the development of their charity's corporate relationships, whether that is by fronting approaches or pitches, or by using their networks to open doors. In addition, they are likely to be the key to future investment in additional staff and training, a new database or perhaps the use of external agencies. At the very least, it is vital that the challenges you face as a corporate fundraiser are appreciated at a senior level and that a pragmatic, strategic and long-term view is taken of this area of fundraising.

You may also find that, to deliver on promises and fulfil obligations to companies, you will be dependent upon the support of a wide range of individuals across your charity. It is therefore important to get key colleagues onside as early as possible by encouraging them to think about how the partnership might work for them and collaborating so that the best offer can be presented to companies. In particular, you may find yourself working closely with colleagues in the communications, public relations or press team; the events team; the finance function; the major giving fundraiser(s); the community or regional fundraisers; and, of course, those who are responsible for delivering your charity's programmes and service delivery.

With good relationships in place across the organisation, you will find it easier to present a broader, more compelling proposition to companies that, in turn, delivers far greater impact and value for the charity and its beneficiaries.

Corporate partnerships as a platform

If they are well planned and well managed, corporate partnerships can act not only as an income generator but also as a marketing platform or hub upon which your charity can promote its broader vision, services, products and brand. This is particularly the case when working with blue-chip companies with large workforces and customer bases, though it is just as feasible on a smaller or local level, as long as the resources to manage the relationship are available. What is certain is that one well-chosen and well-managed partnership, whether local, regional, national or even international in nature, can open up a range of opportunities for collaboration and lead to a step-change in your charity's profile and income.

The following case study highlights what can be achieved if two very different organisations with a clear vision and complementary objectives work together for mutual benefit.

Case study: SolarAid and Yingli Europe

Partnership background

In many African countries, light is produced by dangerous and highly polluting kerosene lanterns which are also expensive to operate: the fuel typically costs families 15% of their household income. Against this background, the charity SolarAid set its mission goal in 2011 to eradicate the kerosene lamp from Africa by 2020.

SolarAid's goal was picked up on by the managing director of Yingli Europe, a wholly owned subsidiary of one of the world's leading solar panel manufacturers, who saw the clear link with the company's own vision of affordable green energy for all. After a prolonged period of discussion, negotiation, trust-building and planning, Yingli agreed to help SolarAid develop and manufacture a high-quality solar light at a price that African families could afford.

SolarAid's approach to achieving its ambitious goal has been not to give solar lights away but to sell them at a fair market price through its social enterprise, SunnyMoney. This strategy, it was felt, would encourage local traders and lead to a swifter distribution of lights than a simple handout of aid.

The cheapest solar light that met the World Bank's quality standards used to cost around $12 – still a high cost for families living below the poverty line. The challenge was to develop a high-quality product that could retail for $5 *and* provide a margin for local traders. SolarAid had already established that families typically spent $1.5 a week on kerosene, and so the charity knew that families would recoup the cost in less than a month.

A collaborative, creative and mutually beneficial approach

After the production of several prototypes, an industrial design team in Manchester, Inventid (appointed by Yingli), finalised the light's design, which incorporated valuable feedback and insight that SolarAid had gathered from African families using other solar lights. In late 2016, the first 10,000 units were manufactured in China and 9,000 were delivered to Malawi, Uganda and Zambia. The $5 lights sold so quickly that another production line was immediately set up.

The remaining 1,000 lights were shipped to the UK and sold for a premium price of £10. It is highlighted on lights sold in the UK that each purchase enables SolarAid to provide a solar light that a family in Africa can buy at a fair market price. SolarAid donors are also offered a solar light if they commit to making a regular gift or a one-off donation of £50. Within months these lights had also sold out.

When SolarAid set its goal in 2011, it was distributing and selling just a few hundred lights a year. Now, SunnyMoney is one of the leading distributors of solar lights to remote rural areas in the countries in which it operates. The new product, nicknamed the 'SunnyMoney 100' (or 'SM100'), is changing lives of families in Africa who live without electricity. Over a three-year period, each light sold enables children to study for an extra 1,000 hours, realises savings of $200 per family and reduces carbon emissions by one tonne.

Key learning points

What is interesting about this project is that SolarAid did not set out to attract a corporate partner to help it achieve its goal and to develop a marketable solar light. Rather, as the charity states:

> We started with the mission and then, once we'd articulated it clearly, a company that shared our values spotted the opportunity for a joint solution to an intractable problem.

> Furthermore, by playing to our mutual strengths, we became greater than the sum of our parts. The production of solar lights was neither SolarAid's nor Yingli's area of expertise, and yet we developed an effective way of working that resulted in an ideal product.

Finally, it is important to stress that this project's success and Yingli's involvement were about so much more than a company's financial support. Without access to its invaluable knowledge of design, development and manufacturing processes, SolarAid would not have been able to create a solar light that could be manufactured at scale, with the risk underwritten.

Not only did this partnership result in the production of the world's most affordable solar light, with the many benefits that that breakthrough entails for developing countries, but it has also been a game-changer by achieving the charity's mission goal of eradicating the kerosene lamp and fulfilling Yingli's vision of affordable green energy for all.

Developing a corporate fundraising strategy

There are a number of key stages to go through before embarking on, or seeking to grow, corporate fundraising. By formulating a clear vision and strategy, giving careful thought to how to package and position the cause, and thoroughly researching each prospect, your charity's hit rate should increase, along with the number of partnerships secured and income generated. What follows is a step-by-step process for developing a well-measured and coherent corporate fundraising strategy that can be tailored to any organisation, and revisited and adapted as necessary.

Step 1: Situational analysis

The first step in scoping out a strategy is to take stock of the current situation and consider your organisation's main strengths and weaknesses – as a charity, as a corporate partnership proposition and as a fundraising team – and how to address or leverage these factors. In the process, it can be useful to consider the following:

The corporate fundraising marketplace in which you are operating:

- the economic conditions;

- the types and numbers of companies in your catchment area;

- the activities of key competitors, and corporate philanthropy trends (such as more strategic company giving and less philanthropy, or increased employee involvement).

The current approach to corporate fundraising:

- team structure and performance;

- income sources;

- the nature of existing partnerships and how they can be developed;

- target companies or sectors to be approached in the future and the reasons for this;

- your charity's positioning and unique selling points generally and in relation to corporate fundraising;

- the corporate fundraising mechanisms (for example, donations, cause-related marketing, sponsorship, employee fundraising and direct marketing) that work best and why;

- a summary of the areas requiring investment.

Past and current financial performance:	• net and gross income; • expenditure; • return on investment; • percentage of repeat/reliable income; • benchmarks against other charities and so on.
All concerns, issues and critical timings that are likely to impact significantly upon:	• current activity; • workload; • plans.
The key internal and external factors impacting your charity's ability to work with companies, including the outputs from strategic planning tools such as:	• the SWOT and PESTLE analyses (outlined below); • internal consultation; • workshops.

There are numerous tools available for helping to define a strategic approach, but in my experience the following methods can help to answer the most important questions and identify core priorities.

Ansoff Matrix

Although primarily a commercial planning tool, the Ansoff Matrix can nevertheless be applied to most charities by providing a framework for assessing their own markets, products, offers and potential growth strategies. By clearly presenting the range of growth options available, the matrix can help charity managers and fundraisers to assess whether to target new or existing markets (or corporate partners) with new or existing products, and the likely level of risk associated with each decision.

Broadly speaking, the four choices defined by Ansoff (see figure 2.1) are:

A: The Market Penetration strategy

This strand of the matrix helps you to consider whether to promote existing products, projects or services to existing markets, perhaps in greater numbers than at present. Could existing products be developed and marketing or promotional activity increased? Or are there ways of ensuring greater loyalty among existing customers or supporters?

B: The Market Development strategy

Should existing products or services be introduced into a new market? This option might involve expansion into another town, region or country; different positioning and pricing of work for companies; or perhaps the targeting of a different business sector. This is a fairly low-risk strategy because the focus is mainly on current products and sales and on marketing strategies with which you are familiar.

C: The Product Development strategy

This strand raises the question of whether to create new products, projects or offers for existing markets or customers. There is a level of risk attached to this approach, since the success of a new product can never be guaranteed. However, this argument is countered by the view that companies are more likely to favour the partner or supplier with which they are familiar.

D: The Diversification strategy

Finally, there is the question of whether to introduce new products or offers into new markets. This is, of course, the riskiest strategy available as it involves the organisation moving some of its focus away from the products, markets and customers it knows best. While the returns from successfully penetrating a new market with a fresh offer ahead of the competition can be considerable, this option would usually be chosen only when there are few alternatives – perhaps when the market or the organisation's market share are under pressure or diminishing.

FIGURE 2.1 ANSOFF'S FOUR STRATEGIES

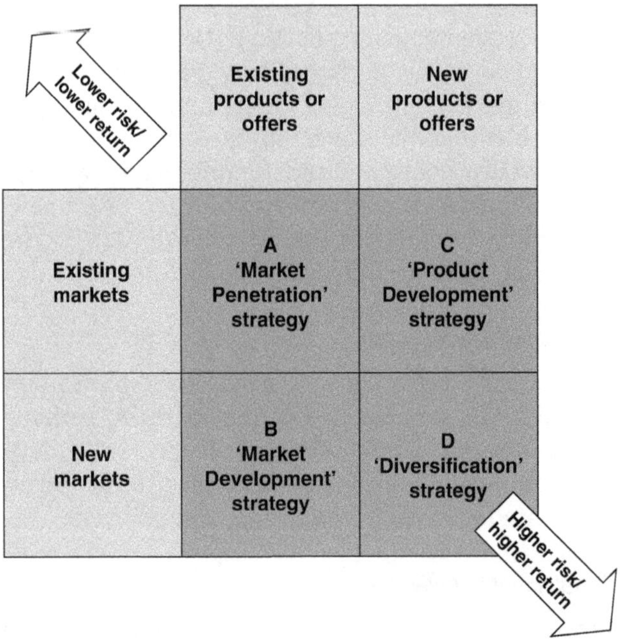

Adapted and reprinted with permission from 'Strategies for Diversification' by H. Igor Ansoff. *Harvard Business Review*, September 1957.

The Boston Matrix

The Boston Matrix is another simple analytical tool; it can be used to help you visualise the probable life cycle of projects, products, clients and donors (as well as colleagues and trustees if necessary!). In highlighting so-called 'cash cows', 'rising stars', 'sick children' and 'dead dogs', it will reveal the aspects of an existing corporate strategy or portfolio that are yielding the best return and those which are likely to require more attention and investment in the future.

SWOT analysis

The dependable SWOT (strengths, weaknesses, opportunities and threats) analysis is a great tool both for unpicking an organisation's or a team's competencies – or lack of them – and for flagging significant opportunities to be grasped and key threats being faced. It can also serve to identify recurring issues (such as poor internal communications and low brand awareness) that could impact on your charity's relationships with companies. With such information to hand, you will be well placed to plan for a range of scenarios and to start scoping out a clear strategic direction.

PESTLE analysis

A PESTLE analysis can help to highlight a wide range of external factors – political, economic, social, technological, legal and environmental (or ethical) – that may have an impact upon working with companies. Most will be outside your charity's control (an economic downturn, or the ramifications of Brexit, for example), but it is still important to be aware of such factors and to think through their possible impact on strategy.

Competitor analysis

There are, of course, thousands of charities and other voluntary organisations operating across the UK, some of which will represent direct competition. By cataloguing the activities of the key players and any overlap in terms of service delivery and/or fundraising and marketing, you will be able to see clearly where your charity has a competitive edge and to build this into your approaches to businesses accordingly.

This exercise can also highlight any complementary activity being undertaken and potential angles for a collaborative approach to corporate fundraising – a strategy which can prove very attractive to companies. A prime example of this new style of consortia corporate partnership is the three-year tie-up between the British Heart Foundation, Diabetes UK and Tesco, aimed at helping people to reduce their risk of type 2 diabetes and cardiovascular disease through simple lifestyle changes.

Step 2: Articulating the strategic vision

By this stage, you are likely to have garnered a good appreciation of the internal and external environments relevant to corporate fundraising, as well as a range of options regarding marketing and positioning.

It can now be helpful to outline what the future will look like for corporate fundraising. This vision needs to be something that encapsulates your charity's opportunities and goals; that inspires and appeals to fellow fundraisers and the wider charity; that is feasible, flexible and focused; and that can be easily summarised. It must also be informed by your charity's overall vision, mission and funding requirements (and the way in which these break down by income stream) and it should be both ambitious *and* realistic. There is little point, for example, in setting the goal of generating £5 million in three years if the only achievement to date is a £5,000 partnership with a local law firm.

The following is an example of a corporate fundraising vision for a large charity:

> The Corporate Partnerships Team will continue to develop into a key fundraising and marketing hub for the charity. It will be generating £2.5 million net for our vital work with homeless and vulnerable teenagers by the end of 2020/21 – an increase of 25% on our current income level. This uplift will be achieved through a combination of integrated, creative fundraising and marketing and by maximising the potential of our corporate relationships at a local, regional and national level.

For a smaller local or regional charity, something along these lines may be more appropriate:

> Corporate fundraising income will double over the next three years, increasing from £175,000 to £350,000. This will be achieved by carrying out more thorough prospect research, by strengthening our corporate offer and case for support, and by maximising the potential of our partnerships with Acme plc and Waitco Supermarket. By playing to our strengths and highlighting the impact of our work locally, we will build a wider supporter base of committed local and regional companies and create additional value for the charity and our beneficiaries.

Step 3: Refining the strategy

The next stage is to start outlining the general direction of travel. Having carefully weighed up all options, the hooks upon which to hang the strategy could look something like this:

(a) Maximise the potential of current relationships and fulfil all contractual obligations

The fact that a new plan is being developed should not impact negatively upon existing corporate partnerships. Any new strategy must take account of, and be able to accommodate, current tie-ups to ensure that commitments to those partners are met and that the relationships are a success. Two key principles of fundraising and marketing which are worth reiterating here are that existing donors and customers are the most important ones and that it is far more resource intensive to attract a new customer or supporter than it is to retain or develop an old one.

(b) Develop new fundraising or marketing activities with current corporate supporters

For the reason given in the previous point, it is likely to be more cost-effective to try to generate additional income from current supporters than to rely heavily on researching and securing new ones. A key objective should therefore be to look at ways of developing existing relationships and bringing supporters closer to your charity.

(c) Develop new relationships through existing networks

There may well be informal opportunities to do this (for example, by talking to your trustees or existing corporate supporters and by endeavouring to gain access to their contacts or networks) or formal ones (such as establishing a fundraising appeal board or corporate panel).

(d) Attract new corporate supporters

Regardless of whether your corporate fundraising function is new or has been operating for years, it is crucial to always be thinking about how to attract new supporters. If all contacts and networks have been exhausted, this will inevitably involve researching businesses and sectors which have clear or perceived links with the charity's work, beneficiaries, brand and locations.

Let us take the example of an international eye-care charity. In seeking new business, the corporate fundraising manager maps out a number of sectors with a relevance to, or resonance with, the charity's work (see figure 2.2).

FIGURE 2.2 TARGET INDUSTRIES RELEVANT TO THE WORK OF AN INTERNATIONAL EYE-CARE CHARITY

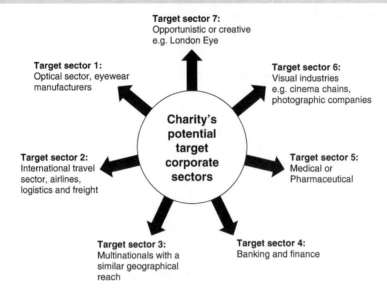

In this way, once you have identified a range of relevant industries or sectors, you can narrow down your targets to a manageable number of companies, which can then be researched and cultivated. This will involve first reviewing each company's activities, businesses, markets, brands and sub-brands, and even their competitors before targeting them with bespoke propositions.

It helps to have a clear understanding of how a target company is structured and of its key personnel. Such information can usually be gleaned from sources such as the company's website, Companies House, *The Guide to UK Company Giving,*[9] Google, social media, local or trade press, or even from a friendly receptionist. Alternatively, your charity's database or board of trustees might reveal connections or knowledge that can be leveraged and shed light on the company's culture and operations.

While some may regard it as rather Machiavellian, this kind of in-depth research, planning and preparation can mean the difference between a well-targeted approach and one that falls on fallow ground. Furthermore, being prospect-focused in this way not only results in a better appreciation of a business's priorities and can improve your charity's positioning, but it can also reveal potential entry points and inspire imaginative angles that can be built into an approach.

Tightening the strategic objectives

Having outlined a clear vision and the possible direction of travel, it is sensible to try to hone the new strategy by setting out four to six objectives – making them as SMART (specific, measurable, attainable, realistic and timely) as possible – that can provide a framework within which to put the fuller strategy.

A larger charity's corporate fundraising strategy could, for instance, be built around core objectives, such as:

By 31st March 2021:

1. We will have increased the income we generate from community affairs and corporate responsibility budgets, Charity of the Year relationships, employee fundraising, corporate foundations, payroll giving and other 'non-commercial' sources to £2.1 million.

2. By better harnessing the power of our charity's brand and by focusing on marketing-led initiatives such as cause-related marketing, sponsorship, affinity deals and licensing, we will have increased the level of 'trading' income to £400,000.

3. We will have adopted a more logical, sector-focused approach to corporate fundraising and new business. We will have secured a minimum of one company partnership worth at least £75,000 in each of the following sectors: banking, airlines, pharmaceuticals and IT.

4. By working more collaboratively with community fundraising, trusts, events and our major donor team, we will have a more strategic, coordinated approach to networking and prospect cultivation that generates more high-calibre leads, income and opportunities for the charity.

Next, outline the main actions required to realise each of these objectives. This should consist of a description of the key activities required in each year of the planning period, along with a summary of the success criteria, outcomes and key performance indicators (KPIs) to be used.

Clearly defined and agreed KPIs are an invaluable component in a strategic plan in the way that they enable you to measure a wide range of financial, qualitative, quantitative and operational impacts of your charity's work. From a corporate fundraising point of view, they can also help to highlight that this area of the charity is about more than just generating cash. With the right KPIs in place, supported by appropriate financial procedures (such as soft-crediting),[10] the wider value provided by your corporate fundraising department to other departments – such as through the recruitment of participants in challenge events, or securing a major sponsor for a gala ball – can be clearly highlighted.

A smaller charity's strategic objectives might focus on the following kinds of issues:

• how to retain, manage and develop existing supporters, with clear outcomes and income targets given for each relationship;

• an overview of the proposed approach to new business development, with an explanation of targets by industry or sector, size, location, giving or corporate responsibility track record, and proposed corporate fundraising mechanism;

• the need for additional investment in the fundraising team – this may be about recruiting an extra fundraiser or a new researcher, or highlighting the need for additional staff training;

• the ways in which the charity needs to prepare itself for the 'growing pains' and demands that a significant corporate partnership can place on a smaller organisation;

• the need to improve the marketing or positioning of the charity's work, materials and funding opportunities;

• the need for greater internal buy-in and support of corporate fundraising, particularly at the senior level – this might also include the need for senior internal contacts (for example, founder, directors, trustees and patrons) and other key colleagues (such as the major giving team and the events team) to open doors and work collaboratively;

• the need to explore ways of boosting the charity's profile, because heightened brand awareness is likely to improve the rate of new business conversion;

• the need for more challenge and networking events and volunteering opportunities to engage current and potential supporters.

Once each objective is clearly defined, outline the main actions required to achieve it and the performance measurements to be implemented.

Step 4: Developing the corporate offer

The starting point for developing the corporate offer is a strong, emotive and businesslike case for support that can be tailored to each prospect. This is a key strategic tool which formally:

- articulates the role of the charity;

- captures its vision, its mission and the essence of its work;

- outlines what makes its approach unique and why it needs support.

The corporate offer will outline the rationale for the approach, the partnership vision and the benefits that can be offered to the target company. Finally, it must also incorporate a compelling 'ask' – i.e. the optimum product, project, proposition or hook, pitched at the right price and aimed at engaging the target.

Focus on product

Most companies these days are not prepared simply to provide free money to good causes, preferring instead to tie their support into a charity's brand or a particular project, service or product. This being the case, how can you position your charity appropriately and decide what to pitch to a company?

A simple analogy is to think of a charity's corporate fundraiser as a shopkeeper who must work hard to tempt people on to their premises. Careful thought must be given to a wide range of issues, such as pricing, positioning, branding and customer care. However, by far the biggest challenge relates to the products and – particularly – what to display in the shop window. What is most likely to catch people's attention and entice them in to browse and sample other wares?

Few charities are fortunate enough to have a product as simple or as engaging as, say, Macmillan's World's Biggest Coffee Morning or Guide Dogs' corporate Sponsor a Puppy offer. However, it is well worth taking the time to develop workable equivalents to these that fully capture the essence of your charity and that help to engage both new corporate supporters and long-standing ones.

Create a product matrix

The main downside to the shopkeeper analogy, of course, is that you can rarely afford to behave so passively. With so much competition, it is a risky strategy to sit back and wait for customers. The charities that are going to succeed in the current climate are those which are prepared to actively seek out supporters by using high-quality and tailored approaches. This will be a particularly important strand of activity if your fundraising team does not have access to effective senior-level networks or other door-openers.

To help clarify your charity's corporate offer, one approach is to take a blank sheet of paper and write down, in a column on the left-hand side, a list of anything that the charity does, owns or has planned which might appeal to a company. This should not only include those activities which are fundable in a traditional sense but also those which could provide more innovative ways to engage companies, perhaps by involving their staff, tapping into marketing budgets or securing gifts in kind.

This list of products and assets might encompass, for example, the names of your main programmes, projects or services, along with flagship events, publications, shops and other embryonic ideas which could provide reasons to enter into dialogue with a particular company.

Along the top of the page, write in headings describing the various ways in which companies could support your charity in relation to each product/asset heading – for example, with financial donations, staff volunteers and gifts in kind. Then put a mark in the matrix where support is most likely, as in figure 2.3.

The back-door approach strategy

If corporate fundraising is about creating unique business propositions that set your charity apart from the competition, it can also help to consider using a less conventional route into your target company. For example, a strong employee-engagement proposal might receive a warmer response channelled through a back-door route into the company. One possibility would be to position it as a solution for the HR team rather than as a more predictable approach to the corporate responsibility or community affairs department. It can also be the case that, by dealing with people who are less used to working directly with charities, fewer of the usual hurdles and standard hindrances are put in your way.

When I was working for Sightsavers, an innovative training project was developed with Sony, involving all of its European marketing and product managers. Sony's UK HR director fully supported the idea (and helped to sell it internally), as she could see real benefits for the business of involving senior staff from several countries in an outward-facing training project, the objective of which was to generate fresh fundraising and marketing ideas for the charity.

In short, the more time taken to identify and thoroughly research each target sector and corporate prospect, and to devise the optimum approach strategy, the greater the chance of a successful outcome and partnership.

The art of crafting successful new business approaches is explored in greater detail in chapter 4.

FIGURE 2.3 CHARITY X'S PRODUCTS AND CORPORATE ENGAGEMENT ANGLES

Charity X's products ⇨	Philanthropic corporate support	Marketing-led support (such as sponsorship and cause-related marketing)	Charity of the Year or staff fundraising	Volunteering or skills exchange	Networking or profile-raising	Trading or earned income	In-kind support
The cause	✓	✓	✓				
Programmes, projects or services							
Older people's day centre	✓	✓	✓	✓			
XYZ campaign	✓	✓	✓				
Youth outreach	✓		✓	✓			
Playgroup	✓		✓	✓			
Mentoring service				✓			✓
Other activities or properties							
Charity shop				✓			✓
Meeting rooms						✓	
Consultancy (training etc.)	✓					✓	
Publications		✓	✓	✓			✓
Brighton Marathon		✓	✓				
Future activities or products							
Quarterly business breakfast		✓			✓		✓
Churches' information pack		✓					
Schools' fundraising pack		✓					
Paris Bike Ride event		✓	✓		✓		
Three Peaks Challenge		✓	✓		✓		
Mobile phone and inkjet recycling		✓	✓				

Conclusion

The shift from corporate philanthropy towards what is generally a more sophisticated and strategic form of engagement – and the need for tangible business benefits to come out of such support – has clearly changed the nature of corporate fundraising. Although the financial and non-financial benefits for charities working in this arena can now be substantial, the same is true of the associated challenges. As such, this is an area of fundraising that will require you to employ considerable thought and planning, and it is certainly not something to be entered into lightly.

You will only reap the rewards from corporate fundraising if you are fully committed and if you are willing to take a long view and a strategic approach. You must also have confidence and clarity about your positioning and niche in relation to the business sector. If it is unclear what you stand for and what you can offer to companies, you will always struggle to make a compelling case for yourself in a crowded and challenging marketplace.

However, as this chapter highlights, if you are ready to invest in this area of fundraising for the medium to long term, if you are willing to take the rough with the smooth and if you are able to navigate carefully through sometimes choppy, shark-infested waters, then corporate fundraising offers considerable opportunities. Even for smaller charities and niche or so-called 'challenging' causes, corporate alliances can – if planned well and managed skilfully – be extraordinarily rewarding on many levels.

Notes

1   Data was collected from latest available company accounts; most year ends were 2011 (74%), followed by 2010 (19%), and 2012 (7%).
2   Catherine Walker, *The Company Giving Almanac 2013*, London, DSC, 2013, pp. xiii–xiv.
3   Cone Communications and Ebiquity, *Cone Communications/Ebiquity Global CSR Study 2015*, Boston MA, Cone Communications, 2015. Interviews were conducted with 9,709 shoppers in 9 countries: Brazil , Canada, China, France, Germany, India, Japan, the UK and the USA.
4   Luke Dubuis, 'Halfords & Re~Cycle Named Winners at Business Charity Awards 2016' [web page], Re~Cycle, 21 April 2016, www.re-cycle.org/news/halfords-recycle-named-winners-business-charity-awards-2016, accessed 13 June 2016. For more information on the Business Charity Awards go to www.fundraisingweek.co.uk/business-charity-awards.
5   Luke Dubuis, 'Halfords & Re~Cycle Named Winners at Business Charity Awards 2016' [web page], Re~Cycle, 21 April 2016, www.re-cycle.org/news/halfords-recycle-named-winners-business-charity-awards-2016, accessed 13 June 2016.
6   *C&E Corporate–NGO Partnerships Barometer*, London, C&E Advisory Services, 2017, pp. 4 and 7.

7   In both business and fundraising, the term 'offer' describes the full package being offered to a customer. It includes the physical product, if there is one, and other factors which together make up the sum total of what is on offer. In fundraising and direct marketing, the 'offer' refers not only to how much is being asked for but also the rationale for giving, such as what the money will be used for and how the donor will feel as a result of giving. In corporate sponsorship, the offer might be made up of tangible benefits along with the expectation of good customer service from the charity and the less tangible warm glow from being involved with a good cause.

8   Figures noted by HSBC speakers at the European Sponsorship Association's Future Sponsorship conference, as reported in 'Future Sponsorship 09 Split over Impact of Recession as Biggest Shake Up for the Industry for 25 Years Predicted' [press release], SportCal, www.sportcal.com/News/PressReleases/36170?size=50, 27 November 2009.

9   See www.dsc.org.uk/gcg for the book or www.dsc.org.uk/funding-website for the searchable subscription website, which contains a company giving arm. Both the book and the website offer detailed information on over 400 companies, including who to contact, any application processes, the company's financial details and number of employees, and examples of organisations the company has supported in the past. They also offer details on companies' preferred methods of giving, including cash donations, in-kind support, employee-led support, sponsorship and/or commercially led support.

10   An arrangement whereby some or all of the income that a fundraiser has helped to raise is recorded within the monthly management accounts. It can act as an incentive for fundraisers to work collaboratively with colleagues across the team and sometimes across other departments, in the knowledge that their contribution is being recognised. Furthermore, it can provide managers with a useful, informal performance management tool, as well as a clearer sense of the real return on investment and added value of different fundraising activities.

CHAPTER THREE

Improving strategy with research and data

Rei Kanemura and Cian Murphy

Introduction

Research, either of the academic or the practical variety, is not a hugely mature field within the world of corporate fundraising. It is often broader than it is deep, with individual research pieces on many different areas rather than a deep focus on any particular topic. This presents a challenge if you are a corporate fundraiser aiming to improve your fundraising strategy by staying abreast of best practice in the sector, and also makes it challenging to present a comprehensive overview of research that has been conducted in the area.

This chapter has the purpose of highlighting findings and trends within this body of research, and what can be learned from this, and alerting readers to the sources of data that are available, whether one-off pieces of research or repeated publications.

We have divided the chapter into three main sections. The first deals with research that is more academic in style, while the second deals with research with a more practical bent. The third section draws comparisons with other countries and outlines what can be learned from research and data sources elsewhere, (mostly) in the English-speaking world.

A note on definitions

We define academic-style research as research that tends to concentrate on the perspectives of companies and corporate philanthropy or that is mainly concerned with theories and conceptual analysis of giving. It is normally published in journals.

Practical-style research, on the other hand, derives from non-academic bodies (including charities, private sector companies and think tanks) and its primary aim is to aid charities in their fundraising. This research emphasises factual analysis, numbers and case studies. It will often be shorter in length and more succinct, and it reflects the needs of its primary audience.

Individual pieces of research may contain aspects of both categories.

Academic-style research in or about the UK

Although it is something of a niche field, there is nevertheless substantial academic research on corporate fundraising and corporate giving, with diversity in both the scope of the research and the findings. Some researchers have taken a predominantly conceptual approach, seeking to determine the impact of the economic climate or of the size of the business, or to examine the public perception of private sector giving. Others have conducted a number of historical analyses, looking at past data on corporate giving in the UK and other countries. While the study of this topic has a long history dating back to the 1930s, the 2000s observed a marked increase in the number of studies emerging in the field.[1]

This renewed academic interest may be attributed to the growth in the importance of corporate giving as a source of charity finance over the same period. For example, a Charities Aid Foundation (CAF) report on FTSE 100 companies[2] suggests that corporate giving (as reported by FTSE 100 companies) increased substantially between 2007 and 2012; the total amount given to charitable causes in both the UK and overseas grew from about £1.3 billion in 2007 to just under £2.5 billion in 2012.[3]

It is not the purpose of this chapter to summarise all of the findings of these studies, but it seems that the starting point for many of these studies can be summarised in one central and fundamental question: what drives businesses to give to or invest in charitable causes? By answering this question, there is the potential to find helpful indicators of which types of company it is best to target and which methods might have the best chance of success depending on the nature of your organisation.

Economic factors

The predominant way of finding out more about what motivates companies to support good causes has been to analyse both historical and existing data to uncover patterns of variables related to corporate giving. In an attempt to identify these patterns, researchers have first looked at the relationship between economic performance and the level of giving. It has been well recorded in this field that a time of economic downturn is often followed by charities reporting a decline in their funding, and it is unsurprising that recession affects companies' ability to give.[4] A company's financial performance affects the level of its charitable giving: if a company contributes a fixed percentage of its profits to charitable causes, a year of poor performance puts significant limits on its charitable capacity.[5] Indeed, the 2016 CAF report on FTSE 100 companies showed a decrease in total giving to charities, which reflected a fall in these companies' revenues and pre-tax profits.[6]

In addition to being largely pro-cyclical (i.e. corporate giving goes up and down in line with general economic performance), a company's level of giving in financial analyses has been shown to relate to a number of other factors. These include spending on research and development, cash flow, profits, lagged profits (i.e. companies which make a high profit in a given financial year will tend to increase their giving the *next year*), low levels of leverage (borrowing), corporate tax rate and institutional ownership.[7] Generally speaking, bigger companies give higher amounts; Amato and Amato, for example, found a positive relationship between financial performance and corporate giving.[8] Thus, when identifying organisations most likely to give substantial amounts to charity, the evidence suggests, on the one hand, that the best approach is to look to a large, profitable company which is spending substantial amounts on research and development, has low levels of borrowing, has high levels of institutional ownership and is operating in a low-tax environment. On the other hand, given the variety of ways in which companies can contribute, it is worth exploring smaller businesses which may give as generously (in terms of percentage of their pre-tax profit) or offer support through services or in-kind gifts. (See 'Learning points from other countries' on page 40.) In addition, Amato and Amato observe that smaller companies tend to have close relationships with the community, which creates local incentives to give.

Societal pressures: social responsibility trend

The levels of giving by FTSE 100 companies grew significantly between the early 1990s and 2012,[9] which cannot be accounted for simply by economic growth. A factor that has likely added to this growth is the increasing social trend where businesses are expected to be responsible for their wider social impact, and researchers agree that this trend can be explained by the rise in importance of corporate responsibility. The idea that businesses should deliver social, ethical and/or environmental benefits while seeking to produce profits is not new, but in the last 25 years or so there has been growing pressure on businesses – especially big, multinational ones – to respond to social issues.[10]

Researchers have suggested that this growing pressure can be explained by stakeholder theory, a model for understanding business management that places corporate philanthropy within a broad framework of agents. In this view, a business independently engaged in a not-for-profit enterprise responds to the interests and needs of a range of stakeholders: not just its employees or customers but also its beneficiaries and charity supporters.[11] Brammer and Pavelin identify a positive relationship between individual company giving and level of company activity in countries linked with poor human rights and civil liberties records. They suggest that, in order to retain stakeholder approval (among customers, shareholders and so on), corporate responsibility activity is required to offset the negative reputational impact of operating in countries associated with poor civil liberties records.

Similarly, globalisation of business has presented big consumer goods companies with the need to address the social, ethical and/or environmental impact of their business. The same researchers, and others, back up this point by highlighting that companies in the oil, mining and minerals industries have been noted to give considerably more than those in other industries. This may be because of the impact these industries make on the environment and local communities, which are often located overseas (in relation to the company's headquarters).[12] (The impact of a business's industry on its levels of giving has also been explored in the body of practical-style research; see 'Top industry givers' on page 36.)

Another example of this trend is the fair trade movement. Whereas it was initially a small and niche scheme, companies such as Coca-Cola, Nestlé and Unilever now invest in fair trade resources, which are growing at a rate of 12% per year.[13] In line with stakeholder theory, researchers have also found a number of social changes that have influenced the nature and pattern of corporate giving. For instance, Low and Davenport suggest that consumers have increasingly become aware of the negative impact of their consumption and ethical implications; these authors argue that ethical consumerism is an important factor behind the twenty-first-century increase in corporate giving.[14]

The nature and limitations of research

In general, the overriding majority of academic researchers analyse the internal mechanisms and financial frameworks of companies rather than charities. At the same time, the bulk of academic research takes a predominantly theoretical, conceptual approach to this topic. This explains why much of the discussion in this section has revolved around corporate *giving* rather than corporate *fundraising*. This business-orientated view of corporate giving is important in understanding the inner workings and financial and managerial mechanisms of corporate charitable activity and, although often theoretical, can point you to markers which may suggest a company ripe for partnership. It can also offer you an overall strategic context for long-term planning.

A useful addition to the field of observational studies of what drives corporate giving would be more truly longitudinal studies. These are observations of individual companies over time that attempt to determine causal factors behind substantial changes in corporate giving, rather than looking at changes in giving in the round over time. Other longitudinal studies that use snapshots of variables that are related to corporate giving in different companies would be useful to have as well.

Most financial modelling of corporate giving has necessarily been driven by large, international organisations due to their stricter financial reporting regulations. Notably, in the UK, these stricter regulations were relaxed through reforms to the Companies Act 2006. Starting with the 2012/13 financial year, companies in the UK no longer have a legal obligation to declare charitable donations. This can pose further problems when evaluating their contributions and trying to build a picture of what a company's giving exactly entails.

Broader analysis of giving by small to medium-sized organisations could also add to the academic debate on corporate giving. Do the same pressures and drivers tend to influence medium-sized national enterprises as they do global FTSE 100 companies?

The academic approach has produced a considerable bias towards theoretical debates on financial performance and corporate responsibility, and a focus on managerial aspects of corporate giving: the role of CEOs and senior managers and the strategic motivation behind corporate giving. Regardless of the size of the company, given that these are questions for a handful of senior managers, the full picture of views across companies is not known. The dominance of theoretical studies is indicative of the paucity of empirical, qualitative studies in academic research and leaves some fundamental questions unanswered.[15] What is the proportion of companies that engage in charitable giving? What is their average income and size? What is the most useful definition of corporate giving – monetary gifts, donations, volunteering or a combination of these? Which industries or sectors have the highest level of corporate giving? What is the relationship between corporate giving and corporate brand?

The absence of substantial academic agreement on these questions has made it challenging for others researching the subject to even agree on what constitutes corporate giving, how it can be measured and how it can be compared between countries. It has also led to a heavy focus on financial support for charities at the expense of other forms of support, such as provision of pro bono help, volunteering hours and gifts in kind.

While some academic researchers have touched upon these issues, it is what we have termed practical research – conducted by charities, think tanks and other public bodies closer to the charity sector itself – that we turn to in order to obtain more comprehensive answers to these questions.

Practical-style research in or about the UK

At first glance the body of practical research on corporate fundraising/giving makes a striking contrast to academic research. The length of each study is usually shorter, and there is a focus on clearly presented facts and figures, not to mention graphs and charts, rather than conceptual analysis. Most importantly, its primary audience is practitioners in charities, and its goal is to help charities to maximise their corporate fundraising.

34

Corporate giving trends

The annual *Civil Society Almanac* compiled by the National Council for Voluntary Organisations (NCVO) records voluntary sector income from the private sector in the UK (including cash and in-kind donations, sponsorship, research, and contracts and subcontracts). The almanac's figures from 2000 onwards show no clear trends but rather indicate an initial decrease year on year from £1.8 billion in 2000 to £0.8 billion in 2003, a substantial increase to £2.6 billion in 2004, followed by steady fluctuations between 2005 and 2014.[16]

CAF, as noted in the academic section, reported an increase in total and median giving of FTSE 100 companies between 2007 and 2012 (see page 31).[17] The latest CAF FTSE 100 findings show a decrease in total giving to charities from 2011 to 2014. However, they also show that the median donation rose fairly steadily between 2009 and 2014, suggesting that a small number of the FTSE 100 companies reduced their giving but that most were still giving at levels similar to those of the preceding years.[18]

Comparing financial data in the UK

'Comparing financial data globally' on page 40 shows the difficulty of comparing financial data across different countries. In fact, differences in methodology can paint very different pictures even within the same country. For instance, research by the Directory of Social Change (DSC) on company giving in the UK looks at corporate contributions from over 400 UK-registered companies. According to findings reported in the latest publication, over £420 million was given in community support in the UK in 2015.[19] Compared with the NCVO figure of £1.9 billion listed in table 3.1 (see page 41), such levels of support from companies may seem relatively low. DSC's figures, however, strictly include only cash and in-kind contributions recorded by what is given by companies, as listed in their annual reports and accounts, or corporate responsibility reports (whereas NCVO's methodology is to use income figures that charities have listed in their annual accounts). In addition, wherever possible, DSC's figures exclude sponsorship, commercially led support, funds raised by employees or customers, management costs and similar expenditures – all these elements are reported on in detail but not reflected in the final figure.

As noted, NCVO's figures record the private sector income that charities list in their annual accounts. These figures include cash and in-kind contributions but also research support, marketing sponsorship and contracts made with charities. The income recorded can include donations from anywhere in the world, not just the UK (as long as the donations are made to a UK charity). In contrast, DSC's research records donations made by UK-registered companies (even if global entities) and, if possible, breaks down the donations further to differentiate between support in the UK and overseas.

This shows how variances in the approach to research can help us see and understand various aspects of corporate giving better but they also hinder meaningful comparisons.

Top industry givers

DSC's *The Company Giving Almanac 2013* highlights that corporate funders tend to assist in areas which are linked to their business, either geographically or by association with a product or service (such as a toy company supporting a children's hospice). Its findings show that, when choosing causes to support, companies tend to favour those that affect the widest possible section of society. The report suggests that these decisions are often tied to companies' marketing and PR strategies and so they look for causes that are more likely to appeal to current and future customers. For example, they are more likely to support the areas of community development, social welfare, education, or children and young people (supported by over 50% of the companies in the sample). Far fewer companies (under 10% of the sample) assist causes that are generally less widely supported, such as equal opportunities, human rights or women's causes.[20]

Findings from this report also show that the financial sector, which demonstrates the highest turnover and pre-tax profit figures of all the corporate sectors defined in the report (including, for example, utilities and telecoms), accounted for the most charitable giving in terms of both cash and in-kind contributions. The second-highest giver was consumer services. The least charitable support was recorded from the technology sector, followed by the healthcare industry as the second-lowest contributor.[21] Similar findings (but with categories broken up differently in some instances) are seen in Institute of Fundraising research which reported that charities received the most support from the finance sector, followed by retail (which corresponds with consumer services). The lowest amount of support was given by the pharmaceutical, utilities and hospitality/leisure sectors.[22]

When creating your corporate partnership or fundraising strategy, it is worth considering the probability of your charity's success in relation to its cause versus the industry the targeted company is in. As *The Company Giving Almanac* points out, while most companies favour community and social welfare, education, and children and young people's causes, there are industry-wide differences: if your charity's cause is in the area of the environment, for example, it might be more strategically sound to specifically target the utilities and oil and gas sectors, which are reported as the strongest supporters of this cause.[23] Another angle to consider strategically is whether you can target an industry that links in some way (geographically or by product or service association) with your cause.

Increases in strategic partnerships

As well as financial analysis, researchers in this area have focused on the changing nature of relationships and partnerships between companies and charities. One notable trend is the increase in strategic partnerships between businesses and charities, defined as deeper, problem-solving relationships that attempt to address core issues and provide direct benefit to service users through the partnerships.

The *C&E Corporate–NGO Partnerships Barometer* regular survey of business and charity employees shows that 79% of corporate respondents say their company has a strategic partnership with a non-governmental organisation – a figure that has increased since C&E's research into corporate partnerships began in 2010. The equivalent figure for NGOs, however, is only 32%, suggesting that they could benefit from taking a more strategic approach to partnerships.[24]

Additionally, research from other countries suggests that, where corporate giving is closely aligned with business interests and structures, strategic long-term relationships seem to be the preferred way forward (see also 'Learning points from other countries' on page 40).

Corporate foundations

nfpSynergy's 2017 report, *Strong Foundations*, looks at the fuzzier area of corporate foundations – charities established and largely funded by companies. The report covers the scale, structure and financial patterns of some of the UK's largest corporate foundations. Little research has been done in this area in the past, and it will be interesting to keep track of developments in this field.

The report highlights that there is generally little opportunity for fundraisers to be involved with these foundations, which commonly lack a grant-application process.[25] It is a significant point to keep in mind that potential growth in corporate foundations as vehicles for corporate giving may disrupt the classic direct relationship between corporation and charity. Such an outcome is not unlikely, given that corporate foundations can be a relatively easy way for companies to fulfil their corporate philanthropy goals and keep their business and charitable activities relatively separate.

Perspectives of corporate executives

One of the great assets to fundraisers of research in this area is the wealth of research from surveys and interviews of executives and others working in corporations, both in the UK (for example, the *C&E Corporate–NGO Partnerships Barometer* surveys, which have been coming out yearly since 2010) and abroad.[26] These pieces of research can provide you and your corporate partners with honest insights into each party's motivations for entering into partnerships and inform your approach to fundraising.

In the 2017 C&E report, 93% of corporate representatives surveyed answered that their aim was to enhance the company's reputation and credibility.[27] While this is to be expected, the survey also shows high rates of corporations seeking innovation and access to people and contacts, suggesting that it is good to emphasise what your organisation can offer businesses in practical terms.

Perspectives of corporate fundraisers

The Institute of Fundraising's *Corporate Fundraising: A snapshot of current practice in the UK non-profit sector* provides insight into the other side of the relationship and highlights perceived best practice among corporate fundraisers. The report provides benchmarks both in terms of finance and in terms of softer measures, such as types of corporate partnership and team structures.

The aim of the report is to provide practical evidence of what makes a corporate fundraising programme successful. It concludes that the vast majority of respondents plan to invest more in corporate fundraising and expect it to be an area of growth.

The report highlights both long-lasting programmes and those with strong internal leadership at a senior level as markers of a successful partnership. As such, it advises cultivating and extending existing partnerships (not simply focusing on new business) to create a corporate fundraising programme that makes a significantly positive impact on your charity. Linked to this, it also recommends creating strategic partnerships – and more proactively proposing them to corporates – in order to raise more for your charity. Respondents noted that a key way to grow effective strategic partnerships is by having strong relationship management and ensuring support from senior leadership.[28]

Carried out in July 2015, this report is a solid overview of how corporate fundraising is conducted in the UK. We hope this research will be updated in years to come.

Perspectives of consumers

A global study by Cone Communications and Ebiquity on consumer attitudes to corporate responsibility highlighted that, for companies in the UK, being seen to be socially and environmentally responsible is crucial for building and protecting their reputation. It observes that, while UK citizens have high expectations that companies should endeavour to do more than simply make a profit, they view companies more sceptically than the citizens of other countries do (57% of UK respondents do not believe that companies try to be as responsible as they can, versus the global average of 52%). UK citizens have to hear about a company's positive efforts before they believe it is endeavouring to be responsible. They are also less likely than people in other countries to take part in a company's corporate responsibility activities.

However, UK citizens are more likely than the global average (70% vs 61%) to donate to a charity that is supported by a company. This tendency towards supporting a charity directly, rather than via a company's corporate responsibility efforts, might be explained by UK citizens' lower levels of belief versus citizens in other countries that companies have made a significant impact on social or environmental issues (15% vs 27%) or that these issues can be helped by buying products (14% vs 29%).

On the flip side, UK citizens are the most inclined, among all the countries surveyed, not to take note of corporate responsibility messages until something goes wrong (59% vs the global average of 50%). Furthermore, although they have a better understanding than other countries' citizens of corporate responsibility terminology, they are more liable to find corporate responsibility messages confusing (71% vs the global average of 65%) and more likely to ignore these messages for the reason of not understanding them (72% vs the global average of 64%).[29]

Companies have to be aware that, to counteract the less than glowing view the UK public has of them, they must take considerable efforts to prove their active engagement in social and environmental issues and that they can indeed make a positive impact. Given the UK public's apparent greater confidence in charities' ability to effect social and environmental change, this suggests that the best approach for companies is to work in close partnership with a charity to take advantage of the positive impact for companies created by these corporate–charity associations.

There are also some crucial learning points for companies and charities working in partnership in the UK. They must:

• communicate in an absolutely clear way and offer proof of how the corporate–charity link or partnership is changing the world socially or environmentally for the better;

• communicate plainly about how consumers' purchases and actions can and do lead to positive social and environmental impact;

• show how the corporate–charity partnership is making an impact independent of the participation of the consumer.

The utility of practical-style research

In terms of day-to-day practice, many of the non-academic research sources are likely to provide you with a much more useful background than the academic sources. Understanding how the market is changing for your organisation as well as other charities provides a useful opportunity to benchmark overall performance against the market. Meanwhile, reports identifying trends in the types of partnership being made between companies and charities help to ensure that you are at the cutting edge when it comes to forming your own partnerships and are making the most of opportunities provided by working with business.

The focus on understanding drivers of corporate giving in this strand of research has been on surveys of executives at large companies, charity sector research on which industries give the most and to which causes, and perspectives from corporate fundraisers and consumers (in addition to executives). This provides a welcome addition to the more theoretical models of the academic research sector. However, more could be done in reports aimed at fundraisers to draw on the experience of academic researchers and to place survey findings within a theoretical framework. While surveys are an important way to uncover the views of relevant individuals, it is important to compare and contrast these findings with the actual financial achievements that corporate–charity partnerships have made. In an ideal research world, the two sets of data would provide a positive feedback loop to one another to deepen our understanding of the factors that really influence corporate giving and partnerships with charities.

Again, it is also often the case that researchers focus on larger charities and corporates, or on partnerships such as the one between Boots and Macmillan Cancer Support, perhaps providing less guidance for small to medium-sized organisations. While non-academic research offers more individual examples than academic research on this subject, more benchmarking and indication of best practice for smaller organisations attempting to develop a corporate fundraising programme could be a useful addition to the area of corporate fundraising research.

Learning points from other countries

There has been little by way of comparative studies of corporate giving in other countries. This is perhaps a consequence of the difficulties in comparing levels of corporate giving across different countries resulting from the lack of an agreed common standard for what constitutes corporate giving. Nevertheless, there are a number of sources of information available on corporate giving in other anglophone countries that you may find useful for finding a new perspective on fundraising practices.

Comparing financial data globally

At first glance, comparing corporate giving between countries could provide a helpful measure of the maturity of corporate giving in a market.

We can identify at least one best guess of the figure for overall corporate giving in each of several anglophone countries, and these are presented in table 3.1 along with sources. Although giving the total per capita is unlikely to be the best way to analyse these figures, as population size is not necessarily directly proportional to corporate income, it is the most practical way in the absence of a consistent measure of national pre-tax profits in each country.

TABLE 3.1 Comparing levels of corporate giving between countries

Country	Total[30]	Total per capita[31]	Source
UK	£1.90 billion	£29	NCVO, 2017[32]
USA	£12.87 billion	£40	Indiana University Lilly Family School of Philanthropy, 2016[33]
Canada	£1.84 billion	£51	Statistics Canada, 2003[34]
Australia	£10.46 billion	£434	Australian Department of Social Services, 2016[35]
New Zealand	£36.81 million	£8	Philanthropy New Zealand, 2015[36]

Table 3.1 clearly illustrates the challenges of comparing financial contributions between countries. Unless we are to believe that Australian companies are over 50 times more generous in their gifts to charities than their New Zealand counterparts, it immediately becomes clear that there are substantial differences in how countries measure corporate giving (even allowing for the fact that there may be more businesses per capita in Australia). Furthermore, the Australian Bureau of Statistics reported the corporate giving figure for Australia in 2012/13 to be AU$863 million; with this in mind, it appears to be highly improbable that there was such a large actual increase to AU$17.5 billion within three years – it seems more likely that this increase was caused, at least in part, by a difference in methodology.[37]

But perhaps there are other ways in which we can learn from the experience of other countries other than by simply comparing finances. Indeed, there are several reports available from beyond the UK that summarise trends in corporate giving in the English-speaking world and beyond. While the financial elements may not be directly comparable, you may still find trends in income and reported drivers of action, satisfaction and innovation in corporate partnerships abroad to be helpful for enhancing your corporate fundraising strategy.

Drivers and difficulties of Australian corporate giving

Although few reports appear to have been written on this subject in Australia in the last decade or so, Adrian Sargeant and Kathryn Crissman's 2006 paper 'Corporate Giving in Australia: An analysis of motives and barriers' provides a comprehensive overview of trends in the first half of the 2000s. Sargeant and Crissman report that corporate giving made up 29% of all giving in Australia in 2005 compared to 7% in the USA and just 3% in the UK – suggesting either a markedly more developed corporate giving market in Australia or simply a more diverse basket of fundraising methods elsewhere.[38]

The report also studies in depth the motivations of companies to engage in corporate philanthropy, as collated through a large-scale and thorough quantitative and qualitative research exercise conducted with Australian businesses. Motivations reported in the study included boosting employee morale, increased publicity, tax relief, and image- and relationship-building; however, for most Australian businesses, one of their motivations to give was altruism.

The findings also suggested that smaller entities and large businesses may experience barriers to charitable giving differently. (These points are worth bearing in mind when targeting potential funders, as such barriers to giving are not necessarily exclusive to Australia.) Many enterprises, especially the larger ones, reported feeling inundated with requests for support. Smaller organisations more often lack established policies and structures for giving and so a barrier for them is the lack of a clear way to make informed decisions when choosing from among the various alternatives. They tend to engage in ad hoc philanthropy as a result. Larger enterprises are more likely to have the resources to employ a more structured approach to these applications.

A more significant barrier for larger businesses is inadequate feedback from not-for-profit organisations. These larger businesses report a desire for transparency and accountability regarding the funds they provide: how exactly the money was used, feedback on the impact the donation had and so on. Showing, therefore, that your charity can communicate transparently on how the corporate's funds are being used and can provide impact reports will put you at an advantage, especially with larger corporate organisations.

Socially responsible millennials across the globe

A more recent research project, *Giving Australia 2016*, alludes to the impact that a new generation of the workforce is having on changing corporate attitudes towards social responsibility.[39] It suggests that millennials as employees expect to be more involved in decision-making in the workplace and want to feel engaged with the employer and the impact the business has.

Such observations can also be found in research by Cone Communications in the USA, which suggests that millennials are more willing than the average American to participate in corporate responsibility activities and more likely to be ready to make personal sacrifices in order to contribute to a wider social impact (such as switching to a more expensive, yet socially or environmentally responsible, brand or settling for a lower salary at a more ethical company).[40] They are also more inclined to voice their opinions to the businesses and want to hear about the businesses' corporate responsibility efforts – 93% feel more positive about companies after finding out what their social and environmental impact is. A global survey by Deloitte confirms these findings and shows that 76% of millennials consider business to be a means of achieving positive social impact and 86% agree that the success of a business cannot be measured solely in financial terms. The findings also suggest that millennials show greater levels of loyalty and have a more positive view of a business when given a chance to get involved in charitable activities at or through the workplace.[41]

A focus on employees – their recruitment, retention, satisfaction and engagement – plays an important role in Australian corporates' decisions to engage in charitable giving.[42] If such a trend is to grow and expand in other countries, this opens up more opportunities for employees to not merely follow the company's set agenda but actually shape and influence the direction the business is taking in its social contributions. Moreover, changing workplace demographics and a growing workforce of socially responsible employees are likely to affect corporate involvement.

Charities should not overlook this shift and must consider the long-term value of building relationships with corporate bodies through their people. In addition, the significant benefit of increased employee engagement and loyalty, especially with regard to millennials, is one of a collection of benefits to highlight when seeking or negotiating a corporate partnership.

Going beyond cash in New Zealand and Canada

Giving New Zealand is a report published by Philanthropy New Zealand every four to five years which looks at total giving in New Zealand broken down into giving by individuals, trusts and businesses. The latest report (in 2014) suggests that corporate giving makes up around 3% of giving in New Zealand, a number that is similar to previous estimates for the UK. Interestingly, New Zealand has seen a decline in income from corporate giving since 2011, although this may be substantially due to a natural fall after the 2011 peak that followed the Christchurch earthquake.[43] In addition to offering financial analysis, the report notes that although relatively low levels of giving in cash might give the impression of modest levels of support, there is evidence that businesses in New Zealand are giving more substantially otherwise – i.e. through sponsorship and in-kind contributions in the form of goods and services.

Imagine Canada has published a range of reports, including *Insights for Strategic Corporate Fundraising* (2010), which details findings from a very broad survey of Canadian businesses combined with qualitative insight and analysis of financial data.[44] The report contains large-scale, yet detailed, information on the propensities of different industries and sectors to donate different amounts, in different ways and for different reasons. It highlights a wide variety of methods in which Canadian corporates assist non-profit organisations and observes that focusing solely on financial contributions can be detrimental to a successful bid. In addition to employee volunteering and professional services, companies can facilitate fundraising from their employees and match staff contributions, and they are more inclined to donate to causes that employees are already engaged with (46% of businesses support causes that employees volunteer for).

This type of observation, seen in many countries, serves as a helpful reminder to explore the many ways in which a company can give.

Ad hoc giving, company size and overcoming funding barriers

In 2014, Philanthropy Ireland published a report entitled *Corporate Giving in Ireland*, which was the result of interviews with key decision makers on philanthropy within companies operating in Ireland. This report suggests that there is little by way of strategy in corporate giving in Ireland, with most companies tending to give in an ad hoc way without long-term planning or strategic goals in mind.

For most domestic companies, the CEO plays the major role in choosing which charities to support; however, employees and their charitable preferences also play a significant role – 53% of companies rely on employees' choices to select recipients of cash donations or other support.[45]

Financial contributions are the most common means of corporate giving in Ireland and the preferred option for small and medium enterprises. Larger and multinational entities, meanwhile, are more open to other forms of corporate giving, such as in-kind donations or employee engagement. The report indicates that there is the potential to engage smaller businesses in a wider range of philanthropy by demonstrating easily applied and managed, and cost-effective, means of supporting charities. This sort of barrier can also be seen elsewhere; Canadian businesses too indicate that their main challenge is a lack of sufficient resources, time and people to respond to and manage requests for support.[46]

These findings suggest that companies with fewer resources to fully explore charitable giving and establish a structured system may require clearer information from charities on the benefits of partnering, and guidance on the mechanisms of how to do so, but nevertheless can be as valuable partners as well-established major givers.

In the Philanthropy Ireland report, funding constraints were noted as the main barrier to engaging in corporate giving by all types of businesses in Ireland. Again, the researchers suggest that demonstrating the many benefits of corporate giving to the business itself (for example, those laid out by Business in the Community)[47] can help a corporate donor to view charitable support as an investment rather than just a donation.[48]

Targeting the right sector

As in the UK market, the finance and insurance sector is the biggest giver in Canada (90% of businesses in this sector donate cash), according to the Imagine Canada 2010 report. However, findings from this research suggest that focusing on a part of the private sector where there seems to be a lot of money flowing may not be the most efficient way to secure support. In fact, as highlighted in the section on practical research, targeting the right sector with the right bid is the key to maximising potential help from corporate bodies.

For example, findings show that intermediary businesses (those operating between the manufacturer and the consumer) are more likely to engage in product donations than manufacturers themselves. Almost 40% of construction and primary industries in Canada offer equipment donations and 43% of all businesses provide free-of-charge services to charities. This amounts to a significant proportion of the private sector that can be helpful in ways beyond direct financial support.[49] This valuable insight into the advisability of targeting the most apposite sector is worth considering in any corporate fundraising strategy.

Influencing from the ground up

An earlier report from Imagine Canada suggests that levels of business giving are, in great part, the result of the overall philanthropic culture of the country.[50] It highlights the findings of a study that show 85% of Canadians make charitable donations and 45% volunteer their time for good causes. Such interests then organically transfer into the workplace through employees and business leaders.[51] Responsible and forward-thinking consumers are also influencing how companies devise their marketing strategies – competition for businesses is not only about offering the best product or service but also about showing that they are socially responsible in more or better ways than their rivals.

In addition, Canadian businesses place a strong value on 'healthy communities' (which is recognised as a good condition for business) and sees corporate giving as means to address this. Of the companies in the sample, 50% reported improving communities to be a motivation for them to provide support, and only a slightly lower proportion (46%) noted maintaining a good relationship with the community as a significant motivator.[52]

This evidence from Canada suggests that effectively engaging corporate support can begin less directly, from the bottom up – through influencing employees and business customers as well as developing a general culture of giving.

A trend towards strategic partnerships

KCI Philanthropy (a Canadian organisation that helps philanthropic organisations) publishes its *Philanthropic Trends Quarterly* four times a year, which looks at various aspects of charitable giving in the country. The latest issue focusing on corporate giving is from 2011, and it touches on the growing trend towards strategic partnerships in Canada.[53] It notes the growing tendency of companies not only to tailor their corporate responsibility activities in a more strategic manner (such as by engaging in partnerships that yield mutual benefits, setting goals, and closely measuring and evaluating the impact the company's support is making) but also to get involved far beyond the signing of a cheque.

This seems to resonate with experience in other anglophone countries. For instance, *Giving Australia 2016* notes that the country's corporate community investment is more orientated towards the business interests of the corporate funder than it is in the USA or Europe. This puts pressure on companies to make sure both that their business interests are satisfied and that their desired social impact is achieved.[54]

In these ways, community investment is becoming a competitive area; it is becoming increasingly important, therefore, to offer innovative means for corporates to contribute in ways that enhance their commercial interests.

Are large, profitable companies really the most generous?

The latest *Giving USA* report (for the year 2015) shows a record year for charitable giving and an increase in charitable contributions by companies. Despite these positive results, corporate giving constitutes the lowest proportion of all charitable contributions in the USA and amounts to 5% overall. This pattern can be seen in other anglophone countries as well.

It is illuminating, however, to compare these overall giving levels with US corporate giving as a percentage of pre-tax profits. From 1975 to

2015, the percentage fluctuated between 0.8% and 1.8% and was low from the beginning of the 2000s, subsequently falling down to 0.8% in 2015 (the same level as in 1975).[55] An increase in donations may not necessarily equate to greater overall generosity (relatively speaking) when considered in terms of giving as a percentage of pre-tax profits. In the UK, research has found that the biggest proportion of corporate giving (90% of cash donations in the UK) is contributed by the top 20% of companies, which tend to be financially robust, powerful global entities.[56] The conclusion from this could be that these financially robust companies are the most generous. This is likely the case in absolute terms, yet it might not be the case in relative terms when comparing the proportion of giving against levels of pre-tax profits. It is worth keeping this in mind to avoid the danger of overlooking the vast majority of the private sector, which gives less overall but potentially equally generously, or perhaps even more so.

Globally reported advantages of corporate responsibility for companies

A study conducted by Cone Communications on consumer attitudes to corporate responsibility observes that companies' efforts in this area constitute a key element for businesses to improve their brand reputation and favourability among customers. According to the findings, consumers from nine countries (Brazil, Canada, China, France, Germany, India, Japan, the UK and the USA) expect vastly more from businesses than just making profits and, as the significance of corporate responsibility increases around the world, look for even deeper engagement.[57]

This study makes some observations that could be used to highlight to companies the potential advantages of partnering with a charity. Combining results from all countries, consumers:

• take note of a company's corporate responsibility activities, in a positive sense, only if that company is clearly exceeding the efforts of other companies (they also notice negative media attention about poor corporate responsibility);

• have a more positive image of a company (93%) if they see it addressing social or environmental issues, and are more likely to trust it (90%) and to stay loyal to it (88%);

• see a greater role for themselves than just paying money to create social and environmental change;

• overwhelmingly believe (91%) that companies must do more than make a profit and must also address social and environmental issues;

• see companies as a means for them to take social or environmental action via buying socially and environmentally responsible products or services (84%);

• will opt, when choosing between two products of similar price and quality, for the product with social or environmental benefits;

• state that they would like companies to offer *more* of these types of socially or environmentally responsible product (90%).

Indeed, some consumers feel so strongly about what is better for the environment and society that they are likely to make some smaller or greater sacrifices, including being willing to:

• be paid less in order to work for a more responsible company (62%);

• consume or purchase fewer products (81%);

• share or borrow products rather than own them (61%);

• purchase a lower-quality product if it would have a better impact on society or the environment than another better product;

• buy a product from a brand they don't know if it has stronger social or environmental commitments (80%);

• pay more for a product that helps to address social or environmental issues (71%).

There are opportunities, therefore, to highlight to your potential corporate partner the public's desire for more responsible product options (their propensity to choose the more responsible product over other products), their high expectations for companies to address social and environmental issues, and their preference for working for a responsible company.

Conclusion

Although there are many individual sources of data and researchers in the field of corporate fundraising and corporate giving, on the whole, research in this area appears a little disjointed. Academic models of giving propensity are built with little reference to the day-to-day experience of charities and fundraisers, while research designed to inform fundraisers and strategists is often interpreted without reference to these very models. What this suggests is that charity personnel looking to increase their corporate fundraising or corporate partnerships still struggle to find practical advice as to how to approach businesses, what types of partnership to build and how to set a realistic financial target.

Research in this area is also limited in a very real way by the lack of a common definition of corporate giving between countries, and even between charities and companies within the same country. It is also important to remember that the public perceptions and the social roles of charities are different in each country, and this may inform the way companies view their corporate responsibility towards charities. This is likely to remain the case in the near future unless common standards for comparison are found.

Financial reports will help you to understand trends in your organisation's income in the context of the broader market – financial models may help you to make your own predictions about what lies ahead for this income stream. Surveys of company corporate responsibility executives provide an insight into how corporate partners view best practice in the field of corporate fundraising. More qualitative research into the features of corporate partnerships is needed, however, to help to inspire fundraisers and company executives alike to find new ways to work together for mutual benefit.

These research and data sources can provide a vital tool for remaining abreast of developments in your field, and luckily in the UK there are institutions such as CAF, the Institute of Fundraising, and NCVO, and companies such as C&E and Deloitte, that produce regular reports. Strategies for raising funds from corporate sources should always be informed by available research to ensure that you are following the most up-to-date best practice and innovations in the field rather than continually reinventing the wheel.

Notes

1   Taha Afshar, *Corporate Philanthropy in the UK and US: The impact of cycles, strategy and CEO succession*, PhD thesis, London School of Economics, 2010.

2   An example of where research overlaps with both categories: the data is taken from the perspective of companies; however, the report is produced by a charity and the style is concise and numbers driven, not conceptual.

3   *Corporate Giving by the FTSE 100*, West Malling, Charities Aid Foundation, 2014, p. 12.

4   *Charities in Recession: A survey report*, West Malling, Charities Aid Foundation, 1993; *UK Giving, 2010: An overview of charitable giving in the UK, 2009/10*, West Malling, Charities Aid Foundation, 2010; *Making the Most of What We Have: Corporate giving in the new economy*, Stamford CT, LBG Research Institute, 2009; Taha Afshar, *Corporate Philanthropy in the UK and US: The impact of cycles, strategy and CEO succession*, PhD thesis, London School of Economics, 2010.

5   Baruch Lev, Christine Petrovis and Suresh Radhakrishnan, 'Is Doing Good Good for You? How corporate charitable contributions enhance revenue growth', *Strategic Management Journal*, vol. 31, 2010, pp. 182–200.

6   *Corporate Giving by the FTSE 100*, West Malling, Charities Aid Foundation, 2016, p. 4.

7   Taha Afshar, *Corporate Philanthropy in the UK and US: The impact of cycles, strategy and CEO succession*, PhD thesis, London School of Economics, 2010.

8   Louis H. Amato and Christie H. Amato, 'The Effects of Firm Size and Industry on Corporate Giving', *Journal of Business Ethics*, vol. 72, 2007, pp. 229–41.

9   *Corporate Giving by the FTSE 100*, West Malling, Charities Aid Foundation, 2016, p. 4.

10   Stephen J. Brammer and Stephen Pavelin, 'Corporate Community Contributions in the United Kingdom and the United States', *Journal of Business Ethics*, vol. 56, 2005, pp. 15–26; Stephen J. Brammer, Stephen Pavelin and Lynda A. Porter, 'Corporate Social Performance and Geographical Diversification', *Journal of Business Research,* vol. 59, 2006, pp. 1025–34; Taha Afshar, *Corporate Philanthropy in the UK and US: The impact of cycles, strategy and CEO succession*, PhD thesis, London School of Economics, 2010.

11   Stephen J. Brammer and Stephen Pavelin, 'Corporate Community Contributions in the United Kingdom and the United States', *Journal of Business Ethics*, vol. 56, 2005, pp. 15–26.

12   Stephen J. Brammer, Stephen Pavelin and Lynda A. Porter, 'Corporate Social Performance and Geographical Diversification', *Journal of Business Research,* vol. 59, 2006, pp. 1025–34; Cathy Pharoah and Catherine Walker, *The Values of Corporate Giving: An overview of models with case studies*, London, CGAP/ DSC, 2015.

13   Cathy Pharoah and Catherine Walker, *The Values of Corporate Giving: An overview of models with case studies*, London, CGAP/DSC, 2015.

14   William Low and Eileen Davenport, 'To Boldly Go: Exploring ethical spaces to repoliticise ethical consumption and fair trade', *Journal of Consumer Behaviour,* vol. 6, no. 5, 2007, pp. 336–48.

15   Meta Zimmeck and Cathy Pharoah, *The Values of Corporate Giving: An update on key figures and trends*, London, CGAP, 2015.

16   Claire Benard, Joy Dobbs, Jack Egan, Lisa Hornung, Veronique Jochum, Marc Lawson, Gareth Lloyd and Nick Ockendon, *The UK Civil Society Almanac 2017*, London, NCVO, 2017.

17   *Corporate Giving by the FTSE 100*, West Malling, Charities Aid Foundation, 2014, p. 12.

18   *Corporate Giving by the FTSE 100*, West Malling, Charities Aid Foundation, 2016, p. 7.

19   Jennifer Reynolds, Jodie Huyton and Carly Hobson, *The Guide to UK Company Giving*, London, DSC, 2017, p. vi. The figure of £420 million is based on the latest available data from companies' annual reports that were published by each company featured in the guide. The financial years of these reports were usually 2014/15, 2015 or 2015/16.

20   Catherine Walker, *The Company Giving Almanac 2013*, London, DSC, pp. 84–85.

21   Catherine Walker, *The Company Giving Almanac 2013*, London, DSC, p. 105, fig. 6.4.

22   *Corporate Fundraising: A snapshot of current practice in the UK non-profit sector*, London, Institute of Fundraising, 2015, p. 21.

23   Catherine Walker, *The Company Giving Almanac 2013*, London, DSC, p. 101.

24   *C&E Corporate–NGO Partnerships Barometer*, London, C&E Advisory Services, 2017, pp. 4 and 11.

25   Megan Williams and Joe Saxton, *Strong Foundations: How corporate foundations raise money and do good work*, London, nfpSynergy, p. 12.

26 For example, Giving Australia received 2,705 replies from companies and conducted some in-depth interviews with key corporate personnel; KCI Philanthropy in Canada provides details in 'The Corporate Giving Issue' (*Philanthropic Giving Quarterly*, vol. 2011, no. 4, 2011) about what corporate donors are seeking in their relationships with charity partners; and Philanthropy Ireland conducted interviews with key decision makers within companies in charge of philanthropy, reported in *Corporate Giving in Ireland: An overview of the landscape*, Dublin, Philanthropy Ireland, 2014.

27 *C&E Corporate–NGO Partnerships Barometer*, London, C&E Advisory Services, 2017, p. 4.

28 *Corporate Fundraising: A snapshot of current practice in the UK non-profit sector*, London, Institute of Fundraising, 2015, p. 42.

29 *2015 Cone Communications/Ebiquity Global CSR Study*, Boston MA, Cone Communications, 2015, pp. 44–45.

30 Figures have been converted both in currency and by inflation to 2017 GBP using 'Converter in the Past' [web page], 2017, http://fxtop.com/en/currency-converter-past.php, accessed 7 July 2017.

31 Population figures are taken from 'Population, Total' [web page], World Bank, 2017, http://data.worldbank.org/indicator/SP.POP.TOTL, accessed 7 July 2017.

32 Claire Benard, Joy Dobbs, Jack Egan, Lisa Hornung, Veronique Jochum, Marc Lawson, Gareth Lloyd and Nick Ockendon, *The UK Civil Society Almanac 2017*, London, NCVO, 2017.

33 *Giving USA 2016: The annual report on philanthropy for the year 2015*, Indianapolis, Indiana University Lilly Family School of Philanthropy, 2016. Figure converted from US$18.45 billion.

34 Michael H. Hall, Margaret L. de Wit, David Lasby, David McIver, Terry Evers, Chris Johnston, Julie McAuley, Katherine Scott, Guy Cucumel, Louis Jolin, Richard Nicol, Loleen Berdahl, Rob Roach, Ian Davies, Penelope Rowe, Kathy Brock and Vic Murray, *Cornerstones of Community: Highlights of the National Survey of Nonprofit and Voluntary Organizations 2003 revised*, Ottawa, Statistics Canada, 2003, p. 28. Figure converted from CA$3.1 billion.

35 *Giving Australia 2016: Business giving and volunteering overview* [fact sheet], Canberra, Australian Department of Social Services, 2016. Figure converted from AU$17.5 billion.

36 *Giving New Zealand: Philanthropic funding 2014*, Wellington, Philanthropy New Zealand, 2015, p. iii. Figure converted from NZ$77.2 million.

37 Myles McGregor-Lowndes, Ted Flack, Wendy Scaife, P. Wiepking and Marie Crittall, *Giving and Volunteering in Australia 2014: Environmental scan/literature review*, Brisbane, Queensland University of Technology, 2014, p. iv.

38 Adrian Sargeant and Kathryn Crissman, 'Corporate Giving in Australia: An analysis of motives and barriers', *Australian Journal of Social Issues*, vol. 41, 2006, pp. 477–94.

39 Sue Smyllie and Daniel Arias, 'Workplace Giving', in *Giving Australia 2016: Literature review*, edited by Wendy Scaife, Myles McGregor-Lowndes, Jo Barraket and Wayne Burns, Brisbane, Australian Department of Social Services, 2016, pp. 136–49.

40 *2015 Cone Communications Millennials CSR Study*, Boston MA, Cone Communications, 2015, pp. 8–9.

41 *The 2017 Deloitte Millennial Survey: Apprehensive millennials – Seeking stability and opportunities in an uncertain world* [PDF], www2.deloitte.com/global/en/pages/about-deloitte/articles/millennialsurvey.html, Deloitte, 2017.

42   *Giving Australia 2016: Business giving and volunteering overview* [fact sheet], Canberra, Australian Department of Social Services, 2016.

43   *Giving New Zealand: Philanthropic funding 2014*, Wellington, Philanthropy New Zealand, 2015.

44   *Insights for Strategic Corporate Fundraising*, Toronto, Imagine Canada, 2010.

45   *Corporate Giving in Ireland: An overview of the landscape*, Dublin, Philanthropy Ireland, 2014, p. 10.

46   Michael Hall, M. Easwaramoorthy and Wyanne Sandler, *Business Contributions to Canadian Communities: Findings from a qualitative study of current practices*, Toronto, Imagine Canada, 2007.

47   *The Business Case for Being a Responsible Business*, London, Business in the Community, 2011.

48   *Corporate Giving in Ireland: An overview of the landscape*, Dublin, Philanthropy Ireland, 2014.

49   *Insights for Strategic Corporate Fundraising*, Toronto, Imagine Canada, 2010, pp. iv–v.

50   Michael Hall, M. Easwaramoorthy and Wyanne Sandler, *Business Contributions to Canadian Communities: Findings from a qualitative study of current practices*, Toronto, Imagine Canada, 2007.

51   Michael Hall, David Lasby, Glenn Gumulka and Catherine Tryon, *Caring Canadians, Involved Canadians: Highlights from the 2004 Canada survey of giving, volunteering and participating*, Ottawa, Statistics Canada, 2006, pp. 9–10.

52   *Insights for Strategic Corporate Fundraising*, Toronto, Imagine Canada, 2010, p. 5.

53   'The Corporate Giving Issue', *Philanthropic Giving Quarterly*, vol. 2011, no. 4, 2011.

54   Daniel Arias, 'Business Giving', in *Giving Australia 2016: Literature review*, edited by Wendy Scaife, Myles McGregor-Lowndes, Jo Barraket and Wayne Burns, Brisbane, Australian Department of Social Services, p. 174.

55   '501(c) Success (National Speaker Series) Giving USA 2016: The annual report on philanthropy for the year 2015', presentation at Ewing Marion Kauffman Foundation Conference Center, Kansas City, Missouri, June 21, 2016.

56   Catherine Walker, *The Company Giving Almanac 2013*, London, DSC, 2013, p.30.

57   Cone Communications and Ebiquity, *2015 Cone Communications/Ebiquity Global CSR Study*, Boston MA, Cone Communications, 2015.

CHAPTER FOUR

Targeting new partners

Rachel Billsberry-Grass

Introduction

To have a chance of securing a corporate partnership and then delivering a successful fundraising activity, you need a robust approach to targeting prospective partners. Thorough research is an imperative: it enables you to understand a company and its business objectives. It will identify how a company has supported charities in the past and uncover key information about corporate decision makers. Armed with such information, the corporate fundraiser can develop a compelling case for support that articulates the reasons why a partnership would be beneficial for both parties.

Research will also enable you to identify opportunities to develop a relationship with the decision makers and influencers at the prospective corporate supporter. The goal is to build personal relationships within a company, developing a mutual trust and understanding that can lead to a far-reaching partnership.

This chapter outlines the various ways in which you can generate leads for new business, how to carry out the research effectively and manage the research process, and what you need to do to make the approach.

Generating leads

Any charity which aspires to be successful in corporate fundraising will need to be very proactive at developing new business. As with any sales-related activity it is vital to generate and maintain a pipeline of good prospects for future approaches. This is especially important to remember if your charity is in the throes of a current fixed-term partnership. It is very easy to become consumed by the work involved in delivering that, at the expense of building new business to replace it.

With thousands of companies out there, the challenge is how and where to start the process of building that pipeline.

Companies that already have a connection with your charity, however small, should be identified first. They will have a higher chance than cold prospects of reaping rewards. You can identify these connections by speaking to staff, trustees and supporters, and by trawling through your charity's database and other past records. These might be companies that have supported your charity in the past, companies with which the board of trustees or other supporters are associated, or perhaps suppliers to the charity.

Taking a strategic approach to business development will allow your organisation to achieve efficiencies. There are several options for how new business development might be approached strategically. Each of these is applicable to any size of charity.

The approach of segmenting, which is suggested in each of the options below, may seem onerous for smaller charities. However, it can be divided between team members or timetabled across the year.

By business sector

New business approaches are often segmented by industry sector. By investing focused resources into one industry, you can achieve a greater understanding of the industry's motivations, discovering the commonalities that can be used in approaches. This knowledge can help save you time – for example, companies in one industry may be more likely to respond to a similar style of approach in terms of proposal structure, images and fundraising ideas, which will help you avoid having to invent something brand new every time. The most notable example of an industry getting behind one cause is Fashion Targets Breast Cancer, which has united the fashion industry in supporting breast cancer causes since the 1990s.

Note that, if you decide to focus on one industry, your charity will be at an advantage if it recruits a corporate fundraiser with experience of working in that area: industry knowledge and contacts are invaluable in building relationships.

Before embarking on this strategy, you will need to give some consideration to the level of competition within the proposed sector. Many companies will seek exclusivity in a relationship with a charity. The company may understandably not want to dilute its own impact by being seen alongside a competitor. For example, a major charity partner of one of the leading supermarkets may find it difficult to even begin a dialogue with another supermarket until the current partnership has ended. This strategy may therefore prove to be limiting in the short term.

By geography

For local or regional charities, or national charities with a strong regional project or presence, it makes sense to segment business development by focusing on companies in a particular geographical area. It will be these companies that are most likely to relate to the charity or project and be committed to supporting it. Many companies will seek out local charities and projects that are providing services in areas where their staff and customers live and work. That may be particularly the case now. Research in 2016 by the Charity Commission shows that three in five people agree they are more likely to trust charities that are delivering services in the local area, and overall the public is more likely to trust small charities (57%) over large ones (34%).[1] This suggests local and regional charities have a competitive advantage that they could exploit.

By company size

Your approach to a prospect that is potentially worth £1 million to your charity will be different from your approach to a prospect worth £1,000, so it is important to segment your business development prospects by company size. In large charities with both a national function and a regional network, it is common for the central office team to take responsibility for the FTSE 100 or 250 companies, with regional staff or volunteers focusing on any company outside this list which is in their locality. While this provides a reasonable framework, it is wise to be flexible. For instance, a regional company could easily become a very significant partner which requires input from the central team, or a large company with a regional head office might be better served by a regional fundraiser. If your charity is small, it is wise to ensure that a good mix of large and small prospects is in hand to spread the risk in the pipeline.

By corporate fundraising mechanism

As corporate fundraising diversifies, so too do the skills that are needed to win and manage particular types of business. A fundraiser with commercial marketing experience is more likely to have the relevant skills for winning cause-related marketing or sponsorship deals. A fundraiser with some human resources knowledge may be able to sell more convincingly the benefits of staff fundraising. For this reason, some charities have segmented their business development activity by fundraising mechanism, focusing on bringing in particular types of partnership.

Given that corporate fundraising is also moving in the direction of broader partnerships that cover several fundraising mechanisms, however, this structure may become less relevant. Nevertheless, having these specialisms within a well-communicating team can be useful, and can demonstrate that your charity has a solid depth of knowledge and experience.

Carrying out corporate prospect research

There is a huge volume of information that you can access about companies, and much of it could be useful. It is tempting, then, to capture every possible detail about a company and very easy to fall down an internet rabbit hole while doing research. To avoid this trap, it is worth focusing on the most pertinent information that a corporate fundraiser might need to ensure research time is used effectively. See below for advice on a sensible process to follow; in addition, finding concise answers to the following questions can help focus your search:

• Who is this company? What is its culture, its personality?

• Which markets does it work in and what are its key business issues?

• Does the company have giving criteria?

• How does it support charities – does it commonly use any particular mechanism from the corporate partnership portfolio (see chapter 7)?

• What is the usual financial value of its charity support?

• Which charities has it supported in the past?

• Does it have corporate responsibility plans for the future? For example, has it already made commitments to provide support to other charities in the future?

• What does it expect of its charity partners – i.e. what benefits does it require or prefer?

• How does the company decide which charities to partner with?

• Who makes the decision, and can you find out anything about that individual or group?

The starting point for research is the company's own website. An increasing number of companies have one or more pages of their website devoted to charitable giving, often as one part of a larger corporate responsibility section. This will offer a picture of which causes the company considers important: is its charity choice heavily influenced by business issues, such as its supply chain? Some companies might focus their support internationally on the communities from which their core product derives. Or are this company's charitable support decisions driven by its workforce and local customers? For example, does it tend to support charities working on mainstream health issues that might affect both staff and customers?

The website is also a window into the culture of the company. As a starting point, what importance does it place on effective marketing? Is the website up to date and contemporary? The website will give an indication of the company's values (explicitly or not) and a sense of its approach to its workforce – formal or more relaxed.

Social media and advertising will give a further insight into the company. Look to see whether the culture portrayed on its website is followed through in its advertising and social media, particularly in its interactions with other people. If the company is proactive, social media in particular is the best way to stay abreast of the company's activities.

The internet, traditional media and social media can all be used to get an indication of the company's reputation and whether a partnership could present risks to your charity's standing in the community. Customers and other commentators will offer opinions of the company and its products on review sites, newspaper articles, blogs and platforms such as Twitter. Although some of these opinions should be treated with caution, taken as a whole, it is possible to get a view of a general public perception, which can be compared against the company's own view of itself. If there are legitimate complaints, look to see whether the company has handled them well.

Looking at industry publications may provide background information; for example, the prospective company may have recently changed advertising agency. This could be seen as an indication for a new direction for the company or product and a potential opportunity for a charity partnership. Other publications and lists, such as the *Sunday Times* 100 Best Companies to Work For, offer further insight into a company's culture, and the *Sunday Times* Rich List can provide helpful information about the owners and managers of a company.

There are a handful of publications and online directories that are useful for corporate fundraisers, including DSC's *The Guide to UK Company Giving* and its sister website.[2] These list many companies and offer an outline of their charitable giving activities. There is now a wealth of business directories, available online or through libraries, from which you can gain financial and legal information about a company and assess the potential risks of a partnership. Through Companies House it is possible to see the latest accounts for all public limited companies, although exemptions from filing make it a bit harder to access the same information about private companies.

Looking at the websites of the company's previous or existing charity partners may provide additional information about the nature of the partnership and the project that was funded.

Further nuggets of information about a company can be gained through business networks and your own contacts within a company or through a personal check. For some companies – for example, retailers, banks and hotels – this is straightforward: a visit can give you a good idea of the company's values, which charities it is supporting and how. You can find out about other companies by observing their offices for a couple of hours from the comfort of the nearest coffee shop or by calling in to reception.

Finally, don't forget to use the telephone. One phone call to a company may prove more useful than several hours on the internet.

Managing the research process

A charity can choose for research to be carried out by its corporate fundraiser, by a specialist in-house researcher or by a prospect research agency. There are advantages and disadvantages to each option, and in many cases a charity will choose a combination of the three. Here are some points to consider:

• Fundraisers should appreciate that, even if there is a research function (within the charity or via an external organisation), it is still a key part of their role to be spotting opportunities and absorbing information throughout their working day and outside work.

• A specialist researcher needs to understand the corporate fundraising process in order to help spot leads and to decide which information is valuable. The role involves far more than simply finding out specific information.

• An agency can save the charity a lot of time and legwork in the initial identification of prospects. Asking an agency to provide a list of company prospects could enable a fundraising campaign to advance more quickly than if this work were done in-house. Many agencies have years of experience of working with both large and small charities and so can offer valuable advice with regard to identifying and researching companies and may be able to make some introductions.

Each option will have associated costs, though these are likely to be higher for using an agency or appointing an internal researcher. However, these costs can be seen as a good investment. Whichever route you take, use clear key performance indicators, and monitor and evaluate progress to ensure the investment is appropriate.

Developing new business

To achieve the greatest success in corporate fundraising, new business development needs to be approached strategically but with the flexibility to respond to new opportunities that arise. Your charity should be looking for any opportunity to meet company decision makers and build relationships.

For that reason, a scatter-gun approach of sending out untargeted letters or proposals is never a good idea. It reflects badly on the charity and, as companies resent spending money on responding to such approaches, the charity is much less likely to hear back from them at all. Time and money will be wasted by the charity and the return on investment of such activity will be low, if not zero.

New business development should be a combination of proactive and reactive approaches.

Some charities are directly approached by companies that are interested in partnering with them. If this happens to your charity, you will need to take time to react and to explore and assess the opportunity. Companies are more likely to directly approach charities with a high profile or that are recognised as experts in a particular field that could provide a commercial advantage. This could include, for example, environmental reporting or the implementation of specific discrimination legislation. A company might be more likely to approach a charity that has provided services for a member of staff or a charity that has been adept at promoting its previous corporate partnerships: the benefits of working with that charity will be obvious to a new prospective partner. It is therefore useful for a corporate fundraiser to work alongside the charity's media team and look for opportunities to promote the work of the charity and the value of a corporate partnership.

You should also be reactive if opportunities arise out of the blue – for example, a chance introduction to a senior manager of a particular company while you are out for dinner, or a new individual donor who is keen to nominate your charity to her company. It is vital to leave some contingency work time to enable you to jump straight on to these opportunities while they are still fresh, exploring the potential for partnership-working.

Making the approach

Having identified prospective companies and carried out the necessary due diligence before investing further time (see chapter 5), the next step is to find opportunities to get a foot in the door and start to build a relationship. Ideally an existing supporter (individual or corporate), a trustee, a member of staff or an ambassador/patron will be able to make a personal introduction.

If not, you could look at opportunities to engage with the company in other ways: perhaps beginning a dialogue on social media that will bring the charity to the company's attention. You could identify networking events that company decision makers might attend and aim to start a conversation.

Some charities use corporate hospitality to engage prospects. An invitation to a special or exclusive event may be attractive to some, although they can be counterproductive if the company perceives that the charity is spending too much money. It is worthwhile using contacts to access experiences that are not usually available on the open market, such as lunch at the House of Lords, or dinner with a celebrity ambassador. This type of experience is much more likely to illicit a positive response, provided it is targeted well: an invitation to London Fashion Week will be more attractive to some than lunch at the House of Lords, for example.

If your charity is able to meet with a company, whether at a networking event or through an introduction, the charity's representatives need to be prepared. The decision of who will lead the approach must be taken pragmatically: it should be the person that the company is most likely to respond or relate to based on the knowledge gained through research.

Ideally this person will be there at the first meeting. Whichever charity representative is able to speak with the company initially, this person should have an idea of what your charity is hoping to get out of a partnership and some information about the company that will help to start a dialogue. It could be as simple as something the company has just posted on Instagram. The most important thing at this first meeting is to listen carefully to what the company says, as ideas for partnership-working might arise through the discussion.

At this initial stage, the aim should be to spark an interest in the company and agree a follow-up, rather than making a direct ask. Ideally the follow-up will be another meeting to continue to build understanding and trust between your charity and the corporate – perhaps a visit to one of the charity's projects. But the company may well invite you to send in some ideas on how you might work together.

There is certainly no one-size-fits-all in corporate fundraising. But, as with many things, relationships are key, so listening well and responding appropriately will be the best way to secure success.

Case study: St Elizabeth Hospice's Charity of the Year partnership with Willis Towers Watson

Willis Towers Watson (WTW) is a global advisory, broking and solutions company. With around 1,400 staff in its town centre office, it is in the top five employers in Ipswich. Each year the Charity of the Year (COTY) is chosen by way of a staff vote.

Charities apply for this partnership in November and a shortlist of four charities is selected by the senior management committee. Each charity is then given a consecutive day in December at the company's offices to engage with staff. The staff vote takes place on the final day of the week.

In late 2016, St Elizabeth Hospice was delighted to be shortlisted as one of the final four charities.

Research and plans

In the weeks before our charity day, we visited the WTW offices to get a sense of the company: what the culture was like, who the people that worked there were and how the space was laid out. We used this information to plan our strategy, develop our communications and make sure we were reaching people effectively.

For example, we decided to have not only a team of staff within the building but also a presence outside the building, including all of the routes from the office into the town centre.

We were also lucky to be allocated the last of the days of the week offered to the shortlisted charities to speak with staff, so we visited the office on the other days to see what the other charities were doing and how they were doing it, ready to make last-minute tweaks in our own plans if needed.

We worked with our marketing team to piece together an in-depth communications plan based on our impressions of the staff from our research and the messages that we, as a charity, needed to promote to the local community. Given the age demographic of the staff, we decided to focus on the story of a young woman called Zoe who had recently died under the Hospice's care, aged just 27. This had the added benefit of educating the local community that hospice care is for all ages, not just for older people.

Zoe's mother, Wendy, helped to produce 'Zoe's Story', a diary of Zoe's last few weeks before her death. This story was told on a postcard leaflet with strong headlines and images. These were then mirrored on T-shirts that were worn by our staff on the day, and on our website. They were also followed through on a social media campaign that we launched at the beginning of WTW's charity week. This campaign would then have a real impact on our pitch day and staff voting day.

Pitch day

Our team was briefed the day before and on the morning of our pitch day. We covered how to approach the WTW staff and how to talk about the work of the Hospice. The focus was on being direct in a professional and efficient manner: our target was to speak to as many members of staff as possible during our allotted four hours, handing out postcards to all.

The team outside the offices visited shops and business premises nearby to put up posters in windows along the most popular routes to the town centre. Inside the offices, the team of one fundraiser, two nurses and Zoe's mother, Wendy, prepared a visually appealing stand and distributed our postcards around all communal spaces.

Result

The day after our pitch, staff were asked to vote in an unusual way: they were invited to donate into one of four buckets each labelled with the name of one of the charities. The bucket with the most money would determine the chosen charity (and all charities received at least a small donation).

During the day we continued our social media campaign to remind staff to vote for St Elizabeth Hospice and included a link to Zoe's story on our website.

A long seven days later, we received the welcome news that we had been chosen as WTW's COTY for 2017. This was the first time we had been selected by WTW and now the hard work begins to make this a successful partnership for everyone.

Conclusion

The work of generating new corporate partnerships can only be successful if there has been some useful groundwork to target potential prospects effectively. Thorough research should be well planned between the team and across the year to build a new business pipeline. You need to be proactive in building relationships with prospects but also allow contingency time for reactively responding to opportunities that arise. The focus should be on building a relationship that is based on mutual understanding and trust: the basis of all great partnerships.

Notes

1   Populus, *Public Trust and Confidence in Charities*, Liverpool, Charity Commission, 2016, p. 5.

2   See www.dsc.org.uk/gcg for the book or www.dsc.org.uk/funding-website for the searchable subscription website, which contains a company giving arm. Both the book and the website offer detailed information on over 400 companies, including who to contact, any application processes, the company's financial details and number of employees, and examples of organisations the company has supported in the past. They also offer details on companies' preferred methods of giving, including cash donations, in-kind support, employee-led support, sponsorship and/or commercially led support.

CHAPTER FIVE

Carrying out due diligence

Lynda Harwood

Introduction

Due diligence is a risk management process that, in the context of a corporate partnership, is made up of the steps a charity needs to take to have a clear knowledge and understanding of the organisation it could partner with. The aim of carrying out this process is to gather enough intelligence to help inform your decision-making on whether your charity should pursue or accept an offer of corporate support. (See chapter 6 for guidance on the decision-making process.)

This chapter outlines:

• how to judge the level of risk to determine the appropriate level of due diligence checks required;

• who should carry out the process;

• the steps of the due diligence process;

• a due diligence evidence checklist.

Note that this chapter does not go into detail on the relevant legislation – this is covered in chapter 13. Furthermore, it is always wise to seek professional advice to ensure that your charity is compliant with the law.

Judging the level of risk

Before you can carry out the due diligence process to the extent required by the Fundraising Regulator and other regulators,[1] you need to anticipate the level of expected risk. Charity Commission guidance notes that trustees must take a risk-based approach to carrying out due diligence. The Fundraising Regulator also states that 'Organisations MUST carry out a process of due diligence, proportionate to the scale of the relationship, before engaging in a partnership'.[2] ('Must' in the Fundraising Regulator guidance means that, although this is not a legal requirement, the regulator treats this as 'a professional standard to be met by fundraising organisations'.)[3]

A 'proportionate' approach means trustees (or the people to whom they have delegated activities – from now on termed 'delegates') carrying out actions that allow the charity to comply with the trustees' duty of not allowing any abuse of the charity, its funds or property to take place. Trustees or their delegates should put in more effort and are required to take certain actions where there is a high-level risk, but they have more discretion to decide what they should do about lower-level risks. In other words, the higher the risks of the potential partnership, the greater the amount of due diligence and monitoring work that must be done to comply with legal duties.[4]

What does carrying out these actions mean in practical terms? It will partly depend on answers to a combination of the following questions:

• What level of financial support is your charity seeking?

• Which aspects of your charity's work might imply a risk of working with the proposed partner? Could, for example, the company's industry directly conflict with the charity's values and an association with it therefore damage the charity's reputation?

• How complex or significant is the proposed project collaboration or partnership?

• What are the timescales for the delivery of the activities?

• What will the likely level of public profile or media interest be in the funding or partnership? (A straightforward one-off sponsorship agreement, for example, would be less visible and attract less attention than a long-term cause-related marketing campaign.)

• How complex are your charity's activities? (The more complex they are, the harder it will be to identify and potentially manage the likely risks.)

• How large or complex is the company? (Note that the sheer size of a company may not allow your research to uncover a totally comprehensive picture of its activities; the aim in this case would be to do as much due diligence as is reasonably possible – enough to allow the trustees to feel confident in associating with the charity's proposed partner and to justify the decision to proceed if necessary.)

• To what extent does the potential corporate associate have the capacity, financially or otherwise, to be an effective partner?

• To what extent does your charity have the capacity, financially or otherwise, to carry out the proposed activities?

• If your proposed project involves any delivery of services by the corporate partner, how easy or difficult would it be for your charity to monitor this delivery?

Generally speaking,

• the higher the amount of money involved;

• the more diverse or complex the nature of the company's or your charity's activities;

• the less stable the company's or your charity's finances;

• the more visible the partnership would be or the more attention it would attract;

• the more the association with the potential partner is likely to damage your charity's reputation;

• the less capacity the corporate partner, or your charity, has for carrying out the proposed activities effectively;

• (or a combination of these factors)...

... the higher the risks will be. Conversely, the smaller your charity is, the more straightforward its activities are and the more simple the proposed partnership is (and so on), the lower the risk.

Note that, while the amount of money involved is significant, this is not the only important aspect to consider, especially given that it is possible for the risk to be high even when only a relatively small amount of money may need to be protected. In that case, it is still necessary to go through certain due diligence stages. For example, if a charity engages in a celebrity endorsement with a controversial figure, the sums involved may be relevant but the potential for reputational damage will also be highly relevant.

To systematically determine the level of risk, choose a risk assessment procedure based on the level of complexity and significance of the proposed partnership. The procedure can range from writing a formal document to having a conversation. If your charity is legally required to be audited, however, it must also make a risk management statement in its annual report. Furthermore, given that the Charity Commission encourages charities that are *not* required to make a statement to do so as a point of good practice,[5] and given that trustees may need to demonstrate later that they are fulfilling their legal duties, it is wise to have at least a basic written record of the outcome of the discussion.[6]

After estimating whether the risk level is overall low, medium or high, you can choose accordingly the depth of due diligence checks that you will need to carry out on your potential partner. This decision informs the level to which you will need to monitor the partnership if it goes ahead. (The following sections advise on the various actions that you can take depending on the level of risk.)

To show how a local charity (which will generally be engaging with a lower level of risk) approaches the due diligence process, the following case study outlines the actions of a children's hospice, Demelza.

Case study: Demelza's evolving due diligence procedure

Demelza is a specialist children's hospice that provides care and support to children and families throughout Kent, East Sussex and south-east London. The charity is similar to many local hospices across the UK: it has a small number of fundraising staff, many of whom perform a mixed-discipline role.

Demelza primarily focuses on local corporate partnerships rather than national partnerships. The hospice often does not meet the requirements of a national charity partnership and, in any case, believes it is currently best placed to work with local partnerships. Demelza feels that very local partnerships are often lower risk and have better alignment with the hospice, and thus they have less need for the involved due diligence processes that many larger, national charities implement.

Demelza carries out an informal due diligence procedure by conducting research on a potential new partnership. This involves basic financial checks to ensure, for example, that the company is solvent; reviewing the company's previous charity partnerships; and examining the press and publicity surrounding the company.

As in many small charities, staff resources and time are limited, which makes it challenging to develop and implement due diligence procedures. Nevertheless, Demelza is aware of its compliance obligations, the importance of protecting the charity with regard to corporate partnerships, and the 'cause and effect' of unsuitable partnerships for the charity and its various departments – given that all areas of a charity are interdependent, the need for unity is paramount. For example, an incident with a corporate partner could create a chain of events which has a knock-on effect for the communications team and require its members' support.

With these points in mind, Demelza is developing a joined-up way of working to ensure all areas of the charity are aware of and support the reasoning behind partnerships and any areas of risk management. In particular, the fundraising team is working towards putting a formal process in place for potential new partnerships, including how to assess partners and the risks associated, if any.

To future-proof due diligence within the charity, Demelza is also beginning to incorporate a due diligence check process into its corporate fundraising policy. Demelza is keen to move away from using several separate policies and will work towards an overarching corporate fundraising policy. This policy will be supported by, for example, cash collecting and media procedures. When this policy is up to date, the corporate partnerships team will also implement policy training for all fundraisers and senior management. Trustees will approve all policy and strategic changes, this being their legal responsibility.

Demelza will ensure its due diligence checks include research into:

- the press and media surrounding potential partners;

- the financials of a company;

- the company's previous charity support;

- partnership communications;

- any potential conflict with other partners.

The procedure for these checks may include annual due diligence check renewals (during which the original due diligence check is updated with any new information) and ensuring the account manager is up to date with all publicity surrounding the company – whether this involves the charity or not.

The next case study outlines the approach of a large, complex charity with a comprehensive due diligence procedure that reflects the higher level of risk this charity faces as a result of complexity and high-profile partnerships.

Case study: the NSPCC's due diligence procedure

The NSPCC is the UK's leading children's charity, preventing abuse and helping those affected to recover. As one of the larger charities in the UK, the NSPCC has a strict and thorough due diligence procedure. It has three layers:

1. **Corporate fundraiser:** the fundraiser completes a 'corporate engagement form', which is a set of 15 detailed questions revolving around ethics, legality, brand alignment, impact on children, values and negative publicity. This enables the NSPCC to gain an initial understanding of the partnership, and the level of due diligence research and potential risk management needed.

This form is then flagged as red, amber or green and passed to the Head of Partnerships to review and authorise. The charity does not progress with potential partnerships marked as 'red'.

2. **Research team:** if the partnership is of substantial value or will generate a significant amount of publicity, then the charity's research team will also become involved in due diligence checks using a range of bespoke tools to find more detailed information.

3. **Director of Fundraising and the trustees:** the corporate engagement forms are often also reviewed by the Director of Fundraising and the trustees, especially if the potential outcome provokes debate. These parties may also have to sign off on the partnership on the basis of discussions resulting from the issues raised by this form.

When completing its due diligence procedure, the NSPCC uses three guiding principles, which are all followed with the ultimate aim of protecting beneficiaries, before going into a more detailed compliance check:

1. **Children:** could what the company does create issues for beneficiaries or clearly contribute towards child abuse or neglect?

2. **Reputation:** would a partnership and/or donations from the company lead to support for the charity being lost or be counterproductive for the NSPCC or the charity sector as a whole?

3. **Ethics:** how is the company's money obtained? Is it obtained legally?

Ultimately, the goal of having guiding principles and conducting the corresponding level of due diligence is to protect charities' beneficiaries. When asked who the NSPCC has a responsibility to for completing due diligence, Ben Swart, Head of New Business at the NSPCC, explained that 'our responsibility is to the children and our donors. We need to know that the partners we work with are ethical and that they can impact positively on both our beneficiaries and our donors.'

Who should complete due diligence?

Everyone in a charity has their part to play in managing risk and carrying out due diligence. However, it is ultimately the trustees' responsibility to ensure that due diligence processes (and monitoring if the decision is made to continue with the partnership) are carried out and that risks are identified and managed. This process is a crucial tool for trustees: it provides the evidence they (or their delegates) need to make decisions that will protect the charity, its assets (including the value of its name and reputation) and its beneficiaries. Ultimately, to meet the requirements of charity legislation, trustees must feel confident with any new partnership and have sufficient control over it. Carrying out due diligence is a way to help secure this confidence by having enough information to hand to make an informed judgement or to review the judgements made.

Trustees may delegate due diligence and decision-making procedures to appropriate member(s) of staff if there is a clear framework in place. However, they must also have a correct level of oversight to hold people to account for how they are carrying out their delegated activities. This does not mean that they are delegating their *responsibility* for due diligence and risk management – they remain legally accountable for these activities.

To have a clear framework and correct oversight, trustees must have sufficient systems and processes to ensure that any arrangements agreed with a commercial partner are in the best interests of the charity. They must also make sure that their charity's systems and processes provide guidance to delegates.

Guidance should advise delegates on the reporting lines and procedures, and how – in terms of content, level of detail, presentation and so on – to provide the right information and advice to trustees. This is the information that will allow trustees to evaluate whether the charity's approach to due diligence (and any corporate fundraising and partnership activities) is compliant with both the charity's agreed standards, including its ethical policy (see page 80), and the standards of best practice and the law.[7] This can include, for example, guidance on reporting procedures for what the Charity Commission refers to as 'high risk and novel decisions', which it states should *not* be delegated. Trustees should instead agree guidelines that will help delegates to assess what is likely to be high risk or novel.[8]

The details of the delegation should be put in writing and must include committee or team terms of reference, job or role descriptions, reporting and decision-making policies and procedures, and so on. Trustees must know that delegates understand what it is that they are to carry out.

The systems and processes must also include guidance that applies when the delegated tasks are being carried out. This includes providing documented feedback on the progress of agreed activities, and how and in which format this feedback should be presented. Due diligence findings and recommendations must be presented at trustees' meetings in the format and detail required by trustees. This allows trustees to monitor and evaluate the agreed activities to ensure that they are being achieved correctly. It also allows them to question anything if needed, request further information and make decisions. After decisions have been made, delegates must continue to update the trustees on monitoring and progress at given trigger points relevant to the risk or at agreed frequencies, say every quarter (see also 'Monitoring the partnership' on page 93 in chapter 6 and 'Delegation' on page 167 in chapter 13).[9]

So, in a model situation of delegation of responsibilities for a new partnership, trustees or their delegates:

1. evaluate the level of risk and hence the level of due diligence checks required;

2. complete initial due diligence research to an appropriate level (with the help of a research team, if available to the charity);

3. carry out a formal decision-making process, comparing any issues or objections against the evidence and the charity's ethical policy to ensure decisions are objective (see chapter 6);

4. follow trustee guidance on providing documented feedback (if nominated people are carrying out the actions);

5. sign off the results of the decision-making process or get them signed off by a member of senior management or the trustees (as appropriate) after any potential risks or concerns have been investigated, analysed and discussed;

6. refer any high-risk or unusual decisions to the trustees, if nominated people are carrying out the actions (following the trustees' guidance on which types of decision are likely to be high risk or unusual).

Then, if the partnership is given the green light:

7. professional legal and finance advice should be sought to help draw up partnership agreements (compliant with legal requirements) and invoice licence fees, if applicable;

8. the reasons to commence the partnership should be confirmed in writing.

(Note that the focus of this chapter is on steps 1 and 2. See chapter 6 for details on carrying out the decision-making process.)

The due diligence process

We have seen that due diligence checks should be proportionate to the size of corporate donation, type of partner and so on. It is useful, however, to reduce ambiguity and doubt with a standard procedure that is clear and structured, outlining what needs to be done depending on the type of partnership and level of risk.

A good practice is to have a template questionnaire or report that fundraisers and other relevant individuals complete. To create a helpful structure for this, you can include steps such as the following, which are adapted from Charity Commission guidance:[10]

1. Who are you dealing with?

• Where is the corporate based?

• What is the legal status of the potential partner? A PLC, private company, entrepreneur or partnership?

• Does it have a parent/ultimate holding company? Who owns it?

• Does it have subsidiaries?

• Is it registered with a regulator, such as Companies House or the Financial Conduct Authority?

• Who are the senior personnel?

• Who in the company or its parent company would you be dealing with? With whom will you be building relationships?

2. What do they do?

• What can you find out about the corporate's business from its website and from internet searches and other sources (such as colleagues and associates)?

• What can you conclude about the corporate's reputation after researching it (and from any research from third parties)? How does the public perceive this company? How valid or credible is any criticism levelled against it (were any allegations proven)?

• What you can gather about the potential partner's core values and ethics? For example, what policies does it have towards its employees and customers that might reveal more about these values?

3. What are the motivations of the parties?

• Is there a potential conflict of interest? For example, has the company offered to be a corporate partner at the same time it is tendering to be a supplier with the charity? (If so, it might be that the company is hoping to gain favour in order to be chosen as a supplier.)

• Does the company want the partnership to be exclusive – i.e. does it want to be the charity's only corporate partner in that industry? If so, would this be in the best interests of the charity or just those of the company?

4. How feasible will it be to deliver the planned activities of the partnership?

• Is the corporate new or a start-up?

• What is the likely corporate partnership portfolio going to be? (See chapter 7.) Would you be in a Charity of the Year partnership? Running events? Licensing your charity's brand? In a sponsorship deal? (And so on.)

• How straightforward would it be to monitor the delivery of the activities in the portfolio?

• Would the potential partner have the ability, including management and technical capabilities, to carry out its end of the partnership deal?

• Would the potential partner have the financial and/or other capacity to carry out its end of the partnership deal or would it be overloaded?

• Does the corporate already have other partners? Would this affect its ability to be an effective partner with your organisation?

• Has it had previous experience of such activities with other charities that demonstrate its ability to deliver them successfully?

• Is it straightforward to get hold of the corporate's key personnel?

It is vital when seeking the answers to these questions to have open and honest discussions with your potential corporate donor from the offset. This helps to avoid confusion and misunderstandings. Their approach to responding is also an indication of their transparency, capacity and reliability.

Note that some of these questions will have already been answered if you have been through a targeting process (as covered in chapter 4), so be sure to take advantage of any research already done.

For more straightforward associations with companies, some of these questions will not be relevant. For example, a basic level of due diligence for any potential association with a company could include the checks done by business information and data companies. These types of report include data on:

• any associations, such as a parent company, subsidiaries or branches;

• the corporate's legal structure and when it was registered;

- the corporate's operations – i.e. types of business;
- the number of its employees;
- a financial summary, including net worth, the most recent balance sheets and key financial information (including assets and liabilities);
- various ratings and risk levels, such as credit and financial strength;
- details of any legal events and any court judgements.

These details can also be found using the company's annual reports and information from Companies House. For other legal structures, such as sole traders and traditional partnerships, however, it is not so easy to obtain such information.

For more complex scenarios, or if the potential partner is in an industry which can be viewed by stakeholders as unethical (which often includes companies in the firearms, alcohol, tobacco and gambling industries), you will likely need to carry out risk assessments, such as a PR and media risk assessment, and then outline strategies for what would be done if something went wrong. For instance, what would the media/communications line be if there were a negative media story about a corporate donation from a gambling company?

You might also need to survey your stakeholders to estimate the consequences of an association with any given higher-risk corporate organisation. This may need to be carried out discreetly, or at a time when agreements are not actively being negotiated, so the charity has a good awareness of the attitude of stakeholders in advance. (See chapter 6 for advice on how to use evidence for or against the acceptance of an offer or partnership to judge objectively and hence communicate consistently.) If it is a low-risk relationship, however, these types of assessment, strategies and surveys will not be necessary.

Differences between what you should ask your beneficiaries and what you should ask your donors[11]

When surveying your beneficiaries, you can ask them directly whether they would want you to partner with a certain company or accept a donation from a company. Trustees, and therefore charities, have a duty to act in the interests of their beneficiaries and so should not seek to alienate them. If the feedback demonstrates that they are overwhelmingly against an association with any given company or industry, this is valid evidence that should be taken into account (along with all the information and evidence on whether to accept or reject that proposal). Similarly, but on the flip side, if your beneficiaries are in favour of what could be deemed a risky proposal, this can be used as grounds to support going ahead with the proposal and to defend this decision if necessary.

The aim of surveying donors is different, however, because you are seeking to find out what the *consequences* of partnering or accepting corporate support might be rather than just donors' opinions on the proposed partnership. This difference occurs because naturally your charity represents its beneficiaries interests, not its donors interests, yet what your donors will do if your charity were to go ahead with the partnership ultimately will affect your beneficiaries and, as such, this evidence is crucial to have in hand. It is appropriate, then, to ask whether your donors' support or likelihood of donating would be affected if the charity partnered with or accepted a donation from any given company or industry. Evidence that support would drop significantly or not be affected at all were an association to go ahead would provide strong support for rejecting or accepting a proposal respectively. In a similar way, the views of staff and any other stakeholders are also immaterial since the evaluation process does not take account of the personal opinions of people (unless they are beneficiaries).

Note that the style of questioning in any surveying process must be open and not leading. If the wording is composed in a way that might invite a positive or negative response to a proposed corporate association (i.e. it is biased by people's personal views), this might influence the outcome and make the survey invalid. The sample must also be large enough to provide a statistically significant result that honestly represents the views or feedback of your beneficiaries or donors.

Checking your due diligence evidence

The following example checklist contains some practical due diligence actions. The results of these checks will help you to determine whether the proposed partnership will be harmful to your charity from financial or other perspectives. They will provide evidence of the suitability of a partner and the likelihood of a successful partnership.

If you use an information reporting service, some of these points will automatically be included in the report. Not all of the points, such as gathering stakeholder evidence and speaking to former partners of the company, will be necessary. What is necessary will depend on the level of risk you have judged there to be based on the complexity of the scenario or level of potential harm to the charity.

Note that, in addition to variations depending on this level of risk, each corporate partnership is unique, so it is a good idea to consider issues and concerns related to your charity and put together a checklist for your particular circumstances to be used to measure progress in evaluating the prospective partnership's suitability.

Evidence checklist

1. Reputational and commercial evidence

☐ We have evaluated, using a PR and media risk analysis, the likely PR and media impact of partnering/receiving a donation.

☐ We have spoken to former partners regarding the impact on their brand of partnering with this organisation and to verify the claims the company has made regarding any such partnerships.

☐ We have valued our charity's assets to determine their commercial value, so as to allow us to evaluate the proposed benefits to our charity against the benefits the corporate will receive. (See page 133 for information on how to value your charity's assets.)

2. Financial and capacity evidence

☐ We have checked the trading status of the corporate organisation, including its parent company and any subsidiaries (ideally it will have been trading for at least three years).

☐ A credit check has been completed.

☐ The company's annual accounts and reports have been reviewed (ideally three years of annual accounts should be available).

☐ We have a list of the company's existing and planned partnerships and have discussed capacity/ability to deliver proposed activities with the company.

☐ We have gathered evidence on the strength of the company's infrastructure and its finances (this will determine whether the company is stable enough to manage a partnership).

☐ We have ascertained what other charity, or similar, partnerships the company is undertaking or is planning to undertake and we are satisfied none of these compromises the suggested partnership with our charity.

3. Legal evidence

☐ Details of any legal events and any court judgements have been gathered.

☐ The company has completed our Modern Slavery Act questionnaire (to check, for example, the welfare of workers in its manufacturing supply chain) and supplied evidence of its recruitment and supply chain processes.

☐ The prospective partner is willing to sign a tailored charity partner agreement, which will need to comply with Charities Act requirements if it is a 'commercial participation' arrangement as defined in that legislation.

☐ Regarding any future agreed percentage of sales, the prospective partner is willing (under Regulation 5 of the 1994 Fund-Raising Regulations) to provide records to establish an audit trail to show the charity has received the agreed amount (other requirements may be needed for compliance but this at least will gauge willingness and awareness of the requirements).

4. Stakeholder evidence

☐ We have received results from surveys/communications with our beneficiaries, donors and other relevant stakeholders.

☐ Evidence of the past impact of partnerships or donations on beneficiaries, donors and other relevant stakeholders has been solicited impartially and collected/recorded.

5. Ethical and regulatory evidence

☐ The decision-making process has been followed: potential objections to partnering with the company – including the parent company and/or subsidiaries – have been compared against our ethical policy, code of business conduct and Charity Commission/Fundraising Regulator guidance. (See chapter 6 for details on the decision-making process and ethical policies.)

☐ We have investigated the level and nature of the prospective partner's corporate responsibility practices.

6. Evidence of the company's previous charitable success

☐ We have investigated the level of the company's history of charitable giving and philanthropic work.

☐ We have communicated with other charities on the level of success of previous or current partnerships with this company.

Conclusion

Good-quality due diligence research is the foundation of making sound decisions. After all, without the right level and quality of evidence, you cannot make good decisions. But, to judge the level of due diligence checks needed, you also need strong risk management procedures, and trustees need to be confident that their delegation processes are clear to ensure that whoever is carrying out the actions and making the decisions is doing so in a way that is compliant with the law.

Having a standard procedure as a basic starting point for due diligence checks will help you to reduce ambiguity and doubt by providing guidance on what needs to be done depending on the type of partnership and level of risk. Remember, though, not to get too bogged down in computer-based research – speaking directly with your prospective partners, and their previous charity partners, can often be more revealing that what you can find out online.

Notes

1   Note that the Fundraising Regulator has responsibility for the regulation of fundraising in England and Wales and in Northern Ireland. In addition, the Scottish Fundraising Standards Panel has responsibility for Scotland, but the Scottish Charity Regulator points Scottish-registered charities towards Fundraising Regulator guidance. Most of the guidance from the charity regulators is derived from or uses similar terms to that of the Charity Commission for England and Wales (the Charity Commission). For this reason, most of the non-Fundraising Regulator guidance in this chapter is quoted or drawn from Charity Commission guidance, but it is nevertheless good-practice guidance for all charities in the UK.

2   'Code of Fundraising Practice' [web page], Fundraising Regulator, 2017, section 12.3, www.fundraisingregulator.org.uk/code-of-fundraising-practice/code-of-fundraising-practice, accessed 8 September 2017.

3   *Code of Fundraising Practice* [PDF], Fundraising Regulator, 2017, p. 2, www.fundraisingregulator.org.uk/wp-content/uploads/2016/06/Code-of-Fundraising-Practice-v1.4–310717.pdf, accessed 8 September 2017.

4   *Chapter 2: Due diligence, monitoring and verifying the end use of charitable funds* [PDF], Charity Commission, 2016, pp. 8–9, www.gov.uk/government/uploads/system/uploads/attachment_data/file/550687/Chapter_2.pdf, accessed 8 September 2017.

5   *Charities and Risk Management (CC 26)* [PDF], Charity Commission, 2010, p. 10, www.gov.uk/government/uploads/system/uploads/attachment_data/file/589944/CC26.pdf, accessed 8 September 2017.

6   For help with evaluating risk, see the Charity Commission guidance documents, *Chapter 2 Tool 1: The risk assessment cycle*, *Chapter 2 Tool 2: Strengths, weaknesses, opportunities and threats (SWOT) analysis*, *Chapter 2 Tool 3: PESTLE analysis*, and *Chapter 2 Tool 4: Risk matrix* [PDFs], Charity Commission, 2011, all downloadable from www.gov.uk/government/publications/charities-due-diligence-checks-and-monitoring-end-use-of-funds, accessed 8 September 2017.

7   *Charity Fundraising: A guide to trustee duties (CC20)* [PDF], Charity Commission, 2016, pp. 4–5, www.gov.uk/government/uploads/system/uploads/attachment_data/file/604684/CC20.pdf, accessed 8 September 2017.

8   *It's Your Decision: Charity trustees and decision making (CC27)* [PDF], Charity Commission, 2013, p. 11, www.gov.uk/government/uploads/system/uploads/attachment_data/file/583855/CC27_new.pdf, accessed 8 September 2017.

9   *Charity Fundraising: A guide to trustee duties (CC20)* [PDF], Charity Commission, 2016, p. 8, www.gov.uk/government/uploads/system/uploads/attachment_data/file/604684/CC20.pdf, accessed 8 September 2017.

10   *Chapter 2: Due diligence, monitoring and verifying the end use of charitable funds* [PDF], Charity Commission, 2016, p. 31, www.gov.uk/government/uploads/system/uploads/attachment_data/file/550687/Chapter_2.pdf, accessed 8 September 2017.

11   The text in this box is based on Ian MacQuillin's advice in 'Appendix 3: Ethical framework for accepting or rejecting corporate support' from the last edition of this book: Valerie Morton (ed.), *Corporate Fundraising*, London, DSC, 2012, pp. 219–220.

CHAPTER SIX

Making decisions, recording and monitoring

Lynda Harwood

Introduction

When your charity reaches the stage of weighing the pros and cons of a potential corporate partnership, you may need to deal with a difficult decision about the confidence you have in the prospective partner versus the income your charity might receive. What might appear to be an incredible income-generation opportunity may – if the issues have not been considered objectively and crisis-management plans have not been implemented – damage your charity's reputation, ultimately putting beneficiaries at risk.

If your charity is considering or eventually decides to work with a corporate supporter, it should be confident and, crucially, open about this relationship. If the partnership could cause staff to feel restricted in carrying out work that is in the best interests of the charity or could make them feel they cannot be fully transparent in their corporate partnership activities, this is an indication of an underlying risk. Of course, an opportunity should not be turned down on the basis of such indications alone – they must be investigated and evaluated objectively.

Ultimately, however, the fundamental touchstone for any decision on a potential corporate partnership is whether it will support the charity's objectives. Fundraising in itself is *not* a charitable activity, so by definition the potential partnership must support the charity's objectives rather than being an end in itself.

When considering a potential corporate partner, you should think about the following questions:

• How can you judge impartially and properly (in accordance with regulatory guidance) which partnerships are likely to compromise the integrity of your charity's values or, conversely, promote the pursuit of its mission and charitable objectives?

• How will you adequately evaluate potential conflicts of interest and loyalty or duty between your charity and a proposed corporate partner?

• How can your charity ensure that it maximises its income, yet does not risk its reputation or cause a loss of public confidence?

This chapter aims to show how to:

• conduct a decision-making process before concluding whether to work with a potential corporate partner;

• record these decisions;

• monitor progress if you decide to go ahead.

Note that this chapter does not go into detail regarding the relevant legislation – for further information, see chapter 13. As noted in chapter 5, however, it is always advisable to seek professional advice to ensure that your charity is compliant with the law.

The decision-making process

To be able to make the best decision, you need some guidelines against which to compare the issues your charity is facing. These guidelines are of course provided by Charity Commission and Fundraising Regulator guidance (and direct professional legal guidance), but another important resource is your charity's ethical policy.

Creating an ethical policy

According to the Charity Commission, one of the main problems that it comes across when investigating charity–corporate partnership cases is where charities 'have failed to establish an ethical policy which can be used to ensure that there is a common understanding of the charity's ethical values'.[1] This highlights that it is advisable to create a clear ethical policy if your charity does not already have one.

In addition to creating a common understanding of your charity's ethical values that will allow everyone to take a consistent approach, an ethical policy (along with regulatory guidance) can be used to test objections and thereby a possible partnership's potential, and/or whether an offer should be accepted or refused.

When putting together an ethical policy, consider:

• any other existing, relevant policies – this helps you to be aware of the overall context, ensure consistency in your charity's position, avoid duplicating existing guidance and therefore use resources effectively;

• that your organisation's values and ethics must be relevant to your organisation's objectives (as outlined in its constitution);

• which industries your charity should not or cannot work with – for example, industries that engage in activities that are directly contrary to your charity's cause, based on what is set out in its constitution;

• the kinds of partnerships or offers of help that the policy applies to (in-kind donations, sponsorship, pro bono work, etc.);

• whether your governing document already restricts or proscribes some types of donation or partnership – it is possible to amend these restrictions if necessary.[2]

Any organisation's policy can include as standard that it will refuse a donation or other association with an organisation in cases where the acceptance of an offer from a company would be unlawful – for example, due diligence research may show that a proposed donation comprises money from a grey-import business (i.e. a business that sells products without the authorisation of the manufacturer) and therefore is, or may be, the proceeds of crime.

The Charity Commission recommends that, along with noting any corporate partnerships, your charity should feature its ethical policy in its annual report and accounts. It is also a good idea to publish the policy on your intranet and website so that all stakeholders, whether internal or external, are aware of it and so internal decision makers can make judgements more consistently by using it.

First introduced in chapter 5, in the following case study the local charity Demelza shares how it approaches potential corporate partners and carries out its decision-making process.

Case study: Demelza's decision-making process

Demelza is a specialist children's hospice that provides care and support to children and families throughout Kent, East Sussex and south-east London. Although corporate fundraising has been a steady income stream for the charity, Demelza has recently refocused its strategy and approach to ensure it is creating and managing great and sustainable corporate partnerships.

As part of this, Demelza is keen to update its ethical fundraising policy to ensure it covers all areas of the charity's fundraising – not just corporate fundraising. From a corporate partnerships perspective, the ethical policy will further highlight industries that the charity can and cannot work with and the reasons behind these decisions. Additionally, Demelza will develop an ethical policy checklist which will complement the charity's updated ethical fundraising policy.

Unlike some high-profile charities, Demelza often approaches potential corporate partners rather than vice versa. Once it has identified a strong corporate partner that is a low risk from a due diligence standpoint, the charity makes the decision on which local companies to reach out to.

Currently, the charity is focusing on identifying potential local 'dream partners' which align with Demelza and will create a mutually beneficial relationship.

Beyond the basic required solvency and legal checks, Demelza's focus when evaluating a prospective partnership is not primarily 'What is the company's financial, ethical or media background?' but rather 'Could this partnership be mutually beneficial?' For example, benefits might include receipt of gifts in kind (for the charity), contacts with potential new partners (on both sides), and promotion and publicity (for the company).

A good example of this is Demelza's current partnership with a building company. The company recently donated household items to the hospice and involved its sub-contractors in funding sensory room equipment for the hospice. In return, Demelza was able to promote the building company's charity work through social media.

The final sign-off on any new corporate partnership sits with Demelza's chief executive, to whom responsibility has been clearly delegated by the trustees. The chief executive will often consult with the Head of Fundraising on the prospective corporate and keeps the trustees appropriately informed. This type of consultation helps to ensure organisational buy-in and support from the outset of the partnership.

To date, the charity has not refused a new corporate partnership (however, it has ended corporate partnerships during collaboration, when potential risks were discovered). Furthermore, as outlined in its ethical policy, Demelza will not work with tobacco companies, deeming this to be against the charity's values. Other corporates from industries which are potentially controversial are reviewed on a case-by-case basis and accepted under advisement from the chief executive, the senior management team and the trustees.

The charity is also working towards establishing procedures to regularly review its due diligence and risk management of a partnership.

Claire Ellis-Waghorn, Head of Fundraising at Demelza, explains, 'We are keen to be as transparent as possible with all our partnerships. We report quarterly to the board and are open about all our corporate partners.' If a partnership launches, the charity reviews the partnership after one year and decides whether to continue it. Claire states, 'We are getting braver with saying "no" to potential or current partners. If the partnership is not proving to be aligned, mutually beneficial and thus strategic, then we have the foresight to not commence or continue with the partnership.'

Demelza feels that it is still risk averse at present and often errs on the side of caution. Claire concludes, 'As a local charity, we feel relatively protected. Every partnership is considered from the highest level and evaluated. However, as with all charities, we do not want to bring our charity into disrepute or disadvantage any of our beneficiaries. That is of utmost importance and the focus for us.'

The objections test[3]

Having gathered all of the practical information necessary to make an informed choice, a decision-making process should be carried out to ensure that personal preference or other inappropriate influences do not sway the decisions made. This is often called an 'ethical check' but this terminology can give the impression that this process of testing objections is subjectively ethical in nature, which it is not. Your charity should compare evidence and objections against the information laid out in its ethical policy, but this process should otherwise be as objective as possible.

For instance, although it might seem acceptable to judge the suitability of a partnership by taking an instinctive approach – 'People will think we've sold out if we partner with this company, so we shouldn't do it' – this not an acceptable method. As outlined by regulatory guidance,[4] decisions on whether it is right to go ahead with a corporate partnership or accept support from a company must *not* be based on, for example:

- your personal moral code;
- the majority view;
- the personal or political views of your PR, HR or policy colleagues.

Instead, decisions should be based on:

- an evaluative system that allows you to decide whether you should seek to partner with or accept support from a company;
- comparisons with your ethical policy, which should reflect your charity's constitution;
- actions that are in the best interests of your charity;

• the Fundraising Regulator's Code of Fundraising Practice (for England, Wales and Northern Ireland) and/or guidance from the Scottish Fundraising Standards Panel;

• Charity Commission for Northern Ireland, Charity Commission for England and Wales and/or Office of the Scottish Charity Regulator guidance.

You should also use the evidence gathered about whether proposed actions are likely to break the law or cause unacceptable risk, including by:

• damaging your charity's reputation, name or brand;

• reducing the future level of financial and other support for your charity.

When imagining a high level of reputational risk, an obviously controversial example that comes to mind is accepting a donation or partnering with an arms company. It might seem, automatically, that the reputational risks would be too high for any charity to consider such a partnership, but this is not necessarily the case. A fundraising partnership (for example, where employees of an arms company raise money for the charity) may not be objected to by beneficiaries given that they may feel employees of any company – no matter its business – should have the right to raise money for the charity. Furthermore, the benefits of the income to the charity may outweigh any evidence of potential negative effects. Note that *evidence* is the key.

While the following process should be considered a crucial element that will influence all decisions regarding a prospective corporate donor, it is not a foolproof set of steps that will provide you with an unequivocally correct answer. This type of framework should only be used as a guide in your decision-making – one that will help you to treat the issues and questions as objectively as possible. Moreover, this decision-making framework (and any framework you use) must be used in combination with the Fundraising Regulator's guidance.

1. List the potential issues

Your due diligence work may have uncovered potential issues. There might also be other, personal, objections that have arisen – we might think that personal objections *should not* arise, but the reality is that they often do, and it is important to take them into consideration so as to evaluate whether they might contain any objective concerns. List all of these objections. (Examples are listed in step 2, below.)

2. Categorise the issues

Decide whether the objections are:

• based on what the *consequences* of working with this company are estimated to be – i.e. based on evidence that the partnership would be harmful to the charity;

• because it would be inherently *wrong* for your charity to work with this company, based on your own set of moral rules or on the personal opinions or moral positions of other people – i.e. you or they may feel that it is wrong for your charity to work with this company;

• a mix of the two.

> Next, list them separately.
> **E** = evidence-based
> **P** = personal
> For example:

I think this company is unethical so we shouldn't work with it. (P)

The company's business activities clash with our mission and conflict with our charity's core values, which reflect our constitution. (E)

The company has recently been accused in the press of promoting its products heavily in developing countries and profiting disproportionately from poorer people. (E)

When we last partnered with a corporate in this type of industry, several major donors withdrew their support. It took us two years to get our major donor income back to a comparable level. (E)

Most of the fundraisers in the department have heard that the company exploits its workers. (P)

Our contacts at the company don't show much enthusiasm for our cause. It seems like they are more interested in the positive effect of associating with a charity. (E + P)

This company is tendering to be one of our suppliers and is hoping to increase its chances of being chosen by becoming a charity partner. (E)

The proposed partnership does not offer enough benefits in return for the use of our charity's assets, especially the use of our name and logo. (E)

3. Test objections against official guidance and the strength of evidence

Compare each objection against your ethical policy and the Fundraising Regulator's Code of Fundraising Practice on accepting or rejecting donations. Consider the following questions:

• Is each objection free of individual or collective personal, political or commercial interests, including your own?

• Is each objection free of personal views on political or ethical issues which are not directly related to the interests of the charity?

If any of the ethical objections are influenced by these conditions, you must drop that particular objection or at least mark it as requiring supporting evidence. For instance, if the fundraisers in the example above want to reject money from a company because they have heard it is unethical, this wouldn't pass the acceptance/rejection filter, given it is a personal belief. For the viewpoint to be evidence-based, this rumour would need to be backed up by evidence from due diligence checks.

To judge which objections are evidence-based, use your due diligence findings and your ethical policy to evaluate what is or is not likely to be in the best interests of the charity by demonstrating objective confirmation or disproof of the potential harmful effects of an association with the company. This could include, for example, evidence (on the negative side) that:

• An undesirable effect occurred in a similar past scenario, such as negative stories in the media that caused the charity's donors to drop their support of the organisation as a result.

• Similar corporate partnerships (with this company, with your charity or between similar charities and companies) worked out badly – for instance, the company was a difficult partner or did not fulfil its agreement.

• The corporate's motives conflict with the charity's aims or interests. For example, the company is seeking to put itself in a good light to gain some benefit from the charity or it is hoping to use the charity's good reputation to gain favour with the general public or other organisations with which the company works.

Conversely, it may be that the evidence gained from the due diligence checks undermines some of the objections. For example, a charity's fundraisers might believe the potential corporate partner operates an unethical supply chain, but evidence from third-party social responsibility monitoring organisations might refute this. Or the accusations against the company reported in the press might turn out to be false when investigated. So, even if the fundraisers still believe the rumour to be true or staff believe the newspaper accusations, the objections are undermined by the facts.

For any objection that passes the test, if you act on this objection and other justified objections by refusing an offer of support, ensure that you could justify this course of action to your regulator as being in the best interests of your charity. Equally, if your charity plans to work with corporates in an industry which is often negatively viewed and could bring harmful consequences to your charity's brand and reputation, or if there is a chance that the prospect partner's reputation could be damaging in some other way, you must have a robust risk management plan to assess the likelihood of negative media coverage and create strategies that, if the negative publicity were to happen, will mitigate it and support the charity's continuing work.

Deeper considerations about the prospective partnership

If the proposed partnership hasn't been ruled out by the objections test, a series of questions and further considerations should be researched and answered to help determine whether the partnership would be truly viable and beneficial to the charity – both financially and from other perspectives of value.

These are points that should be agreed with the company before the partnership commences to remove room for error and misunderstandings.

The following list is not exhaustive – further points may apply to your organisation.

Expectations and compatibility

• Are the expectations the company has for what we can bring to the partnership reasonable?

• Are they a fair exchange for the value that we will receive from the company?

• Are our objectives for the partnership similar or complementary to the corporate's?

• Are these objectives achievable?

• How will partnership objectives be communicated, developed and implemented? What does the company expect us to deliver and vice versa?

• What benefits do we and our corporate partner expect to gain respectively from the relationship (e.g. financial, gifts in kind, influence, raised profile or improved reputation)? Are these benefits equally weighted on either side? (See also the point in the following section regarding HMRC's rules on tainted donations.)

• Will these benefits help us to achieve our charitable objectives?

Financial and legal considerations

• Will the proposed partnership provide income for our charity?

• What is the minimum income guarantee that can be agreed from the partnership?

• Is the return on investment to the charity worthwhile?

• Are there tax implications for either party?

• Are HMRC's rules on tainted donations (a purported donation in return for a commercial advantage) relevant? (See also chapter 13, which covers legal and regulatory issues.)

• What is the legal nature of the arrangement? For example, is it a genuine collaboration, a commercial participation or trading involving the charity's brand? What implications does that have for the arrangement and the charity?

• Is the partner happy to sign a partnership agreement (and pay a licence fee) or a commercial participator agreement (depending on partnership type)?

Resources, marketing and materials

• Which types of resources will we need to commit – for example, PR support, celebrities, social media strategy or other resources?

• How will our charity's brand be used?

• Will we have approval of all marketing and communications materials?

• How will the partnership be communicated?

• Will a licence fee need to be completed and paid for? (See 'Charities, trading and tax' on page 164.)

• Are there review processes in place for marketing and fundraising materials?

• Will both organisations sign off on the materials?

• Does the corporate organisation plan to publicise the relationship? If so, how?

The next case study outlines the approach of a large, complex charity with a comprehensive decision-making procedure that reflects the high level of risk this charity faces as a result of complex and high-profile partnerships.

Case study: the NSPCC's decision-making and review procedures

Due to high awareness of the NSPCC, the organisation is contacted weekly by sole traders, small and medium enterprises, and other interested parties that are keen to engage in, and benefit from, the NSPCC's reputation and brand. This means that the charity is very aware of the value of its brand and understands the worth and importance of this as an asset. It is vital that the NSPCC has a decision-making procedure to ensure it chooses companies that fit with its ethics and values and that will not bring the charity into disrepute or endanger the lives of children.

When making the decision to work with a corporate partner, the NSPCC aims to ensure minimal risk to the charity's reputation and its beneficiaries. It also aims to ensure that the huge amount of time and resources needed to deliver corporate partnerships is spent on the right ones.

The NSPCC decides whether to work with any given company based on the evidence gathered during the due diligence process and on evaluating the benefits for both the charity and the company using a clear set of criteria. An example of a prospective partner which the charity refused was a loan company (which could be viewed as encouraging families to take loans). Even though the company was willing to reach the potential financial targets of the partnership, the NSPCC did not progress with the partnership as it was judged, based on evidence from due diligence research including the types of customers that the company was trying to target and a public relations risk management assessment, that the association with the company was likely to damage the charity's reputation and ultimately its beneficiaries.

A corporate engagement form (outlined in chapter 5), along with a 'new partners' checklist (including a partnership agreement) is completed by the corporate fundraiser who also, along with the Head of New Partnerships, has the responsibility of completing and reviewing all the relevant partnership documents before passing them to the Head of Partnerships for final sign-off. In addition, the partnership documents are presented at trustees' meetings, as required by the board, and they are regularly spot-checked by the charity's audit team. When a partnership has been approved and is ready to begin, the partnership account and the responsibility for carrying out due diligence check renewals is passed on to the account-management team.

Although in many cases it is important for charities to be risk averse, there have been examples where taking a calculated risk (through effective risk management) has paid off for the NSPCC. For example, the charity's partnership with O2 was initially viewed as risky due to mobile phones being seen as negatively contributing to child beneficiaries' quality of life through bullying and harassment. However, using risk assessments and research from its due diligence process the charity objectively predicted that the benefits of the potential partnership would likely outweigh any risks. The partnership has since evolved into a successful, long-term collaboration that focuses on educating children and parents about staying safe online.

Nevertheless, there are industries that the NSPCC will not work with, as outlined in its ethical policy, which allows the charity to make a decision on whether to partner without the need to conduct a full due diligence process. These industries include alcohol, loans, tobacco, arms, pharmaceuticals and any industry which promotes violence.

Making the final decision[5]

After going through the decision-making process and having considered the deeper considerations, the best course of action to take should be clear. A great way of testing whether you have made the best decision for your charity, however, is to imagine coming face to face with one of your beneficiaries or an inspector from your charity regulator: would you be able to say to them, hand on heart, that your charity made the best decision for its purposes and beneficiaries? This type of thought experiment, reflecting on the results of the decision-making process and your evidence-based reasoning, allows you to review your charity's justification for any decisions made.

This can help to avoid making the mistake of switching back and forth between evidence-based and personal-opinion-based justifications. Imagine, for example, that a charity turns down a donation from a company that conducts animal experimentation because the trustees fear negative media coverage. The public reason given by the charity for the refusal, however, is because it believes that animal experimentation is morally wrong (even though the organisation is a children's charity and its purposes and ethical policy do not directly clash with this company's practices). The charity attempts to make a defence in public that is based on a personal justification – that animal experimentation is morally wrong –

when in fact the charity's real concern was an evidence-based position based on a fear of negative publicity.

Rather than having tied itself up in contradictory knots and having damaged its reputation as a result, the charity would have been much better off – and compliant with official guidance – judging its position using a pre-defined process. That way it would have known which option to take based on the objective best interests of the charity and how to defend its position were negative publicity to arise. The decision of what would be in the charity's best interests may not have been clear-cut, but the plan of what to do in either case (whether accepting or refusing the donation) would have been transparent and unwavering.

Keeping records

It is a good idea to record due diligence research, the results of decision-making, and the final decisions made as evidence for future general reference, and in particular for trustees. Dedicated folders on any given partnership that can be referred to at any time are useful, including details on:

• the reasons for agreeing to go ahead with the partnership;

• a summary of the history of the partnership so far;

• any issues found in the due diligence research, including the sources where the information was found;

• the results of any risk assessments;

• any precautions taken as a result of the issues flagged by due diligence research or risk assessments;

• the location of the most recent due diligence checks;

• the background of the agreement/contract;

• how the charity is continuing to ensure that the partnership is in the best interests of the charity – i.e. what the reviewing processes are for oversight and control of partnerships, which may include results of a quarterly audit, for example.

The records should, of course, include the agreement itself.

Practical points on making agreements

To comply with charity legislation, there must be a written agreement between a charity and a commercial participator before certain types of partnership can be embarked upon. In fact, whether or not charity legislation explicitly requires it, a clear contract is always a wise control measure. In addition, the Charity Commission recommends that charities should not allow companies to solely draw up any agreements and further says that 'if a commercial partner will not agree to a charity's reasonable terms we would expect the charity to go elsewhere'.[6]

Your charity should, therefore, be in control of the process to ensure that any agreement is correct and in the charity's best interests. Remember that you are more likely to be aware of charity legal requirements than the corporate is.

For details on the legal ins and outs of commercial participation agreements and a definition of this type of formal agreement, see chapter 13. The chapter includes guidance on the legal statements that should be made by commercial participators, the tax implications of these relationships and arrangements regarding the use of a charity's brand by a corporate.

However, a few practical points that will help to ensure a smooth partnership include recording in writing:

• the types of activities that will be carried out and the corresponding timescales;

• the conditions for success – for example, including key performance indicators;

• how each partner's compliance with these agreements will be monitored;

• a strategy for what the consequences will be if any of these agreements is broken, including get-out clauses to end the partnership within the terms of the agreements.

It is also important to record how the two parties will communicate and provide feedback, including:

• details on the communication channels through which the partnership will be conducted;

• the process that will allow the charity to proofread marketing materials and approve in advance any use of its name and logo;

• which types of fundraising tactics are and are not acceptable for the company to employ;

• if the proposed activities involve the company's employees carrying out activities in association with the charity, (a) how training will be given, (b) how the effectiveness of these activities will be evaluated and (c) how feedback from beneficiaries and outcomes will be communicated;

- when the review periods for the partnership will be and how the partnership will be reviewed.

Finally, financial issues should be recorded, including:

- who is responsible for the costs of the partnership (for example, corporate partners normally agree to pay for materials);

- the minimum income guarantee that it has been agreed the charity will receive from the partnership (based on the value of the association);

- how the company will provide any documentation or evidence to support the agreement – including (if applicable) details of revenue generated and an audit trail – and when such details will be supplied.

Additionally, just as the level of complexity of the potential partnership and the size of your charity and the company will determine the amount of due diligence required, it will also determine the level of detail and length of the partnership agreement.

Monitoring the partnership

If your charity decides to go ahead with a partnership, it must be monitored closely. As noted in the previous section, it is helpful to decide on particular review dates in order to make the monitoring process systematic.

The originally completed due diligence checks (of the type outlined in chapter 5) will need to be periodically reviewed, and therefore these reviews should be factored in as a continual, budgeted cost. It is not wise to rely solely on the initial research given that corporate partnerships progress and evolve: what may have been an acceptable charity partnership ten years ago could be viewed entirely differently today.

It is normally the responsibility of the account manager of the partnership to review due diligence checks annually and complete reports (if necessary). It is their responsibility to ensure all concerns are considered and that the evidence as to why the charity is satisfied to continue with the partnership (and this may be so in spite of some concerns) is robust, up to date and accurate. The account manager should also ensure, in line with the trustee communication policy, that the trustees are kept informed.

If any negative impact to the charity is observed, this must be addressed immediately. For example, if your charity's donors do in fact desert your charity in droves and this can be linked definitively to the partnership, then you have reason and a responsibility to end the relationship. It would no longer be in the best interests of the charity to keep it going.

Equally, it is important to review what the impact would be on the charity's income were the partnership to end.

Much of what will need to be monitored will be related to what is in the partnership agreement. For example:

• If a percentage of the sales of a cause-related marketing product has been agreed, the charity will need to monitor that it is receiving books and records to establish an audit trail and demonstrate that it has received the agreed amount.

• Monitoring will need to examine whether the company is using your charity's name in the agreed, contracted manner.

• If part of the agreement involves the company's employees carrying out activities in association with the charity, you will need to monitor the quality of delivery and training and also receive sufficient evidence of feedback from beneficiaries, such as questionnaire data, and other evidence on outcomes.

Overall, it is crucial to monitor the impact of any given partnership: is it ultimately providing a benefit to your charity and furthering its objectives? And what are the opinions of your beneficiaries: how aware are they of any given partnership and do they feel that it is credible and beneficial?

Conclusion

To deal with a potentially difficult decision about whether to go ahead with a prospective partner, you need the right tools to be able to objectively judge and decide whether the partnership would be in the best interests of your charity and would support its objectives.

Ensuring your charity has an ethical policy that everyone is aware of is one of the crucial tools against which to judge any objections that arise against a prospective partnership. By following a set process that is recorded for the benefit of trustees and your regulator, you can avoid any errors of personal judgement, which can send charities in the wrong direction and can cause embarrassing or damaging results.

Finally, when a decision has been made to go ahead with a partnership, the process doesn't end there. It's essential to monitor progress against what has been agreed with the corporate organisation. In addition, you must ensure that the due diligence checks that were originally carried out are refreshed, and any subsequent decisions that have been made must be reviewed in the light of any new evidence, and possibly reversed if necessary.

Notes

1   *Charities and Commercial Partners (RS2)* [PDF, version 07.02], Charity
     Commission, 2002, p. 2, www.gov.uk/government/uploads/system/uploads/
     attachment_data/file/284729/rs2text.pdf, accessed 8 September 2017.
2   This list is based on best-practice guidance. Note, however, that at the time of
     writing guidance is being transferred to the Fundraising Regulator; the guidance
     that includes advice on writing ethical policies available at the time of writing is
     Donation Acceptance and Refusal Policies and Processes Guidance, London,
     Institute of Fundraising, 2013.
3   This full section, 'The objections test', is adapted from Ian MacQuillin's original
     text in 'Appendix 3: Ethical framework for accepting or rejecting corporate
     support' from the last edition of this book: Valerie Morton (ed.), *Corporate
     Fundraising*, London, DSC, 2012, pp. 217–220.
4   See *It's Your Decision: Charity trustees and decision making* [PDF], Charity
     Commission, 2013, www.gov.uk/government/uploads/system/uploads/
     attachment_data/file/583855/CC27_new.pdf, accessed 4 September 2017, and
     'Code: Legal appendices' [web page], Fundraising Regulator, 2016,
     www.fundraisingregulator.org.uk/code-of-fundraising-practice/legal-appendices,
     accessed 4 September 2017.
5   Ideas and examples in this section, 'Making the final decision', have been
     adapted from Ian MacQuillin's original text in 'Appendix 3: Ethical framework
     for accepting or rejecting corporate support' and 'Take it or leave it: corporate
     fundraising ethics' from the last edition of this book: Valerie Morton (ed.),
     Corporate Fundraising, London, DSC, 2012, pp. 51 and 217–220.
6   *Charities and Commercial Partners (RS2)* [PDF, version 07.02], Charity
     Commission, 2002, p. 22; see also pp. 19 and 21, www.gov.uk/government/
     uploads/system/uploads/attachment_data/file/284729/rs2text.pdf, accessed
     8 September 2017.

CHAPTER SEVEN

Choosing a corporate partnership portfolio

Rachel Billsberry-Grass

Introduction

A corporate partnership portfolio is made up of the fundraising activities that a company chooses to engage in during a charity–corporate partnership. Given that most companies are strategically motivated to engage with a certain cause for the business benefits they can gain, these activities will be the ones most likely to help the company achieve its business objectives. The portfolio can be formed of just one activity, but in the past decade or so I have noticed a trend towards broader-ranging partnerships which include several different fundraising activities.

It is of course also crucial for charities to think strategically about corporate fundraising. To address the basic question 'Is corporate fundraising right for us?', you will need to consider some factors. For example, is your charity willing to invest in building a corporate fundraising programme? Would having a corporate fundraising programme help to move your charity closer towards achieving its mission? What balance does it need between unrestricted and restricted income? What return on investment do you expect – and over what period? What ethical issues may arise from working with companies? And how much (if any) influence over projects can a corporate partner be given?

This chapter explores some of the diverse activities that make up the corporate fundraising portfolio. Its aim is to provide the information required on each of these activities to help your charity evaluate which will be worthwhile engaging in with a corporate partner. Furthermore, it aims to help you decide which combination of activities would, on the one hand, allow your corporate partner to achieve its business objectives and, on the other, create the biggest impact for your charity and its beneficiaries.

Charity of the Year

In a Charity of the Year (COTY) partnership, a company adopts a charity for a defined period, commonly for a year (hence the title), and puts all of its philanthropic efforts into raising money for that charity.

Traditionally, a COTY partnership focuses on staff engagement with the charity. This can be through fundraising activities organised by employees, often involving customers and suppliers, and also through staff volunteering opportunities with the charity. The range of possible activities is wide – from head-shaving to quiz nights and from glamorous balls to marathon runs. Companies can use such activities to generate healthy competition between different departments or regions. Some COTY partnerships may also present other opportunities to a charity, such as sponsorship or cause-related marketing promotions.

A COTY partnership can demonstrate to staff, customers, suppliers and the general public that a company has a strong community focus and is socially responsible. This is particularly so if the company matches the funds raised by staff or supports the partnership in other ways, such as allowing staff to fundraise during work hours. The enhanced reputation that the company gains can contribute to improved staff morale and therefore retention, and to positive customer and supplier relationships.

Research by the Centre for Charitable Giving and Philanthropy reports that companies recognise the value of corporate philanthropy and of involving staff in the choice of charity from the perspective of promoting good staff morale and increasing the success of recruiting, developing and retaining good staff.[1] For these types of reasons, members of staff throughout a business might be involved in the choice of charity partner. Although the partnership itself might be managed by a community affairs team or communications department, and often staff vote for the final charity from a shortlist provided by senior management, a panel of staff sometimes judges the shortlisted charity pitches and makes the final decision. Some businesses make the decision even more democratic by inviting all staff to vote for their choice of charity from a shortlist of nominations put forward by colleagues. The same research from the Centre for Charitable Giving and Philanthropy notes that, while a company's management team is more likely to choose a charity partner that has a good business fit, shop-floor staff are inclined to choose an organisation with which they have had personal experience (such as a palliative care or cancer charity that helped a relative) or that has a naturally popular cause, such as one that helps children. In this way, both senior management and staff recognise that people are most likely to vote for the major players in the charity world: the charities that are best recognised and that have the most obviously compelling causes. The next most important factor recognised by staff is whether the charity offers activities that inject fun into the working week and put managers and staff on a level footing.[2]

To apply to become a company's COTY, you will usually need to write a proposal and then, if your charity is shortlisted, you will be invited to attend a pitch presentation and/or the shortlist will be put to a staff vote.

Your written proposal and formal pitch presentation usually need to address such things as:

• how your charity's regional staff will work with individual branches of a business;

• what media support and celebrity involvement you can offer;

• some ideas for new and exciting fundraising activities;

• what volunteering opportunities you can offer to build engagement with the staff;

• whether there are guaranteed places in major events, such as the London Marathon.

Having a strong elevator pitch is vital: the decision makers need to quickly understand and be motivated by your charity's cause or the project that the partnership will raise money for. But, in addition, it is a good idea to look for ever more original and creative ways to get noticed, both at the pitch presentation and by promoting your cause to staff who have a vote. Possibilities include a service user who can tell an emotive story, a celebrity ambassador, original fundraising ideas mocked up for the panel and samples of merchandise.

Although some companies have a strict no-campaigning rule, others will allow you to promote your cause to staff before and on the day of voting. If this is an option, you can canvass your charity's supporters and trustees in advance ('Do you know anyone who works at this company?') to ask them to use their contacts to highlight your cause. They may also be willing to tweet their support of the charity's partnership bid or otherwise spread the word on social media – this is especially helpful if they happen to be well known. If you are permitted to be there on the day of voting, you can ask any celebrity supporters to be present, hand out free branded gifts as aides-memoires or bring your cause to life using videos, talks from users, demos from experts and so on.

The highest-profile COTY partnerships raise millions and are likely to feel unachievable for the majority of smaller charities and for less well-known causes. However, there have been some examples of the underdog winning a major staff vote because of a perfectly articulated need and well-executed campaign. Carers Trust, for example, pipped Scope (a considerably larger charity) to the post with a staff vote to become the Co-operative Group's COTY for 2013. Although the charities were not permitted to canvass staff, Carers Trust's success, according to its corporate fundraising manager, was a result of communicating with staff via their intranet with a compelling short description of the charity and a photo of beneficiaries, and soliciting the help of the company's vice-president, Hilary Devey from *Dragons' Den*, and a high-profile supporter,

Martin Sheen, both of whom tweeted their support for the charity.[3] In addition, many smaller companies choose to support local charities. I have also noted a growing trend for national companies to choose to work with smaller charities either solely or as part of a group or consortium. Sainsbury's, for example, allows individual stores to choose their own local COTY partner.[4] Nevertheless, COTY partnerships remain a difficult proposition for many charities, so it is worth weighing up the probability of success and doing a cost–benefit analysis. How can you increase your chances of success? Is your charity, for example, more likely to win a COTY partnership that *doesn't* include a staff vote and instead is decided by a panel of senior managers? (This might be the case for charities with less name recognition or with what might be considered unpopular causes, since they may benefit from the opportunity to pitch their cause and the strategic benefits of the partnership to a small group of dedicated people rather than rely on a popular vote.)

Your cost–benefit analysis will need to take into account that a COTY partnership can require significant expenditure for both parties if it is to be managed effectively. Companies naturally have high expectations of charities when it comes to delivering a partnership. For example, you might need to provide large quantities of support materials, such as leaflets, T-shirts, collecting boxes, sponsorship forms and jointly branded promotional material. The staff resource requirements may also be substantial. You will need a member of staff to be the account manager of the partnership. It is common with larger COTY partnerships for the account manager to be based at the corporate's office at least part time. Support from marketing and communication teams, from regional staff and sometimes from the most senior people in the organisation is also necessary in many partnerships.

Much of this investment occurs up front, before the fundraising activity has even begun. The investment and income may span two financial years – a risk that your charity's finance department and treasurer may need to be convinced to take on. This risk can be mitigated by negotiating a contracted guaranteed minimum donation and asking the company to underwrite the initial investment costs.

In choosing a COTY, some companies look for volunteering opportunities for their staff. This can be a challenge for some charities, particularly those working internationally or with vulnerable people or children. You will need to make a judgement call: is it worth investing in developing volunteering opportunities to win a COTY (and potentially build longer-term volunteer or financial support from staff)? Or is it best to avoid partnerships that demand them?

By their very nature, COTY partnerships have a definite timescale, but with good management it is possible to build lasting relationships. Your charity may be involved in an extended partnership, a sponsorship deal or a cause-related marketing opportunity or may be adopted again sooner than expected. However, as the number and size of adoptions that a charity has rarely follows a regular pattern, there can be major budgetary implications of partnerships. You will need to consider how your charity will manage peaks and troughs in income as a result of this irregular pattern and ensure that future fundraising projections and targets do not become unrealistically inflated as a result of a one-off partnership.

It requires time and investment to pitch for and then run a COTY partnership. It can result in a highly lucrative return on investment, but it is sensible to focus on pitches where your charity has a good chance of success, which might mean choosing not to pitch for other opportunities. (For more information on preparing for a successful pitch, see chapter 9.)

Cause-related marketing

Cause-related marketing (CRM) is where a company uses a good cause to help market a product or service – for example, by donating a sum of money to charity for each unit sold. Companies and brands that utilise this method commonly do so as one part of their marketing mix, and the decision to use CRM will sit with a brand manager.

In the UK, CRM was championed by Business in the Community in the late 1990s and early 2000s. Research undertaken by Business in the Community found that consumers are more likely to purchase a product which supports a charity than one which does not, provided that other factors, such as price and perceived quality, are the same.[5] Naturally, therefore, a company wanting to undertake a CRM partnership will be looking for a cause that can drive sales: something that has a particular resonance with the company's target market, or something that can offer some other clear benefit, such as defined routes to market or leverage with a major retailer.

Charities such as Comic Relief and Children in Need, which have guaranteed television coverage, celebrity support and wide mass-market appeal, tend to attract several major CRM deals. The same is true of breast cancer charities during the high-profile Breast Cancer Awareness Month.

Companies are increasingly looking at adapting this mechanism to support smaller or more niche charities. For example, the company Lush sells Charity Pots, which raise money for a wide variety of small, grassroots organisations working in the areas of animal protection, the environment and human rights. Money raised from sales of the Charity Pots goes into a fund, which is given out in grants. Each of the Pots features the details of one of the grant recipients, which helps customers to appreciate the value of their purchase.

Unless your charity has a particularly high-profile brand and, as such, has strong leverage, it would be highly unlikely for a brand manager to respond to an unsolicited approach. Most CRM partnerships come about as a result of an introduction or recommendation, targeting by a brand manager to identify a charity partner, or the development of an existing relationship. With marketing campaigns usually planned some 18 months or more ahead, if your charity is interested in pursuing a CRM partnership, it would need to consider this as a medium-term investment of time and effort.

Given the high public profile of promotions, there are reputational implications for both parties. Your charity should carefully consider which company or product it is willing to work with and be sure that an appropriate price is negotiated: aim to secure a guaranteed minimum donation where possible.

A CRM partnership is considered to be a trading activity, so you will need a commercial participator agreement if your charity enters into such a partnership. You will also need to examine your financial arrangements for VAT. As the primary motivation in most CRM partnerships is the business benefit rather than any particular charity project, income is usually unrestricted, which simplifies the relationship, particularly if a charity's trading company is involved in the relationship.

Licensing

Licensing is a contractual agreement between two entities (in this case, usually a charity and a company) in which the licensor permits the licensee to use a brand name, patent, image or other proprietary right in exchange for a fee or royalty.

There are a number of ways in which licensing agreements can be used within a charity–corporate partnership. For example:

• The charity sells a licence to a company to use its logo on a product or as part of a partnership such as COTY.

• The charity creates an image in addition to its logo (such as BBC Children in Need's Pudsey Bear) and generates income from the sale of the licence to use the image.

• The company gives the charity a licence free of charge to use an image, such as a cartoon character for use on a pin badge or on fundraising materials, to raise money for the charity.

Licensing agreements can be complex. As with CRM promotions, if your charity takes this route it will need to take care to protect its reputation as well as to ensure fair and enforceable financial arrangements. Promotions that involve licensing will usually be competing in a commercial market, so you will need a solid business case that takes this into account.

If your charity has specialist knowledge, intellectual property or a strong brand identity, licensing may be an appropriate income-generating or business development activity even if it does not fit within the scope of a fundraising operation.

Sponsorship

Sponsorship is another way that companies can support charities. Normally it is led by the brand or marketing manager.

In common with CRM partnerships, sponsorship is one part of a marketing programme which seeks to achieve clear marketing objectives and is planned over a year in advance. Unsolicited approaches for sponsorship will most likely fail, so if your charity wants to target particular companies with an idea, it should be looking to approach one whose interest in the charity is already known.

The majority of sponsorship deals relate to sporting events or teams, but sponsorship is also an important income generator for the arts and other charitable causes. By sponsoring a cause, corporate brand managers aim to demonstrate and communicate the values of a brand and build trust in the brand for the future. Companies approach sponsorships by identifying causes that will help them to achieve their aims relating to sustainability, education, well-being and community through projects which fit with existing major sponsorships. For example, some companies are incorporating sponsorship of causes into their major sport-sponsorship programmes, such as a grassroots football project alongside a major football team sponsorship.

The fee paid by a corporate sponsor is unrelated to the cost of the activity being delivered by the charity. Rather, the value is based on the benefits that the company will receive from the sponsorship, both tangible (such as 100 tickets for the event that is being sponsored or branding opportunities on all marketing collateral) and intangible (such as the value of the association with a well-known and respected charity).

If your charity goes down the sponsorship route, it is important, therefore, that it is really clear on what benefits it can offer – its own brand value, its audiences and its access to media contacts, celebrities and other high-profile individuals – and that these are tailored to the prospective sponsor's perspective.

These should all be taken into account when pricing a sponsorship opportunity, alongside consideration for other similar sponsorships and the equivalent cost of advertising.

Sponsorship can offer benefits in addition to income. The association with a well-known brand and its existing marketing activities will enable you to achieve a much greater reach and help you to build loyalty for your charity among the brand's customers.

A robust contract will be needed to define the terms and scope of any sponsorship agreement and the exact benefits that your charity is committing to offer. As with CRM, the charity needs to consider whether it should use its trading company and whether there are any VAT implications. Once the contract is signed, the risk that you won't receive the agreed income should be low, but there is always a reputational risk if a mismatched partner is chosen, and a legal risk if your charity does not deliver the contracted benefits.

Sponsorship deals have the potential to last several years. It is worth finding a sponsorship opportunity that will last in order to build a strong brand association between your charity and your corporate counterpart.

Project funding and donations

While partnerships nowadays tend to be more commercially motivated, some companies still take the traditional route of making a donation to support a particular aspect of a charity's work. Sometimes a donation is made through the company itself, but a number of companies channel their charitable support through a grant-making charity, usually referred to as a 'corporate trust' or 'foundation'.

A corporate trust is governed independently of the company, although its giving criteria may be very similar to the company's (and therefore it is useful for the charity to demonstrate a fit with the company, whether that is with regard to values, goals or other factors in common). In other cases, though, the trust is managed independently and sets its own clear criteria for giving. Corporate trusts are often used to ensure focused giving which has some continuity, and sometimes they are set up to support less mainstream causes.

Whether your charity is seeking funding through a corporate trust or directly from the company it is linked to, you will need to provide specific information about your charity's work, such as details of the project (including costs and outcomes). The income from corporate donations and grants is most likely to be restricted, so requests for funds will need to be justified. Like other grant-givers, many corporate donors prefer to support brand-new projects and may try to influence the development of those projects. Therefore, if your charity is able to plan the development of new services alongside a corporate fundraising strategy, it will have a strong platform on which to build corporate donations. Be wary, however, of developing out-of-budget projects – at the expense of in-budget priority projects – simply because the funding is offered.

The investment needed to undertake this type of corporate fundraising is relatively low. As with fundraising from grant-making charities, success relies on thorough research, well-developed applications or proposals for funding, and excellent feedback on how the funding is being used and the process for managing the funds.

Once a company has agreed to a donation, provided it is credit-worthy, there is a relatively low risk that it will not pay. If it has agreed to several interim donations, your charity should request a letter of agreement or contract to secure the future funds. This is particularly important if the donation is to fund a new project over forthcoming years, as your auditors (or independent examiner) will be keen to see evidence of the agreed funding.

Some companies have a policy of supporting different charities each year, so if your charity receives an initial donation there won't be the immediate prospect of being funded again the following year. Nevertheless, this scenario still provides an opportunity to engage the company, build on the relationship and potentially secure ongoing donations in the future.

Internally, the charity needs to consider the respective roles of trust fundraisers and corporate fundraisers to decide who should manage the relationship with corporate trusts. Given the skill set required, corporate trusts are usually part of the trust fundraiser's portfolio. Another important internal consideration is how to maintain good communication between the trust fundraising and corporate fundraising departments (or, indeed the individual trust fundraiser and corporate fundraiser in smaller organisations) so as to maximise cross-selling to other forms of corporate support.

Payroll giving

Although there are mixed views regarding the effectiveness of payroll giving as a fundraising mechanism, it can be a useful product to have in your corporate fundraising portfolio. Payroll schemes may be pre-tax (in which case the company will need to contract with an agency which will process the donations and give full tax relief to the donor, i.e. the employee) or post-tax (which can be managed by the company and which means your charity can benefit from Gift Aid). You may have the opportunity to promote payroll giving directly to the company's staff, or in some cases the company will manage promotion of the payroll giving scheme itself.

Once a payroll giving donor has been recruited, some charities choose to manage these donors alongside other individual donors recruited through other means, such as direct mail, whereas others feel a bespoke strategy for donor stewardship is more appropriate for the unique relationship between charity, donor and company. Many charities choose to invest in promoting pre-tax payroll giving because it is an excellent source of unrestricted income, because attrition rates are generally low and because it insulates the charity against any tax changes.

General fundraising, events and employee-led support

There is a wide range of general fundraising activities which are appropriate for companies, in addition to the specific mechanisms mentioned so far. These include social events, sales of pin badges, sales of Christmas cards, charity collection boxes, raffles and lotteries, and raising money at corporate hospitality events.

Team or challenge events are a popular way to involve company staff with your charity and can prove to be a useful entry point for a broader future relationship. There are a number of opportunities for companies to compete against other corporate teams in endurance or high-adrenaline events while raising money for their chosen charity. A company team might do its own event, such as a Kilimanjaro summit, taking a group of people from across the business.

This type of activity can be organised by the company itself or by the charity. Events can be time-intensive to organise, so if you choose to go down this fundraising avenue you will need to agree a target return on investment and a clear plan to achieve this target.

Strategic partnerships

In the past decade or so I have observed a growth in charity–corporate strategic partnerships. The defining characteristic of these partnerships is a mutually agreed commitment to address or in some way focus on a particular issue (such as social, health or environmental issues) that will provide a strategic business benefit to both partners. For example, improving the healthy eating habits of women could reduce the onset of certain illnesses, thereby reducing pressure on a health charity's services. The charity will be keen to promote healthy eating habits to women, as will a company which has a healthy-option brand to sell.

If you embark on a strategic partnership to target a particular sector, both partners will have greater strength working together to achieve mutual aims: the company benefits from being associated with a prestigious charity, and the charity benefits from the commercial buying power and reach of the company.

In many cases, your charity will receive a financial benefit from the partnership. This could derive from any of the mechanisms discussed in this chapter but is not usually the primary focus of the partnership. In a *strategic* partnership, it may be the case that your charity considers the other benefits gained from the partnership to have an equal or higher value than a financial injection.

Charity–corporate partnerships are usually built on a mutual recognition and understanding of each other's aims and objectives. Ideas will thrive in a culture of openness that involves listening to the company, being honest about issues that your charity is facing and exploring potential solutions together.

Case study: strategic partnership

Environmental charity WWF and retailer Marks & Spencer (M&S) worked together for more than ten years in a strategic partnership which aimed to protect and maintain natural resources used in M&S products and conserve habitats and species at risk around the world.

The partnership supported M&S's 'Plan A' ethical and sustainability programme, and most recently focused on three areas important to M&S's supply chains: seafood, cotton and fresh water. WWF's environmental experts and M&S's sourcing specialists worked side by side on projects related to these themes, and M&S provided funding where relevant to cover the cost of activities. Examples of the work the two organisations delivered together are as follows:

• **Seafood:** As a signatory to WWF's Global Seafood Charter, M&S committed to working alongside WWF and other stakeholders to safeguard marine wildlife and habitats. As part of the charter, WWF supported M&S to advocate for reforms in government policy and to ensure its wild-caught and farmed seafood products are from sustainable sources. WWF advised on and facilitated M&S Fisheries Improvement Projects, designed to move fisheries towards verified sustainable practice.

• **Cotton:** Working alongside the Better Cotton Initiative, M&S and WWF supported farmers in India to develop ways of producing cotton that used less water and fewer pesticides, which is better for the health and economic viability of cotton-farming communities and the environment. The partnership also helped M&S to achieve its commitments to increase the amount of sustainably sourced cotton in its products.

• **Fresh Water:** WWF supported M&S to identify food-supply chains at risk as a result of poor quality or scarcity of fresh water from rivers and streams in key sourcing regions. By working with M&S and many other stakeholders, WWF's ultimate aim was to improve the health of key river basins around the world. Supporting the development of water-stewardship methodologies has been a shared objective, and the partnership has moved this agenda forward with projects and shared points of learning.

Alongside projects related to its supply chains, M&S contributed significant funding to WWF's conservation programmes around the world. Over £2.7 million was raised through the M&S Forever Fish campaign, which included donations to WWF's marine conservation programme via carrier-bag sales. The intention was to reduce carrier-bag use while also raising money for WWF. In addition, M&S has supported WWF's work on elephant conservation in India and forest conservation in Borneo, and WWF is one of a small number of charities that benefit from the M&S Sparks customer membership card scheme. Every time a customer uses their Sparks card, M&S makes a 1p donation to the charity chosen by the customer.

WWF and M&S recognised they couldn't solve the huge challenges the environment faces from issues such as unsustainable use of natural resources, pollution and climate change on their own. A key ambition of the partnership was therefore to develop and trial approaches that could be adopted by other businesses in order to achieve positive results for nature on a larger scale. The two organisations developed a close and honest relationship over the years, and partnership activities were carefully planned to ensure they supported both M&S's and WWF's strategic goals. Impacts and outcomes were closely monitored and the partnership delivered many successes. It can therefore be seen as a true example of strategic collaboration which meets both business and charity objectives.

Conclusion

There are many ways in which you can work together with a company, and what will work well for one organisation might not work well for yours. To develop a robust and convincing case for support, you need to take time to understand what a company needs and realistically assess what it can offer a corporate partner. By taking a pragmatic view of its strengths, your charity will have a much greater chance of success and avoid wasted time chasing unsuitable partnerships.

Notes

1   Beth Breeze, *Corporate Philanthropy on the Shop Floor: What drives employee fundraising?* [working paper], Canterbury, Centre for Charitable Giving and Philanthropy and the University of Kent, 2013.
2   Beth Breeze, *Corporate Philanthropy on the Shop Floor: What drives employee fundraising?* [working paper], Canterbury, Centre for Charitable Giving and Philanthropy and the University of Kent, 2013.

3   'Analysis: When charity partnership is decided by a staff vote' [web page], *Third Sector*, 9 December 2014, www.thirdsector.co.uk/analysis-when-charity-partnership-decided-staff-vote/fundraising/article/1322426, accessed 13 June

4   'Sainsbury's Local Charity of the Year' [web page], 2016, www.sainsburyslocalcharity.co.uk, accessed 2 May 2017.

5   *Brand Benefits: How cause related marketing impacts on brand equity, consumer behaviour and the bottom line*, London, Business in the Community, 2004, p. 6.

CHAPTER EIGHT

Corporate volunteering

Serena Castiglione

Introduction

Corporate volunteering is a key way in which businesses can engage with charities, and is seen by fundraising professionals as a growth area in terms of investment in and income from this form of fundraising.[1] It continues to grow in size and complexity and it is expected to expand significantly. While it is recognised as a valuable opportunity, corporates and charities often have divergent needs in this area. It is particularly challenging for most charities because of its scale and its demands in terms of resource and organisational readiness.

This chapter explores these challenges. It examines the ways in which some charities have addressed them successfully and developed a corporate volunteering offer[2] that is sustainable, mutually beneficial and impactful.

The business case for corporate volunteering

The benefits of volunteering for corporates are proven and almost universally acknowledged, especially among large organisations. A *Deloitte Volunteer Impact Survey* found that millennial employees who work at companies that offer employee volunteer programmes or activities were more likely to rate corporate culture as very positive, more likely to feel very loyal towards the company they worked for and more likely to be very satisfied with their employer.[3]

Employee engagement and loyalty are more important now than ever in a time when the 'ethical millennials' – i.e. millennials who care deeply about ethics and social responsibility and are vocal about their desire to work with ethical organisations – are bringing higher expectations to the workplace. They seek reward in ways that are not just financial. According to a survey, 77% of millennials are involved with charities or 'good causes' and 30% describe themselves as 'active volunteers/organisers'.[4] They also want to be personally involved with companies' corporate responsibility activities and to feel that they can make a positive impact and have more influence on societal problems via the workplace.

The benefits of corporate volunteering go beyond staff engagement and corporate reputation. For example, corporate volunteering is increasingly recognised as a useful way to enhance staff development.

In fact, research from the Chartered Institute of Personnel and Development (CIPD) identifies a strong connection between employee volunteering and learning and development. A CIPD survey of HR professionals indicates that 70% believe that volunteering can form a part of staff development plans and 79% think that volunteering provides a personal development opportunity for employees.[5]

A mismatch of supply and demand

According to other CIPD research, 70% of the UK's FTSE 100 companies have an established corporate volunteering programme, 23% of all private sector organisations have a scheme and 13.3% of people in paid work participated in corporate volunteering schemes between 2013 and 2014.[6]

However, a 2015 report by Good Values and the Institute of Fundraising on corporate fundraising found that the majority of charities find employee volunteering challenging. A third of them either did not have an employee volunteering offer or felt that it was weak, and only 7% of charities in the report said they had a fully developed corporate volunteering offer.[7]

A mismatch of needs

One of the key drivers of corporate volunteering from an employer's perspective is staff engagement, and consequently employers regard team-building as an important area of focus.

This often means that employers favour volunteering models that involve team and challenge-style activities rather than individual volunteering opportunities. As such, they frequently require charities to offer group activities, in many cases for a large number of people in a single day.

Corporates also face obvious constraints in terms of time. Offering paid time off to staff to volunteer can present difficulties in terms of managing workload, especially for small and medium-sized businesses. While there may be buy-in at a senior level, often middle managers are concerned about the day-to-day realities. A survey by vInspired found that over half of managers are concerned about the financial and time costs of allowing their employees to volunteer.[8] Offering volunteering opportunities on an ongoing basis is therefore much more challenging than offering one-off activities.

And, of course, there is the factor of cost. Companies face the cost of staff hours spent volunteering, and larger companies also have to factor in the cost of providing dedicated internal resources that will source and manage the programme internally and externally, and monitor outcomes.

While it is clear from the research that companies draw significant benefits from engaging in employee volunteering programmes, these come at a cost, so they are aware of the need to manage resources effectively.

Charities, on the other hand, need to build capacity to deliver for their beneficiaries above all else. Everything they do needs to bring them closer to their mission. This means they need to focus on increasing their income, the awareness of their cause, their reach and their efficiency. They need to base their volunteering offer on what they really need to do to achieve their strategic objectives. Most of the time, this will not be offering one-off, unskilled team-building activities for large groups of people, such as repainting walls or gardening.

It is no surprise, therefore, that a survey of 111 UK charities of various sizes found spectacular discrepancies between the volunteering support that charities want and what they receive. The most common type of corporate volunteering they receive is work on unskilled team projects; however, less than a third of charities say they want this. Charities state that their top needs are fundraising, pro bono support, business skills, supporting and developing beneficiaries, and awareness-raising.[9] They are also three times more likely than corporates to favour ongoing support over one-off volunteering support.[10]

Additionally, particularly at times of huge scrutiny and focus on value for money, charities find it difficult to justify the time, effort and cost of delivering and managing corporate volunteering opportunities if the programme they offer to companies for the benefit of corporate volunteers does not further the aims of the charity in any proven and significant way.

As this chapter has noted, cost is an issue for companies, but corporate volunteering is clearly by no means cost-free to charities either. Many of them charge corporates a fee to cover their costs, and that is often met with reluctance or even incredulity on the part of corporates.

To complicate things, charities often feel obliged to offer volunteering opportunities to their existing corporate partners for fear of damaging relationships or of reputational damage. In other cases, however, they see corporate volunteering as a potential point of entry to larger, more beneficial income-generating opportunities. In this way, they treat corporate volunteering almost as a cultivation tool that does not in itself necessarily have to further the cause in the immediate term.

The charity case for corporate volunteering

While the business case for volunteering is amply researched and documented, the charity case for corporate volunteering is far from proven. The sector has yet to undertake a rigorous analysis of the benefits of corporate volunteering: impacts are often not measured, and the full potential to support charities to realise their mission is, most of the time, left unexplored.

Corporate volunteering is still regarded as a matter for fundraising teams to manage, as this is the area in which it offers obvious benefits. However, as long as it is driven mainly or even solely by fundraising needs, it will struggle to realise the full impact it could have on charities as a powerful engagement tool to develop relationships and even win new business.

While the benefits to charities of corporate volunteering have not been formally recognised, the power of corporates cannot be underestimated. The private sector employs 26.4 million people in the UK – that is 82.9% of all working people.[11] Companies reach every single one of us, every day, through their immense communication channels and through the things we buy, the papers we read, the programmes we watch and the conversations we follow on social media. They drive innovation in technology, communication, health care and many other fields. They are also keen to be, and to be seen as, problem solvers of social issues. They position themselves no longer as observers and funders of the great work charities do but as active participants, and, despite the challenges highlighted, they are often willing to put their scale, their reach, their knowledge and their human capital to great use. However, corporates' familiarity with the challenges that charities face may be limited, and they may not realise how they could best support charities in their work.

Charities, on the other hand, are unsure of what to do with all this potential capital. They know that what corporates offer does not always suit their needs. However, they have not developed alternative requests apart from financial support. They struggle to turn down offers of volunteering support and are not sure about what they could ask for instead.

Harnessing the benefits of corporate volunteering

If you are looking to make the charity case for corporate volunteering, it is essential that its value is assessed at a strategic level for your organisation as a whole. By taking the opportunity to explore it at a high level, you can further its possible impact on your organisation's capabilities and operations and create truly beneficial corporate volunteering engagement. How might corporate volunteering increase not only resources but also awareness, brand recognition and the brand credibility of your organisation? How can it ultimately have a long-term impact on your charity's ability to deliver its mission?

To help answer these questions, it is worth considering what charities have done to realise the power of corporates and to drive change by working with them in many areas beyond fundraising, such as influencing or community engagement. For example, Stonewall has worked successfully to address LGBT inequality in the workplace by developing the Stonewall Workplace Equality Index, a benchmarking tool that employers can use to measure their progress on LGBT inclusion.[12] In 2016, Mind developed a similar engagement model, the Workplace Wellbeing Index, to promote and support positive mental health in the workplace.[13] Many international development charities also work with corporates to influence business behaviour and practices that affect children in developing countries. These charities have recognised that the impact of corporates is immense and have driven change by working in partnership with them.

Corporate volunteering should be no different: it is just a mechanism of engagement and it has the potential to unleash huge levels of resource to charities when approached strategically. The following case studies highlight how three charities have done just this. They have started to develop corporate volunteering models that are rooted in the needs of their organisations, recognised as strategically important internally and therefore suitably resourced. They are also tailored in their format to the needs of corporates.

Case study: the ambassador model – Dementia Friends

Dementia Friends is an excellent example of success in the strategic development of a corporate volunteering offer. But it is much more than that: it is a flagship initiative to raise awareness of dementia.

With the number of people living with dementia set to rise to over 1 million by 2025, Alzheimer's Society was acutely aware that communities in the UK needed to be better equipped to support the needs of people living with dementia. The charity was determined to tackle the stigma and loneliness that people with dementia experience so it set out to create a movement of dementia-friendly people and communities.

The initiative was set up with the financial support of the government, which provided funds through the Department of Health and the Cabinet Office for the first two years.

Right from the start, it was identified that corporates were a key audience and potential major drivers of the programme. Corporates were offered the opportunity to engage their staff in dementia-awareness sessions which would allow staff members to become Dementia Friends. Staff could then receive further support to become Champions and go on to recruit new Dementia Friends.

The benefits for corporates were obvious: this programme allowed them to offer meaningful, simple volunteering opportunities to their staff that provided the additional business benefit of giving staff support in dealing with customers who had dementia. This was particularly relevant to staff working in retail, call centres and pharmacies, for example. It was also a very relevant and much appreciated addition to corporate well-being programmes, as

Dementia Friends allowed staff to be better equipped to deal with family and friends who had been affected by dementia.

The programme was led by the community engagement team, and the initial corporate approaches were made by an agency funded by Public Health England. The corporate partnerships team at the start was not fully involved but the organisation soon realised that engaging corporates in this potentially huge programme of change required a joined-up approach where relevant members of any given department should come together to work as a team.

The corporate partnerships team worked together with the community engagement team to identify, target, cultivate and deliver the Dementia Friends corporate volunteering programme. Together they exceeded their target of achieving 1 million Dementia Friends and have now set themselves a new target of achieving 4 million Friends by 2020.

A suitably resourced team of 33 members of staff develop, deliver and market the programme. Corporates have embraced the programme enthusiastically: almost all of Alzheimer's Society's corporate partners offer Dementia Friends to staff, and one key partner, HSBC, already has over 12,000 customer-facing staff signed up. While it was never developed as a corporate engagement tool, the programme has also become a powerful initiator of new partnerships with big-name corporates, such as Celesio UK (which includes LloydsPharmacy) and Iceland Foods.

The impact has been significant. A survey conducted in 2016 highlighted that 72% of Dementia Friends felt more confident interacting with customers with dementia since becoming a Friend. A similar percentage also felt more confident interacting with family and friends with dementia.

The number of Dementia Friends is close to reaching 2 million. Over half a million of them were recruited through employers – 28% of the total reach.

In 2014, Dementia Friends launched an online video which allows people to learn, via people's personal stories about their experiences with the condition, about what it's like living with dementia. This allows more flexibility for corporates whose staff can familiarise themselves with the condition and the Dementia Friends service online rather than needing to attend an information session in person. The service will continue to develop and adapt to reach more audiences.

Case study: the remote befriending model – Call in Time

Age UK's Call in Time model is simple: telephone befriending for corporates. Employee volunteers call a lonely older person for half an hour each week to give them much-needed company. To help fund Call in Time, corporate partners make a donation to Age UK, which enables their employees to take part in the programme and receive training and support.

Call in Time was created through a meeting of minds. Help the Aged (which, along with Age Concern England, formed Age UK in 2009) was developing services to tackle loneliness in later life. Loneliness has devastating effects on health and it is, in fact, worse for people than well-known risk factors such as obesity and physical inactivity.[14] The figures are truly alarming: 1.2 million older people are chronically lonely.[15]

Help the Aged was also looking for meaningful, cost-effective ways to maximise on the growing number of requests they were receiving for corporate volunteering opportunities.

Meanwhile the Zurich Community Trust had been successfully piloting telephone befriending at a local level, with Zurich employee volunteers making weekly friendship calls to lonely older people. The trust approached Help the Aged with a view to partnering on a national level and rolling out the programme to engage additional corporate partners.

Together, Help the Aged and Zurich Community Trust launched Call in Time, initially on a small scale, adopting a test-and-learn approach. This allowed them to keep refining aspects of the programme such as recruitment of volunteers and older people, training and the charging structure for corporate partners. Once Age UK was ready to launch Call in Time, Zurich Community Trust helped the charity to secure additional corporate members.

The model is perfectly suited to the needs of the corporate sector: it is simple, truly meaningful and not time-consuming. In addition, it addresses business challenges, particularly in the financial and utilities sectors. Customer vulnerability is a challenge for businesses in these sectors, and Call in Time is a highly successful way to help their employees understand and empathise with older, vulnerable customers. Call in Time continues be largely a self-funding programme. All corporate partners make a donation for each employee they have in the programme per year. In return, they receive training, reporting and ongoing support. It has been embraced by some of the largest businesses in the UK, including Bloomberg, British Gas, Nationwide, Prudential UK and Santander.

Most of Age UK's current corporate partners get involved in Call in Time, and the volunteers tend to be the charity's strongest fundraising advocates too.

Like with Dementia Friends, Call in Time's offer is complemented by Age UK's strategic partnership propositions, including the help they offer businesses to understand vulnerability and opportunities presented by the growing older market. Call in Time is often a point of entry to wider, higher-value corporate partnerships.

The programme is supported by a dedicated team at Age UK that helps with internal recruitment drives, trains volunteers and matches them with older people based on common interests, then provides all-round support.

Members of the team make calls when volunteers cannot, and they also provide 'wrap-around' support, beyond the weekly call. This is where the team assesses the older person's needs and requirements in order to create a plan that will allow the team to provide the person with the practical and emotional solutions they need. Operationally, this is vital.

For Age UK, Call in Time is more than a nice-to-have corporate volunteering ask; it is one of Age UK's core national services and therefore is run by a dedicated, expert programme team. Given that the team is responsible for considerations like safeguarding and wrap-around support, its expertise is of paramount importance.

Age UK also set up rigorous measurement and monitoring processes and tools, incorporating the LBG measurement framework for measuring the value and impact of corporate community investment.[16] These processes measure the numbers of older people and volunteers involved in the programme, minutes of contact and, most importantly, the impact on older people, focusing primarily on measuring how much the intervention reduces their sense of loneliness. To do this, the charity uses the UCLA Loneliness Scale (a widely recognised model for measuring loneliness), surveying members when they enter the programme and at intervals throughout. Age UK also measures the impact on employee volunteers by surveying them annually to ask how their involvement in the programme impacts on their personal development, including how it affects their skills and their attitude towards their employers.

The corporate partnerships team focuses on business development, manages the company relationships centrally and produces all of the corporate-facing reports and contracts.

The team now aims to support 10,000 older people by 2020 through Call in Time by rolling it out as a public volunteering proposition also. It sees digital innovation as key to this goal and so the team is working to improve automation of the user journey and is currently looking at piloting web-chat and video-call befriending.

Case study: the structured model – Macmillan Cancer Support

Since 2012, Macmillan has reviewed its corporate volunteering strategy and made significant changes to its programmes. The charity is now one the leaders within the sector in this field.

Up until 2012, the main corporate volunteering offer was Paint and Fix, a programme of decorating and gardening projects offered as team-based activities to all corporate partners and non-partners. The programme was driven by corporate requests and not by organisational need. It was a resource-intensive programme: Macmillan's services are set within partners' buildings so locations had to be identified at the homes of people affected by cancer or in clinical settings. The return on investment was very poor, as the time taken to deliver this programme far outweighed the benefits.

Then, in 2012, the corporate partnerships team developed a new, bold corporate strategy that recognised the pivotal role that volunteering could play in adding value to partnerships. In addition, the organisation recognised that, in order to realise its mission of reaching and improving the lives of the 2.5 million people living with cancer in the UK, it had to call on the support and the resources of volunteers. Consequently, it developed a new volunteering strategy for the whole organisation.

The task was to create a sustainable, impactful volunteering offer that provided real value to both corporates and Macmillan, and reflected the strategic priorities of the whole organisation.

The charity reviewed its practices, evaluated its needs and, armed with this new understanding, created new volunteering roles, such as skills-sharing, community engagement and influencing roles, to meet these needs.

Macmillan also increased the resources available to the corporate volunteering team by adding two members of staff. Furthermore, it created a tiered system that allowed the team to focus on top-priority corporate partners who were working with Macmillan on high-value, mutually beneficial relationships. This enabled the team not to spread its resources too thinly.

The corporate volunteering team developed a suite of tools and materials to measure both volunteer experience and charitable impact, and corporate partnership satisfaction. It also took steps to ensure its model met Macmillan's volunteer quality standards.

Above all, the team focused on working with other departments across the organisation to ensure that the outcomes of corporate volunteering would benefit other teams and ultimately the whole organisation.

As a result of this strategic and systematic approach, corporate volunteering engagement has increased by 76% since 2012. It is completely rooted in the needs of the organisation and is resourced sufficiently so that it can be delivered.

Key learning points

Start with a plan

In order to make a positive impact, it is paramount to consider the needs and priorities of your charity as well as its capacity. Doing so will provide you with the fertile ground required to start to develop a corporate volunteering strategy that truly delivers. If you are currently delivering corporate volunteering opportunities, it is worth reviewing to what extent they add value to your organisation. If they do not, be prepared to say no to corporate requests and create your own offer.

Leverage the value of corporate volunteering

Employers fully recognise the value that corporate volunteering programmes offer them in terms of staff engagement, staff satisfaction and skills development. As a result, many of them will be prepared to pay for corporate volunteering opportunities that match their needs and deliver impact for both sides.

Consider whether you can deliver

Corporate volunteering is often resource intensive. Be prepared to be forensic in assessing the cost and time required to deliver your programme. Be open to the option of being selective about what you offer and to whom. If a programme is very resource intensive, consider offering it only to priority partners or consider a model that is more manageable.

Go beyond fundraising

To plan and deliver corporate volunteering effectively and to monitor its true impact, you need to have a one-team approach. To achieve this, you will need to sell the potential benefits of it to other teams within your charity and, most importantly, to the senior leadership.

Conclusions

Corporate volunteering has huge untapped potential and is likely to grow in size. When the scope of corporate volunteering is freed from the shackles of income generation and broadened to encompass activities that are truly valuable for both the corporate and your organisation, it can be a key vehicle for furthering your charity's key strategic aims.

The case studies in this chapter have a number of factors in common. In all of them, corporate volunteering engagement is driven by the mission, the strategy and the objectives of the charity. The programmes in these case studies were not conceived as engagement tactics to develop relationships with potential funders and were not developed as points of entry for financial support (although they have ended up generating significant levels of financial support too). They involve decision-making at a strategic level and have a focus on impact. They also require investment and long-term thinking and, most importantly, a genuine belief that corporates are legitimate and powerful partners in the business of making the world a better place.

As the case studies illustrate, if you want to make a deep impact with corporate volunteering, your charity will have to develop an offer that is rooted in its organisational priorities and break the boundaries of internal teams. You will need to be imaginative about developing models that work for corporates' agendas and ways of working, and explore the potential for technology to connect people. Your charity will need to invest and resource its offer adequately and develop robust ways to measure long-term impact.

Notes

1   *Corporate Fundraising: A snapshot of current practice in the UK non-profit sector*, London, Institute of Fundraising, pp. 38–39.
2   'Offer' is defined in endnote 7 in chapter 2.
3   'Executive Summary', *2011 Deloitte Volunteer Impact Survey* [PDF], www2.deloitte.com/us/en/pages/about-deloitte/articles/citizenship-deloitte-volunteer-impact-research.html (PDF report listed under the heading 'Employee engagement'), Deloitte Development, 2011, p. 2, accessed 14 June 2017.
4   *The 2017 Deloitte Millennial Survey: Apprehensive millennials – Seeking stability and opportunities in an uncertain world* [PDF], www2.deloitte.com/content/dam/Deloitte/global/Documents/About-Deloitte/gx-deloitte-millennial-survey-2017-executive-summary.pdf, Deloitte Touche Tohmatsu, 2017, p. 14, accessed 14 June 2017.

5   *From Big Society to the Big Organisation? The role of organisations in supporting employee volunteering*, London, Chartered Institute of Personnel and Development, 2015, pp. 9–10.

6   *On the Brink of a Game-Changer? Building sustainable partnerships between companies and voluntary organisations*, London, Chartered Institute of Personnel and Development, 2015, p. 4.

7   *Corporate Fundraising: A snapshot of current practice in the UK non-profit sector*, London, Institute of Fundraising and Good Values, 2015, pp. 8 and 25.

8   Anne Gammon and Gavin Ellison, *Volunteering is the Business: Employers' and employees' attitudes to workplace based volunteering*, London, vInspired, 2010, p. 3.

9   *Employee Volunteering*, London, Three Hands, 2015, p. 7.

10   *Employee Volunteering*, London, Three Hands, 2015, p. 9.

11   Figures are for December 2016 from *Statistical bulletin: UK labour market: Mar 2017*, www.ons.gov.uk, Office for National Statistics, 2017, p. 10.

12   'Workplace Equality Index' [web page], Stonewall, 2017, www.stonewall.org.uk/get-involved/workplace/workplace-equality-index, accessed 14 June 2017.

13   'Workplace Wellbeing Index' [web page], Mind, 2017, www.mind.org.uk/workplace/workplace-wellbeing-index, accessed 14 June 2017.

14   Julianne Holt-Lunstad, Timothy B. Smith and J. Bradley Layton, 'Social Relationships and Mortality Risk: A meta-analytic review', *PLOS Medicine*, vol. 7, no. 7, 2010, e1000316.

15   M. Marmot, Z. Oldfield, S. Clemens, M. Blake, A. Phelps, J. Nazroo, A. Steptoe, N. Rogers, J. Banks and A. Oskala, 'English Longitudinal Study of Ageing: Waves 0–7, 1998–2015' [data collection], UK Data Service, 2016, https://discover.ukdataservice.ac.uk/catalogue/?sn=5050, accessed 13 June 2017. Figures extrapolated using the latest estimates of the national population from the Office for National Statistics in order to determine the total number of lonely elderly people.

16   LBG was formerly known as London Benchmarking Group. For more information on this measurement framework, see www.lbg-online.net.

CHAPTER NINE

Pitching

Paul Glazier

Introduction: today's context

If you have successfully built a relationship with a company through effective engagement, proactive asks or a formal application process, you may be invited to pitch your partnership ideas directly. In today's corporate fundraising context, pitches can take place in various settings. For example, you might be asked to make a formal pitch to a large audience, or a pitch might be much less formal and involve a meeting with a small number of representatives from the company or even be a telephone conversation. When you are entering a pitch scenario, it is important to identify and acknowledge that it will involve selling the benefits of partnering with your charity. This chapter takes you through the necessary preparations and planning steps for a successful pitch.

Types of pitch

Charity of the Year pitches

Companies of all sizes and across diverse sectors have Charity of the Year (COTY) partnerships, which are often led by a set application process. With greater competition in the charity sector and companies becoming more aware of what they are looking for, companies are increasingly using pitches to choose their charity partners. A company will want to know how a charity will fulfil its tailored criteria and whether the charity can deliver on its commitments. A pitch is also a good opportunity to get a sense of how a charity operates and how the cause will motivate the company's staff and customers. It is also a chance for the members of the pitch panel to meet the people they will be working with.

Commercial pitches

As well as working in COTY partnerships, companies are working with charities in increasingly varied commercial ways through activities such as brand association, sponsorship and cause-related marketing. These partnerships are not based on philanthropic objectives and often have little to do with the corporate responsibility or community affairs teams within a company. It's important to remember that, when pitching for commercial opportunities to a company, charities may also be competing with non-charities.

If you have the opportunity to pitch for a commercial partnership, it is unlikely to be through an official process. It is likely to be a result of your charity actively approaching and building strong relationships with the identified company. These pitches may be perceived to be less formal than COTY pitches but they are no less significant and require the same level of preparation. For commercial opportunities, a company's criteria, motivations and objectives are likely to be very different from the charity's and so you will need to put yourself in the company's shoes to pitch in a way that will show the panel what solid benefits an association with your charity can bring.

Strategic partnership pitches

Another type of pitch is for strategic charity partnerships with companies. Increasingly, charities and companies are looking to work together to achieve joint and long-term strategic objectives. Even though these types of partnership often involve the most complex collaboration, there will commonly still be an element of pitching ideas and the business benefits of a potential partnership. Because you will be looking to find mutual strategic overlap, the teams you may need to pitch to may be extremely diverse. The development of strategic charity partnerships is also likely to take the longest amount of time and potentially need the highest amount of internal resources compared with other types of charity partnership.

Time and resource investment

With all this in mind, you will need to realistically consider how successful your charity can be in these different pitching approaches. Will the pitching process allow your organisation to play to its strengths to secure corporate partners? Has your charity historically been unsuccessful in this area, particularly with COTY opportunities? If so, how much time and resources is it worth investing in a COTY process, which may include not only a pitch but also a staff vote? From a commercial perspective, do you have brand credentials, fundraising products and events that will be of commercial value to companies? If you are looking to gain a strategic partnership, can you identify companies which have similar strategic objectives to your charity?

All charities have limited resources and so corporate fundraisers should focus their time and efforts on developing the opportunities which can ultimately deliver the biggest impact for their beneficiaries. It may be better, for example, to take a strategic decision to focus on commercial pitches and opportunities rather than on COTY pitches.

If your charity does decide that pitching opportunities are of strategic importance, then it needs to plan and prepare in such a way to put itself in the best possible position to secure support from a corporate partner.

Before the pitch
Researching the company

It is likely that you have already researched the company as part of the engagement process (naturally, it is very important to fully research the company with which your charity is proposing to work in partnership). Desk-based research should cover the company's employee and customer demographics, financial stability, marketing activities and competition, as well as other charities the company has worked with. This initial in-depth research will provide the necessary foundations and insight to inform the preparation of your pitch.

At this stage, you should also research who will be on the company's pitch panel, or attending a meeting, and gather relevant information on key decision makers. Researching the panel members' roles and personal motivations may reveal what information and criteria they will be looking for in the pitch. For example, marketers will be interested in marketing opportunities and PR professionals in PR opportunities. This also allows you to identify with whom you should be building strong relationships before the pitch.

It is also important to carry out due diligence on the company as a whole in order to acknowledge and mitigate any potential risks of working with the company. Your charity may have its own ethical policy or ethics committee, and you should work within the bounds set by these (see chapters 5 and 6 for more information on due diligence and ethical policies).

Building strong relationships

After carrying out the initial research, you can then identify opportunities to engage and build strong relationships with the key decision makers before your pitch. This could be as simple as meeting regularly with key contacts or inviting individuals to visit a service or project before the pitch to demonstrate the impact of your charity's work. If key contacts are unable to meet you in person, there may be an opportunity to send interesting and pertinent information about an area of work or marketing activity that may be of interest to the individual or company. If you have existing corporate partners, this offers a great opportunity to introduce one of your contacts as an advocate of your charity and share how you've already delivered a successful partnership.

Depending on the significance of the opportunity, you may need to develop full cultivation plans and look to build relationships up to a year in advance of an ask. A cultivation plan is simply an intentional and agreed list of interactions (such as phone calls, meetings, invitations to charity events and information sent in the post) that you are planning in order to engage with a company.

Understanding the pitch criteria

Once you have developed a relationship with the company, the next stage is to understand the pitch criteria and what the members of the panel or key individuals are expecting to see. It is important to commit time to this stage before starting to create the presentation itself. Even the most visually impressive presentation with the most confident of presenters will be wasted if the prospective corporate partner's criteria or business objectives are not being met.

To ensure you are well prepared, you will need to clarify any assumptions you may have made (for example, what the company's top priority is for working in partnership with a charity), and, if necessary, discard them if they are wrong. Without doing this, you can waste your time and effort in the wrong places and on the wrong criteria. Companies set out increasingly clear criteria and over the years have got better at articulating what it is they are looking for from a charity. The stronger the relationship your charity has with the company, the better position it will be in to fully understand the company's criteria and objectives.

Understanding the business objectives and motivations of a company for a commercial pitch is just as important. Often for a COTY opportunity, you will have gone through a proposal or application stage prior to the invitation to pitch; it is essential to gather as much feedback on this as possible before going into the pitch. There are simple questions you can ask that can provide valuable insight. For example: what elements did the company particularly like about the application? What did it have concerns over? Which areas of the application would the company like further information on in the pitch?

The company's previous and current charity partners can also hold a wealth of information, and many corporate fundraisers are happy to share their experiences with their peers. When communicating with a fellow corporate fundraiser, be sure to target your questions rather than asking for a broad overview. By doing so, you are likely to have more success in understanding what secured the partnership for them. Two good questions to ask are what the company would have specifically liked more of from the charity and what the charity was unable to deliver.

The pitch structure and content

When preparing the presentation, it is wise to structure it around the company's set criteria and objectives so that the panel members do not have to search for important information. An excellent pitch needs to be simple, have a clear structure and be easy to follow. The method of 'tell them what you are going to tell them, tell them, and then tell them what you have just told them' works well to keep people's attention and remind the audience of the key parts of the pitch.

Having taken the time to provide criteria, pitch panels will most likely have specific checkboxes that they are looking for the pitch to satisfy. Much like in a job interview, members of the panel will be listening out for key elements, so make it as easy as possible for them to pick these key points out of your pitch. Focus on benefits to the company and continually ask yourself: what does the point I am delivering mean to this company? If possible, the pitch should be enhanced by using some real examples. It is easy for a charity to make broad statements about what it has delivered for a company, but such statements become more powerful when backed up with evidence.

Choosing your pitch team

The person leading the pitch preparation needs to carefully plan who will be on the pitch team and understand how different people and styles will complement each other. Having built up a knowledge of the company's pitch panel and criteria, and decided the key messages to deliver, it should be easier for the pitch leader to select the winning combination of pitch members. This is because the leader will fully understand what the company wants to see and who will best deliver these messages.

In my experience, there is value in mirroring the company's own panel in terms of both job specialisms and seniority. This may mean thinking beyond the corporate fundraising role or team. If the aim of the corporate partnership will be to raise funds for a specific charity project, the responsible project manager could be best suited to bringing that section of the pitch to life. If you are pitching a commercial opportunity and a key driver for the company is positive PR, consider including PR professionals in the pitch team who can demonstrate how your charity will deliver on this objective.

It can work to have a beneficiary as part of the pitch team to communicate your charity's cause more authentically. However, increasingly companies are looking for those charities that can create synergy with their business and can help them to deliver their wider objectives, so the beneficiary role may be less relevant in the pitch. It is also important to consider the impact that being on a pitch team may have on a beneficiary. For example, how would they feel should the charity not be successful? In my experience, a video of a beneficiary or charity service can be just as emotive and achieve the same objective. Whoever is involved in the pitch, it should always be the responsibility of the project lead to provide a full and clear brief. Each person should be clear about their role and the key messages to be delivered.

Pitch slides and technology

If you are using pitch slides, they should be developed once the previous stages have been completed and the members of the pitch team know exactly what they are going to be delivering. Pitch slides are there to support what the presenter is delivering and must not detract from this delivery in any way. Strong images work well, particularly as they can often convey a key point and result in fewer words being needed. If there is too much text on show, the panel will read that rather than listen to the presenter. Also think about how the pitch slides can be brought to life with quotes and by using emotive and tailored video content. As part of the planning process, make the time to do creative brainstorms to explore how you can align your charity's brands and values with the company's and generate creative partnership themes and messaging.

If you're using technology in your pitch – such as slides, a projector, a memory stick or video content – make sure you are extremely well prepared. Have back-up options and pre-empt any problems in case the technology fails. In this eventuality, it is important to remain calm and remember that this has happened to everyone at some point. It is advisable to move on to a back-up plan promptly rather than wasting time trying to fix equipment.

Practise, practise, practise

Practising is arguably one of the most important aspects of pitch preparation for both formal and informal pitches and is often overlooked by charities. It is vital to practise any pitch, in full, and several times in front of an audience. Speaking to an empty room is simply not the same.

It is not until the pitch team members have practised the pitch that they will find out what is working and what is not. An audience can feed back what they understood to be the key messages and the pitch team can make sure these meet the company's criteria and satisfy the requirements for the initial qualification stage. Even if your pitch is going to be informal and in a meeting setting, the pitch team should still go through the same rigorous process of practising.

Just as important as practising the actual pitch is practising potential questions and answers. At the end of nearly all pitches (formal or informal), there will be a question-and-answer session. This can be even longer than the actual pitch, and if the pitch team does not practise the charity will be at a major disadvantage. A good way to prepare is by providing the mock audience with questions to ask at the end of the rehearsal. Practising answering tricky questions will help to ensure that there are no surprises on the day. In addition, encouraging the mock audience to come up with their own questions can help make the practice session as realistic as possible – the real audience won't, after all, be asking you questions from your prepared list. If the pitch team is short of time, the most challenging questions should be practised first. Remember that the question-and-answer session is an opportunity not only to answer the question factually but also to sell another benefit of working with your charity which may not have been covered in the main pitch.

Another aspect to agree before the pitch is who will be answering which questions. It can look unprofessional and confused if all members of the pitch team are trying to answer or follow up each question with additional information.

During the pitch

Verbal and non-verbal communication

The individuals on the pitch team need to consider the delivery of the pitch and how to influence the panel through verbal and non-verbal communication. They will need to be conscious of eye contact, tone of voice and body language and potentially adapt their delivery style to the culture of the company. The pitch could be in a very formal environment, so it may be appropriate to mirror this in your delivery style or you may even want to counteract this formality with humour or by inviting more interaction from the panel. However, it is worth trying to find out what the expectations are of the company when it comes to delivery style. You may want to do this by asking key contacts directly or speaking to a previous charity the company has supported.

It is very important to build a relationship with the people being pitched to as quickly as possible. Eye contact is a key way to do this: good eye contact builds rapport and trust and encourages a level of engagement throughout the presentation. Consider whom to focus on during which parts of the pitch. For example, who from the panel will most want to hear about PR? Who needs to be engaged more when the pitch turns to financial information? The pitch team needs to make sure they are engaging the correct person on the panel when delivering a message.

When pitching, some people prefer to have notes with them. This is fine, but if it is your preference be sure to keep your eyes up when talking. Think 'load, aim, deliver' – give yourself a prompt by reading the notes (load), look at who this point is for (aim) and then speak (deliver). Pay attention to body language: the body language of the person speaking will communicate emotion and confidence to the audience. Also, effective use of tone, volume and speed of voice will help you to come across as passionate, knowledgeable and enthusiastic about the content you are delivering and the prospect of a potential partnership.

When members of the pitch team are practising, they should ask for feedback not only on content but also on verbal and non-verbal communication. If you have enough time, it could be useful to invest in formal training or to use practice techniques such as videoing rehearsals: watching yourself giving a presentation is one of the most effective ways to learn about presentation style.

Case study: BMW Group UK and Macmillan Cancer Support

The car manufacturer BMW Group UK has a two-year COTY partnership which aims to raise £200,000. The formal process of applying is an initial staff nomination followed by a formal pitch and then a staff vote.

After some initial research, Macmillan Cancer Support decided this would be a suitable opportunity to pursue because of the significant monetary and wider partnership value on offer. Macmillan also felt that the application would be an effective use of time and resources because previous experience indicated there was a reasonable chance that, with the right preparation and commitment, it could be successful. This type of COTY opportunity also fits within Macmillan's corporate strategy.

Macmillan initially undertook desk-based research. The BMW Group UK website contained lots of useful information. Macmillan then looked to build relationships with decision makers at BMW Group UK by using Macmillan's local networks near the company's head office in Farnborough.

After a successful nomination, Macmillan was invited to pitch. To fully understand BMW Group UK's pitch criteria, the New Business Manager at Macmillan, who was leading the pitch preparation, had several telephone conversations with a member of the BMW Group UK's charity committee. This opportunity was open to all charities. Questions that Macmillan's New Business Manager asked covered topics including BMW Group UK's broader motivations for working with charities, the demographic of the company's workforce, dealership engagement opportunities, what fundraising has worked with BMW Group UK's shift workers in the past, and information on previous charity partnerships. From this research, Macmillan learned that BMW Group UK wanted the charity partnership to focus on employee engagement, health and well-being and to demonstrate local impact. Macmillan also found out that the BMW Group UK pitch panel would be mostly made up of the company's internal communications colleagues.

Following insight-gathering and relationship-building, Macmillan could start developing the pitch. After an initial brainstorm, the partnership theme was decided, which was 'BMW and Macmillan, the ultimate partnership'. This was based on BMW Group UK's own slogan: 'BMW, the ultimate driving machine'.

The pitch was structured around three key sections, which were in turn based on BMW Group UK's criteria. The first was an introduction to Macmillan and how cancer was a cause that would resonate with BMW Group UK's employees. In this section, Macmillan used emotive case studies to build the case for support and gave the pitch a community focus. The second section focused on how Macmillan would engage all of BMW Group UK's employees in the partnership with a focus on health and well-being initiatives, fundraising ideas and volunteering opportunities. The final section was on partnership delivery and covered partnership support, how to recognise and thank BMW Group UK's employees, and how the partnership would deliver local impact.

Once Macmillan had decided on the pitch structure and content, clear, bold and image-led PowerPoint slides were used to reiterate key messages. The pitch team focused on the business benefits to BMW Group UK throughout the pitch and included existing Macmillan corporate partner quotes to back up statements and add credibility.

As Macmillan knew that the BMW Group UK pitch panel was going to include employees working in the company's communication team, Macmillan's pitch team mirrored this expertise by incorporating the charity's Director of Communications, the New Business Manager and the potential Partnership Manager. Each person had a clear role to play in the pitch and had key messages to communicate. The pitch and question-and-answer session were practised three times in front of an internal Macmillan audience and this allowed the pitch team to become comfortable with the content, prepare potential questions and practise non-verbal communication. The pitch team agreed in advance what individual questions they would answer in the question-and-answer session, focusing on subject knowledge and additional benefits of supporting Macmillan.

To add an element of creativity, Macmillan created a small 3D replica of a BMW car made of card. On the car was the partnership title and the three key reasons why BMW Group UK should choose Macmillan. The aim of this leave-behind was for Macmillan to remain memorable after BMW Group UK had sat through a day of charity pitches. For the end of the pitch, Macmillan had also created a bespoke video of three nurses from Frimley Park Hospital, close to the company's head office, to provide a direct call to action to the panel and demonstrate the tangible difference the partnership would make. This video resonated with the BMW Group UK panel members who had links with the hospital.

After a successful pitch, Macmillan made it through to the staff vote and BMW Group UK's employees went on to choose Macmillan as the company's next charity partner. Even though Macmillan successfully made it through to the staff vote, the pitch team took the opportunity to ask for feedback to help the charity improve future pitches. BMW Group UK fed back that Macmillan's pitch was well structured, clear and professional. BMW Group UK was impressed that Macmillan had taken the time to understand what was important to BMW Group UK as a company and then addressed each of these areas during the pitch. BMW Group UK loved the leave-behind and liked the fact that Macmillan had used local nurses in the pitch to articulate impact. Macmillan believes the pitch was successful because the charity was committed to the opportunity, was fully prepared and tailored the pitch to meet BMW Group UK's own objectives.

After the pitch

Pitch follow-up

Once the pitch has been delivered and the follow-up questions have been answered, you may have the opportunity to ask the panel questions. The team should consider giving the panel what has become known as a 'leave-behind' – i.e. any kind of document, visual or even object that you can leave with the members of the panel that will make it easy for them to remember the key elements of the pitch. If you do use a leave-behind, make sure it is relevant and informative and does not come across as gimmicky or frivolous. (See the pitch case study above to find out more about the use of a leave-behind for BMW Group UK.) You may also want to follow up with additional information, such as links to particular websites, videos or relevant documents. In a more commercial setting, the budget holders or other decision makers may not be present, so any leave-behind or additional information can help the panel to sell the proposition on your behalf.

Pitch feedback

Whether your charity is successful or unsuccessful, you should always ask for feedback. It is extremely important to find out why a pitch was unsuc-cessful. Gleaning useful feedback can be difficult; however, if your charity does not receive constructive criticism, it will not be able to improve in the future. You should directly ask the members of the pitch panel why your pitch wasn't successful and what elements didn't meet the panel's criteria or objectives. However, you may also need to use more tactical questioning to draw out feedback. One approach is to ask what it was that the panel liked about the successful pitch(es). This can be easier for panel members to articulate. It is also worth noting that an unsuccessful pitch is not the end of the road with a company. It can lay down the foundations on which to build a relationship, and it can be a prompt to think about other opportunities to explore with the company in the future.

If your charity is successful, it might not occur to you to solicit feedback, but it is still important to do this, particularly with a COTY opportunity, as the pitch may not be the last stage; there could be a staff vote or canvassing stage next.

Conclusion

This chapter has aimed to show the level and rigour of preparation needed to deliver a winning pitch, no matter what type you are taking part in – formal, informal, COTY, commercial or strategic. If any of these stages are skipped or shortcuts are taken, there is a good chance you will be unsuccessful.

As your pitch team becomes more experienced in pitching, there can also be the temptation to recycle ideas and formats, but this can be a big mistake. Every pitch needs to be fully tailored to an opportunity and to match the company's objectives. Because of the amount of time, resources and tailoring which your charity would need to commit if successful, it is vital when aiming to secure corporate partnerships that you focus on the partnerships which have the best opportunity to deliver the highest return.

Pitching can be daunting but it should also be enjoyable. Pitching to companies provides a fantastic opportunity to work collaboratively with the rest of your organisation. It is your chance to deliver inspiring, innovative and potentially life-changing partnership ideas which can go on to have a significant impact on your charity's beneficiaries.

CHAPTER TEN

Negotiating

Paul Glazier

Introduction: today's context

Following a successful pitch or partnership development phase, your charity may enter a negotiation with a company. The types of negotiation a charity may enter vary greatly because of the breadth of a charity's activities and the types of partnership opportunities. For example, you may be negotiating with a company on the minimum level of financial underwriting of a commercial partnership, the resources your charity will invest as part of a fundraising partnership (such as a Charity of the Year partnership), or even an area such as naming rights for a capital build project.

However, in all circumstances you should personally and as a team acknowledge that you are entering a negotiation with a company. This is because, at the negotiation stage, you are no longer selling or pitching to the company. It is now about agreeing the terms of the partnership, not generating demand. Just like pitching, negotiations can take place in formal and informal settings, depending on the circumstances. You may even find yourself negotiating new areas within an existing long-term partnership.

In my experience, the strategy which is the most effective way of conducting negotiations is the win-win strategy. The win-win negotiation method is the preferred option among the other styles (win-lose, lose-win and lose-lose). This approach is favoured by charities because they often want to develop long-term, committed partnerships in which one party sees the other as a partner instead of trying to gain the maximum advantage. Essentially you should approach a negotiation not as a battle, but as a way for both sides to achieve their objectives. The aim is to achieve mutual value, build relationships and trust between the two organisations, and seek out common goals.

Preparing for the negotiation

As is the case for a pitch, preparation is vital. You must go through the appropriate planning steps to achieve a successful negotiation. The rest of this chapter highlights some important areas to consider. It is crucial to note, however, that the art of negotiation is a huge subject and countless books are entirely devoted to the subject. With this in mind, I encourage you to read more around the subject and the different techniques and, most importantly, to use them in practice. There are some excellent negotiation courses your charity can invest in too.[1]

Understanding your charity's value

Negotiating can be a complicated and daunting prospect for anyone, and this is particularly the case if your charity is dealing with a big corporate organisation. In my experience, charities often feel that the power is with the company, but this is an incorrect assumption that can make you feel that to secure the partnership you must agree to what the company wants, even if it is not what your charity needs.

For this reason, you must be mindful of your own psychology within the team: are you entering the negotiation as equals with your corporate counterparts? A true partnership should be balanced from the start. If you go into the negotiation with a mindset of being somehow inferior, or with a need to be overly accommodating, you are unlikely to achieve a win-win partnership.

It is important to understand that charities have a right to negotiate and that their assets are objectively valuable in a commercial sense. As such, it is crucial to ascertain what your charity can offer and find out why the company wants to form a partnership. There are many benefits your charity can provide to a company through association, and your goal is to negotiate real value back from the company, in cash, resources, expertise or in-kind support. Once you understand what these assets are and their worth, you can use them to make up your negotiation moves (i.e. your planned actions in the negotiation; see 'Preparing your moves' on page 138) and trading points. They will also inform your LIMit model (see 'Determining your limits' on page 137).

Valuing assets

Determining your charity's value is crucial. However, one of the most challenging areas of commercial proposal creation, pitching and then negotiating is *what value to place* on both the charity's own assets and the various partnership opportunities and assets. Values are likely to vary between the individual opportunities, and you will need to consider variables including the assets offered, brand values and target audiences reached. You also need to be aware that the value you place on an opportunity should not be based on how much money you need to raise or how much something is costing the charity, but instead on the opportunity you are offering the company and the associated benefits.

When developing commercial opportunities (i.e. cause-related marketing and sponsorship), you may want to structure your valuation around the **tangible value**, the **intangible value** and the **market value** of the opportunity. In combination, these three elements should help you to determine your charity's value to its partners and the fees you may charge.

The **tangible value** of the opportunity might include the actual cost a company would need to pay for the measurable benefits the charity is offering. To quantify a sponsorship fee for an event, consider, for example, how much a company would have to pay for X number of tickets to attend. This is then a quantifiable benefit for tickets that can be included in the sponsorship package. Another measurable benefit includes how much it would have to pay for the opportunity to advertise within an event programme – the sponsor would then receive a certain amount of advertising space worth £X as part of the package.

The **intangible value** represents the wider value of being associated with the charity, a particular event or individual opportunity. This can be difficult to quantify but takes into consideration the benefit to the company through association. The intangible benefits the company may receive include enhanced brand reputation, recognition and a reinforced positive image from the link with your charity's brand. For example, your charity has 'brand equity', which is the value of your brand based on the public's perception of your charity. If your charity is well established and is trusted by the public, it will have a higher level of brand equity. Third Sector's Charity Brand Index and YouGov's CharityIndex[2] can potentially be useful as confirmation of the level of public trust in your charity, but, if your charity is not in either of these indexes, its brand equity can be valued based on how people perceive the charity in the local community or how it is perceived by its beneficiaries. This could be achieved by, for instance, quantifying feedback from beneficiaries (from surveys or other sources) or determining how often you are positively reported on in the local press.

If you have a high level of brand equity and you are negotiating the use of your logo and brand (for example, in a cause-related marketing campaign), it is highly likely that this use will improve the perception of the company's product, which in turn has been shown, from data on previous charity–corporate tie-ups, to increase product sales.[3]

The third element is researching **market values**: it is very useful to find out what companies are paying for other commercial or partnership opportunities with charities and non-charities. You can also look to find out what other charities are charging for comparable opportunities. If a company weren't working with your charity, how much would it be paying to achieve the same objectives?

If a company is offering value to your charity that isn't cash, it can be equally challenging to determine the value of the assets, resources and expertise the company can deliver back to the charity. To help determine the real value you can place on pro bono support, access to communication channels and gifts in kind, you need to understand first whether what the company is offering actually meets an identified partnership or organisational objective. Then, you need to determine how high in priority these objectives are and how the partnership and value the company is offering will be measured against these objectives. If what the company if offering as part of a negotiation does not meet any of your objectives and can't be measured, you should not place value on the offering as part of the negotiation and should be very cautious when trading it as part of your moves.

It is important to remember to be as consistent as possible in your valuations and what you ultimately seek to charge or receive from a company, including across different opportunities and with different partners. If companies can see you are being inconsistent in your valuations, it is likely to create a sense of mistrust and ultimately will devalue what you may be trying to sell.

Choosing your negotiation team

Research has found that negotiating in teams achieves better results, including a higher level of information exchanged between the parties and a better level of accuracy in judging the other party's interests than when individuals negotiate alone.[4] This is partly because by working as a team you can learn more about the other party's priorities. With this in mind, it is well worth having at least two people who can form your charity's negotiation team.

When putting together the team, it is important to decide who is leading the negotiation preparation as it will be this person's responsibility to bring all of the different elements together, including the members of the negotiation team, the table of moves and any templates to record moves. This person must also organise the practice sessions (these elements will be outlined in the following sections). In addition, make sure you assign clear roles and responsibilities to individuals in preparation for when you enter the actual negotiation situation (whether formal or informal, in person or over the phone). You should have at least one lead person who can put forward your proposals and summarise the other side's proposals (see 'During the negotiation' on page 140), and then someone to record the discussions, offers and agreements made. (The lead person should not also record proceedings – this would detract from how effectively they can negotiate.) Like with pitches, you may want to mirror a company's negotiation team with specialisms and seniority (see 'Choosing your pitch team' on page 125). You may want to include someone in a senior position who can lend weight to the team in circumstances when the negotiations become particularly challenging, but be careful not to deploy senior people if it will undermine your own negotiation authority and position.

Being clear on your objectives

Once you have agreed your negotiation team, it is important to make sure everyone in the team is completely aligned on the objectives before entering the negotiation, even if different internal teams have their own key objectives. To help set your objectives, as the negotiation specialist Gavin Kennedy recommends, it is important to clarify your interests – i.e. *why* you want what you want from a negotiation. To do this, he suggests asking yourself many 'why' questions to drill down into your motivations (i.e. 'Why do we want to do X?') and then continuing to ask 'Why?' to any given answer until you reach the most fundamental reason.[5]

A charity has a natural advantage in knowing its interests thanks to its inbuilt central motivation for everything it does: its mission. Any partnership that a charity develops therefore must be in line with its corporate strategy and ultimately with its charitable objectives. In addition, the reasons for partnering should have been explored as part of the pitch preparation or partnership development process. Nevertheless, it is a good exercise for the negotiation team to remind itself of the whys of partnering with the company and to check that its motivations are indeed serving the charity's beneficiaries.

Once the team members fully understand their objectives, they are then able to prioritise these.

Including more than just cash objectives

Remember that a company can deliver more than money to a charity, and often it is those areas that are of a lower or no cost to the company that can add real value to the charity. As part of the negotiation, you can ask for something that's valuable to the charity but doesn't cost the business much. Not only does securing these areas provide added benefits but it is also a great way of developing more sustainable and long-term partnerships. Those companies which are more closely involved with a charity's work and fundraising events are less likely to end their support.

It is good to explore these sorts of benefits with relevant colleagues. For example, an objective could be that the company's marketing or customer communication channels will be used to promote and drive registrations for one of your fundraising events. Another objective could be to harness the company's expertise in an area that could transform one of your projects.

Determining your limits

Once you have a list of prioritised objectives, it is important to have a clear idea of where there is room for movement between what your charity ideally wants and the least amount that it could accept from the deal. The LIMit model, originally conceived by Gavin Kennedy, is a useful tool for a negotiation team to use and structure its thinking.[6] This mnemonic can help the team to track the limits of the charity in terms of the best- and worst-case scenarios.

• Like: This category includes all of the things your charity *ideally* wants as a result of the negotiation, including your desired highest financial commitment from the company and the less important objectives that it would be nice to have. If you were unable to attain them all, it wouldn't stop you from agreeing the partnership. It represents the best deal possible.

• Intend: These are the significant objectives that your charity would like to achieve in the negotiation, including your intended financial commitment from the company, but again not to the point where you would reject the partnership if these objectives were not reached.

• Must: This is the absolute minimum your charity can accept from the negotiation, including the minimum financial commitment from the company, to prevent you walking away from the potential partnership. It represents your bottom line.

The LIMit model can prove extremely useful, no matter how formal or informal the negotiation/conversation may be. I recommend using a LIMit document that is shared with stakeholders to agree what is collectively desired and needed from the negotiation and signed off by them before the negotiations begin. In my experience, this is one of the most useful documents when going into a negotiation: it allows the members of the negotiation team to have clearly in their minds what they are going to ask for, where there is room for manoeuvre and what their walk-away point is.

It is crucial to know the walk-away point because, although all partnerships involve some level of compromise, there is always a possibility that a satisfactory agreement cannot be reached. The negotiators need to know at what point the partnership (or aspects of the partnership) no longer offers sufficient value to the charity compared with the resources or benefits the charity is offering. The real danger if you go beyond your walk-away point is the risk of costing your charity money, or building a partnership that doesn't deliver the desired value to your beneficiaries. A bad deal is worse than no deal.

If you are clear with your own team before the start of the negotiations about the charity's walk-away point, this will help to avoid any possibility of agreeing a deal that cannot offer your charity enough. Although it can be a difficult decision to walk away from a potential partnership, you can always leave the door open to further negotiations.

Being clear on the company's objectives

You also need to ascertain, as far as is possible before the negotiation, what is valuable to the other party: the objectives that the company wants to achieve. This can be uncovered through conversations that the negotiation team has with the company before going into the negotiation. In addition, use your knowledge about the company from a combination of research and any direct conversations to date. Try to uncover the company's priorities, the audiences it wants to target, its interests and so on. You can also use information gathered from your investigation and due diligence processes, including any intelligence previously gathered from the company's reports, websites, marketing activities and so on. For example, what current commitments (whether corporate responsibility commitments or those otherwise relevant to the negotiation) does the company have? Does the company want, for instance, to increase its employee volunteering opportunities? Ideally, speak directly to any company contacts you have to probe into what the company's objectives are.

Once the team has a list of the company's likely objectives, put them in an estimated order of priority. Also consider what further information you would like to elicit from your counterparts and therefore what questions you could ask.

Preparing your moves

Having listed both the charity's and the company's priorities and objectives, the negotiation team can compare its objectives with the expected objectives of the company. How do they compare with the priorities you have identified for your charity? Where do you anticipate these priorities will converge? And where are there likely to be differences in priority that will create debate and will need an agreement to be reached? This questioning process allows you to highlight the negotiable issues – i.e. where there is room for manoeuvre – and predict which likely points of contention will need to be prepared for.

Once your priorities and objectives are clear, the moves then need to be planned and you will need to think about how these might be exchanged or traded. Ideally, the first move should be to address your most important objective, and the proposals should become smaller throughout the negotiation. I find the following format – as developed by negotiation consultancy, The Gap Partnership – to be a helpful format for planning negotiation moves:[7]

If you ...	Then we ...
Agree to a fundraising target of £X	Will provide a dedicated account manager to manage our partnership
Agree to sponsor our fundraising event for £X	Will allow your logo to appear on the following event assets ...
[and so on ...]	

This clearly outlines the team's priorities and its first move. Being systematic in this way will allow you to ensure that your charity can secure what it really needs from the partnership before moving on to any finer negotiation points. Alternatively, in the least desirable case, it will allow you to walk away from the possibility of partnering if the company cannot agree the minimum amount. The LIMit document works in combination with your planned moves so that it is clear how far the negotiating can go before you walk away. For instance, your charity's ideal objective might be £50,000 for the sponsorship of an event (its Like figure) with an Intend figure of £40,000 and a Must amount of £30,000 as a minimum.

The table of moves that you create can also be used to practise conditional 'if... then' scenarios in the preparation phase, as outlined in the following section.

Practise, practise, practise

Like with pitches, the negotiation team should take the opportunity to practise before entering a negotiation with a company. This gives you the opportunity to become comfortable with the situation and get used to responding to questions that may be asked. For example, it is very useful preparation to:

• work out some 'what if?' scenarios and role-play them: have colleagues – who should be briefed on the likely priorities and concerns of your potential partner – sit in as the corporate negotiators;

• try out a scenario using your prepared moves and actively use open questions (see 'During the negotiation' below) to move the conversation along;

• practise accurately summarising the other party's proposals in order to, among other reasons, ensure that you're all on the same page (see 'During the negotiation' below);

• role-play your 'if... then' conditional scenarios using the prepared moves table to become accustomed to or hone your trading and bargaining skills.

Of course, no negotiation is the same and none will ever go exactly to plan. Nevertheless, planning and practising are crucial to prepare the members of the negotiation team to perform at their best and to build the confident mindset that is crucial for success. To paraphrase an astute aphorism: when under pressure, you don't rise to the level of your highest hopes; you fall to the level of your preparation.

During the negotiation

As your charity is likely to want to develop long-term relationships, it is usually most effective to conduct a negotiation in a friendly, collaborative style rather than an uncomfortably formal or aggressive one. Negotiating is about having a two-way conversation, and the focus should be on finding a way to make things happen that works in the best combined way for both parties.

How the members of the negotiation team conduct themselves in the early stages of the negotiation is crucial as it will set the tone for the negotiation. At this early stage, be wary of using aggressive language: you risk reaching your walk-away point unintentionally and leaving yourself with nothing left to negotiate. However, adopting a constructive style does not mean being overly accommodating and undervaluing the charity.

Remember to listen a *lot* more than you talk – often, the more your side listens, the more the other side reveals and the more information you can gather for your own use. Build rapport in simple ways, such as by smiling, being relaxed and talking in a positive tone of voice – these approaches alone can help to put people in an optimistic and collaborative frame of mind.

Furthermore, Gavin Kennedy and other negotiation experts emphasise the importance of using open questions in a negotiation – especially those starting with 'what' or 'how'.[8] By using these types of questions, you can avoid completely the need to say 'no' and instead demonstrate understanding, get the other side speaking more, and keep the tone friendly and collaborative. An example of a 'what' question might be 'What are your priorities?' And an example of 'how' question might be 'How do you feel about the issues we have raised?'

The ability to summarise your corporate counterparts' proposals well is another crucial skill. Before responding to any proposal, clarify whether you've understood it by summarising it as accurately as you can: the aim is to invite your counterparts to confirm that what you've said is correct. This has a reassuring effect on the other side by assuring the negotiators that you understand both them and their position well. Summarising can also serve to simplify complex issues and can help to focus and progress the negotiation. You can use this technique to bring to light any concerns that have been picked up on during the discussions or to affirm the company's positive motivations for partnering with you.[9]

While you may plan for a collaborative, win-win approach, the members of your team may come up against a company using a competitive negotiation style. In this case, they would need to adapt their style if they are to make sure their charity's objectives are met. If you find yourself on the receiving end of an aggressive negotiation style (with more of a win-lose approach or a short-term mindset) in which unacceptable proposals are made, you may need to use your walk-away point.

Recording agreements

In some situations, there can be multiple areas which are being negotiated at the same time. To record offers, counter-offers and what is being agreed during a negotiation, I have found following table – as developed by The Gap Partnership – to be very useful.

Point of negotiation	Yours	Theirs	Yours	Theirs	Agree
Sponsorship fee for an event	£50K	£30K	£40K	£35K	£40K
X					
X					

The last step of the negotiation is formalising the agreement. After a negotiation, you should follow up in writing with a comprehensive summary of all the agreements you have made, ensuring there is no ambiguity. Following this, you can then draw up an appropriate partnership agreement or contract. (For more on agreements and contracts, see chapter 13.)

Conclusion

This chapter has illustrated that just as much preparation and thought are needed for negotiating as for the pitch stage. But, by being able to negotiate effectively with companies, you will be in a strong position to develop long-term, committed and mutually beneficial partnerships. By failing to negotiate properly, you are more likely to develop partnerships which do not fully meet your charity's or the company's objectives, and these partnerships are more likely to be short-lived.

Following any negotiation, I would recommend taking the time to capture all the things you have learned from the negotiation process and what you could have done differently. This is because negotiation is a skill and one that you need to continuously develop to be a successful corporate fundraiser.

Notes

1   See, for example, the Gap Partnership training courses at www.thegappartnership.com/training.
2   These indexes are put together as a result of surveys conducted by Third Sector (www.thirdsector.co.uk/charity-brand-index) and YouGov (https://yougov.co.uk/find-solutions/brandindex/charityindex).
3   *The Business Case for Being a Responsible Business*, London, Business in the Community, 2011.
4   Reported by psychologists Leigh Thompson, Erika Peterson and Susan Brodt in 'Team Negotiation: An examination of integrative and distributive bargaining', *Journal of Personality and Social Psychology*, vol. 70, no. 1, 1996, pp. 66–78.
5   Gavin Kennedy, *Perfect Negotiation*, London, Cornerstone Digital/Random House eBooks, 2011, at location 226.
6   See Gavin Kennedy, *Kennedy on Negotiation*, Brookfield, Gower Publishing, 1997, p. 37.
7   See www.thegappartnership.com/insights to read free negotiation articles by The Gap Partnership.
8   Gavin Kennedy, *Perfect Negotiation*, London, Cornerstone Digital/Random House eBooks, 2011, at location 392–414.
9   Gavin Kennedy, *Perfect Negotiation*, London, Cornerstone Digital/Random House eBooks, 2011, at location 416.

CHAPTER ELEVEN
Managing the corporate account

Beth Courtier

Introduction: a shared vision

Too often, there is a focus on the differences between partners rather than on the areas of mutual benefit and the additional value that can be gained from a partnership. A corporate–charity partnership is no different from any other customer relationship: it is about understanding the needs of your customer, identifying opportunities, delivering solutions and building on your relationship to gain a greater understanding through ongoing dialogue. And, as with any relationship, communication is at its heart.

A corporate–charity partnership built on a shared vision, an agreed way of working together and a genuine desire to make a positive difference can transform the lives of the charity's beneficiaries and positively impact on society more widely.

What can be more motivating than a partnership which has, at its heart, the aspiration to make a genuine impact on some of the neediest in society? Work simply does not get any better.

Account management and good relationships
Structures and remits

While having an account-management structure and formalised processes does not guarantee a successful partnership, these elements are critical in understanding how you will work together with your corporate partner to drive and achieve a shared vision. The size of the account team and the seniority of its members are not in themselves important; what is important is having the appropriate level of support given by both parties.

The account team does not need to be static; it can and should draw in the relevant people at the appropriate times. A successful partnership is about how both parties make the best use of those resources to which they have access. Corresponding account managers from the charity and corporate sides are responsible for maintaining the relationship with the other party, but the remit of the relationship does not need to be limited to the confines of the corporate responsibility or corporate fundraising departments. Rather than leading on every activity, your charity's account manager and their corporate counterpart can explore opportunities across both organisations by encouraging the direct engagement of other parts of the respective organisations and by brokering and making introductions.

Bear in mind, however, that while some great activities should and will be generated, developed and delivered outside an account team, the account leads in both organisations are those who have the broadest experience and greatest influencing opportunities through existing contacts, and who genuinely seek to add real value and longevity to the partnership. Therefore, they should be consulted on and involved in any partnership activity even if they are not leading it, as ultimately they are responsible for making sure that activities generated from other parts of the organisations are harnessed and delivered effectively.

Commitment to the partnership

Your charity will want its corporate partner to know that the charity is committed to and passionate about the partnership (and vice versa). For this reason, your account lead must convince their corporate counterpart not only that they are personally committed to the partnership but also that the organisation is committed. Indeed, everyone involved must sustain a high level of commitment to and energy within a partnership: partnerships are an investment by both organisations and they should not fizzle out at the end of the contract period (as too often happens).

Constructive feedback and generation of ideas

A sound relationship between account managers should allow both parties to give feedback on both positives and negatives. The positives are certainly easier to communicate, but the negatives are equally as important. Where there is a significant partnership – for example, in terms of longevity, funds raised or integrated working – broader issues should be raised by a partner organisation. Being a good account manager is about understanding key stakeholders and communicating well. Significant changes in organisations can have a direct impact on partners, and they would certainly rather hear about these from their contacts than through a third party or even the press.

In addition to formal meetings, ongoing dialogue and introductions to others can often result in unexpected opportunities or new possibilities. Informal introductions can result in the stimulation of new ideas. It is a good idea to look at how all parts of your organisation could benefit from your corporate partner's engagement.

Handover processes

A frequent cause of frustration is where an account manager leaves and there has been no proper handover or succession planning. Neither organisation will feel like a valued partner when a new account manager asks the other organisation's account lead to explain the partnership, what it has done and what the plans are. It is important, therefore, to have a proper handover process to fully brief your new account manager before they meet the other organisation's account lead.

It is always hard to say goodbye to a good account lead, but with any departure of a lead contact you will have the opportunity to bring in someone new who will have different ideas and see potential for new opportunities. With the correct processes in place for a good handover, this can be a very positive scenario.

Project management and good relationships
Project management processes

Account management is about people and personalities, and inevitably results in informalities. Nevertheless, however small or large a project, you should always have formal project management processes and an appropriate contract in place. Clear meeting structures, reporting procedures and review dates are important, not to demonstrate the principles of good project management but to provide a structure and a way of reviewing progress and measuring success. This ensures a focus on objectives and, critically, makes certain that everyone is kept informed and has opportunities to learn from one another. In addition, free web-based project management systems such as Freedcamp (freedcamp.com) can be useful tools to keep all parties in touch and aware of any actions they need to carry out and of what progress has been made.

Assessment and measurement

Measurement is essential, and so both partners should try to measure everything they do, as everything should have some impact. To assess best use of efforts and a return on investment, in terms of both time and money, this is clearly critical. Some things are undoubtedly more difficult to assess, but that should not stop you or your corporate partner from trying if it is relevant (just because something has not been costed or measured before isn't a reason not to look at it). But measures need to have relevance: trying to come up with a figure for something that you cannot measure will only create data that is accurate, unrepresentative and of no value to anyone.

One development I have noticed is the way that charities and companies are increasingly recognising and measuring in-kind gifts in addition to income from their fundraising activities. Don't forget to include how these almost endless opportunities for additional value – volunteering and access to products, services, rooms, suppliers and so on – are making an impact.

Learning from each other

As in any good relationship, both organisations should be able to learn from each other. Your charity will undoubtedly have different processes and different reporting and measurement procedures from those of your corporate partner, but these can be reviewed and mutually modified in a way that works well for each party. If you both recognise that you do things differently, this will allow you to work through the issues and identify the common ground.

If you were to tell a partner organisation that you have to work in a certain way as this is how your charity has agreed it works with all of its corporate partners, it is likely that the organisation would bristle. Partner organisations don't want to be thought of as 'just another corporate'. It is much better and more effective to agree on an individual basis how your organisations are going to work together.

Reciprocity in contracts

Contracts and service-level agreements are critical in formalising partnerships; however, one size doesn't fit all. Both your charity and your corporate partner need to recognise any legal obligations and established processes, but open dialogue remains crucial and so, if any issues arise, they must be raised at the first opportunity.

In a good partnership, the contract does not consist of three pages of obligations for one partner and none for the other. It is important to make sure that the balance is right and that both sides are happy with what is expected of them. In addition, it is best not to use a set agreement with multiple corporate partners. Just as not all charities are the same, neither are companies, so a new agreement should be drawn up for each separate partnership that is tailored to the specific needs and expectations of that partnership.

Review dates

While partners need to sign up to a shared vision, the flexibility of being able to review this vision is critical: organisations change, the environment changes and the world changes. At worst, these changes can frustrate plans and progress, but they can also present new opportunities. In any partnership, particularly longer-term ones, you need to build in expectations for change and make new plans accordingly. On the other hand, beware of changing plans to avoid delivering outcomes that are difficult but crucial to achieve.

Working with competitors

Corporate–charity relationships are often complex, but additional layers of complexity are created when there are multiple companies or even multiple charities involved. Understanding the different relationships is important in order to understand opportunities and potential conflicts.

While a company will expect and want your charity to work with other companies, it will not necessarily want to be on stage with a competitor or support the same activities. Similarly, sometimes you will need to work with another charity. This might not be your first choice and it won't necessarily be straightforward, but a review of the value of being involved will put things into perspective. After all, it is better to share resources than to have nothing at all. Success when working with competitors is about looking at where the shared interests lie, taking joint ownership and being very open.

Motivating employees

In looking at relationships, wider stakeholders – and employees in particular – need to be considered. Employees are the key: corporate responsibility and charity teams are generally small and need to galvanise people across the business to deliver on objectives. There should be an opportunity to engage every member of a company, whether by using their professional skills, fundraising efforts, personal connections or other assets.

Many employees will cite their engagement with charity activities as their career highlight, feeling that they have really made a positive difference and been rewarded by what they have done. This experience has prompted many to take on additional volunteering and some to pursue a career change. But employees also need support and need their efforts to be recognised, not only by their own organisation but also by the charity they have supported.

Making relationships last

There are sometimes expectations that successful partnerships, based on their success, will continue after the contract period. And they often do. But it is wise not to base expectations purely on success and hope. At the start of a partnership, you need to discuss an exit strategy to manage expectations and to help in succession planning. If an existing partner cannot extend its support, work with that organisation to see whether it can help to secure another partner or support an incoming partner with a handover.

The best partnerships, however, are not defined by the length of time or the size of the partnership; they are about what has been jointly achieved as measured against the shared vision.

The following case study illustrates a successful long-term partnership in terms of both achievement and longevity.

Case study: Comic Relief and BT

This multi-decade partnership began in 1985. As one of the largest grant-giving charities in the UK, BT helps Comic Relief to support tens of thousands of projects around the world through fundraising efforts centring on both Red Nose Day and Sport Relief. The partnership works, and continues to work, because of the synergy that both organisations have created through their joint relationship-management effort. This is accomplished by:

● having dedicated account teams both at BT and at Comic Relief;

● hosting regular meetings to discuss how to improve the relationship;

● increasing meeting frequency during campaign windows;

● conducting project visits (both in the UK and internationally) so that BT's people can engage with Comic Relief and to drive awareness;

● engaging in mutual collaboration on technical projects.

BT's support is far-ranging and includes fundraising (short term and long term, with a focus on sustainable fundraising), strategic and technological support, and the recruitment of volunteers.

The length of the partnership is clearly unique, but what is more significant is the extent of the support provided by BT. The two parties have worked on a diverse range of activities together, and BT has cemented support for the charity across the company. This has allowed the partnership to make a genuine, lasting difference.

BT's ongoing support since the 1980s includes:

● providing the MyDonate fundraising platform at call centres, enabling secure and commission-free donations during telethons;

● providing the network-management technology that ensures volunteers can seamlessly process all calls on Comic Relief telethon evenings;

● enabling its staff to volunteer and fundraise through employee activities and by supporting celebrity challenges;

● allowing Comic Relief to use BT Tower's 'Information Band' (a prominent LED display system) as a promotional tool free of charge.

In addition, between March 2007 and March 2016, BT helped Comic Relief to raise £28.8 million through public fundraising and donations via MyDonate.

Conclusion

Building a great relationship between your charity and its corporate counterpart can make the biggest difference in creating a successful partnership. It will allow the partnership to bring about long-term sustainable benefits thanks to having the flexibility to create opportunities and embrace change. To build this type of relationship, you need to have a shared vision – and a genuine commitment to achieving that vision jointly through agreed ways of working – and ongoing, open communication. It is critical to form good relationships and to keep these relationships strong, using structures, processes and competent account management.

CHAPTER TWELVE

Recruiting and structuring a corporate partnership team

Valerie Morton

Introduction

This chapter explores the various ways to structure a corporate partnership team and how to recruit and retain the best fundraisers.

Structures for corporate partnership teams

There is no right or wrong way to structure a team. The key is to structure to deliver the corporate partnership strategy, ensuring that team members are clear about their individual roles and responsibilities so that they may achieve the overall objectives and targets. The structure of a corporate partnership team will depend on factors such as your charity's overall fundraising strategy and its corporate partnership strategy, the size of your organisation, the number of current partnerships and the investment strategy for growth.

Evaluating current team structure and roles

Team structures and responsibilities generally evolve over time due to preferences, the details of specific partnerships and other specific needs at the time. Therefore, it is important to step back and evaluate your current team's structure and roles. Look at both immediate needs and long-term needs for the next three to five years.

Here are some of the questions to consider:

• Are the team's current structure and roles enabling the team to achieve its strategy and fulfil the needs of the organisation?

• Are the team members clear about their specific roles and responsibilities and how these all fit together? Are donors clear about whom to contact?

• How does the team spend its time on a day-to-day basis? How much time are team members spending facing externally (for example, meeting current partners or new prospects)?

• Is there an effective split between time spent on current partnerships and time spent on new business, such that income can grow over time?

• How much time are team members spending doing work which could be done by someone else, such as a volunteer or intern (for example, research or sending out materials)? Is there enough support within the team?

• Are there opportunities for team members to progress their career within the team or organisation or will they need to leave for the next step up?

• What are the barriers to successful fundraising and achieving more income?

It can be beneficial to develop a checklist covering all aspects of the team structure, such as capacity for new business growth, supporting and expanding current partnerships, and career progression for team members or a structure to allow future growth and expansion. With any change in structure, it is essential to communicate clearly with the team throughout the process and involve them in discussing possible options where they are available.

Short-term contracts are an option and may be an easier way to gain approval for the expenditure budget or to test a new position. Although use of such contracts has become more commonplace, the benefits should be considered alongside the principle that corporate fundraising success is due in no small part to the development of relationships. You will need systems in place to ensure that relationships are managed well and continuity is maintained if personnel change.

Corporate team structure options

There are a number of options to consider when developing a corporate partnership function. These include:

• **A sole corporate fundraiser within a fundraising team:** common in small- to medium-sized organisations and when starting to test corporate fundraising and partnership opportunities.

• **'All hands on deck' approach:** a few corporate fundraisers with responsibility for both managing partnerships and generating new business. Often used for small corporate teams.

• **Separate teams for partnerships and new business:** the best approach with this structure is to have clear processes when any new partnerships gained are handed over from the new business team to the partnership team, or to involve them early on in discussions so that corporate partners do not get too accustomed to one person. In larger corporate teams, there may be a few layers, with team leaders of sub-teams and account managers to manage larger partnerships.

• **Sector-focused approach:** account managers and new business teams are structured around certain key sectors, such as finance, retail and technology. This allows you to recruit fundraisers with specific sector knowledge, often from the corporate sector, who can seek new opportunities.

• **Product-focused teams:** teams have responsibility for specific areas of corporate fundraising, such as commercial activities (sponsorship, affinity marketing, licences, trading activities and non-commercial activities), employee fundraising, payroll giving or corporate foundations. It is important to have a coordination process and to provide clear points of contact if corporate partners want to have multiple funding streams.

• **National and regional corporate teams:** many organisations have regional or community teams which are responsible for securing income from local companies and/or supporting a national partnership at a local level. There are many opportunities for both as long as roles and responsibilities and ownership of income are clear. Good coordination between the teams is essential to ensure that the teams' activities are synchronised to support one overall corporate fundraising and partnership strategy.

• **Managing a major partnership:** if the charity is successful in being chosen for a major partnership, you will need to recruit additional resources to maximise the opportunity (see 'Increasing resources to manage a specific partnership' on page 156).

Larger teams may also have a research-function, product-development or programme person to source suitable projects for funding, either within the corporate team or within fundraising.

A factor driving any structure is the need to be client focused – looking at which structure will result in the most successful development of new partnerships and the effective management of existing partners. Given the relatively high turnover of corporate fundraising staff, the structure needs to ensure companies have a comparatively seamless relationship with your charity even if a central member of staff leaves.

The key to success with any team structure is being very clear about roles and responsibilities. You will need to continually review and change these as partnerships are gained or expanded, or as they end. Developing a team is similar to developing a new car model – even if the underlying components remain the same, it still needs a test drive and may need modifications.

Providing a support resource

As part of the team structure, it is important to provide a support resource through an assistant role, a personal assistant, volunteers or interns. This role can help to ensure research is completed and provide general support to a corporate partner, such as via distribution of materials. This will enable the fundraiser(s) to focus on directly interfacing with companies.

An intern programme can be a valuable way of gaining resources and allows the intern to gain experience in the charity sector. In addition, it can provide existing team members an opportunity to gain management experience and learn new skills.

Intern positions typically last between two and six months, and can be part or full time. To develop a role description, you will need to define the specific tasks required. For example, would the person provide additional support to the whole team or support a few key partnerships? Would they need specific skills in a particular area, such as social media? It can be beneficial to give an intern a specific project to lead during their internship in addition to day-to-day duties as this will make the intern role more attractive and also avoid the risk of the role becoming that of a dogsbody.

Case study: Breast Cancer Now

Breast Cancer Now was formed in 2015 from the merger of two charities: Breakthrough Breast Cancer and Breast Cancer Campaign. The new charity had bold ambitions and corporate fundraising was identified as an area of strong potential growth. Both pre-merger charities had some fantastic long-standing partnerships, although income from companies was heavily reliant on product sales and a few key corporate partners. The corporate team members in place post-merger had limited experience of other income streams, such as strategic partnerships (where there is a mutually agreed commitment to address or focus on an issue that will make a deeper impact and provide a strategic benefit to both partners), corporate foundations and employee-engagement partnerships. Clearly there was potential to grow income by developing a strategy for diversification. In order to do this, Breast Cancer Now needed to develop a team structure that would allow it to develop new types of partnerships and the tools and expertise required to succeed.

The challenges the charity faced were multiple. Firstly, the pre-merger charities' corporate partnership teams had not won any large new partnerships for the previous five years. New business income was almost exclusively made up of incoming low- to mid-value cause-related marketing partnerships (where the company uses the charity's cause to help market a product or service, for example by donating a sum of money for each unit sold). The managers of new business were also managing existing small accounts as well as working on new business.

Secondly, the account-management team had no distinct areas of specialism. The vast majority of partnerships were retail focused and commercial (i.e. cause-related marketing partnerships rather than employee-related activities such as Charity of the Year), so the team had little experience in other types of partnership. Also, the team was made up of four managers and two executives with very little admin support.

Thirdly, an over-reliance on commercial partnerships had meant that the team had not developed the tools necessary to win other types of partnership that require deeper engagement opportunities (such as volunteering) and fundraising products that engage employees (such as dress-down days).

Finally, the biggest corporate campaign for the charity, Fashion Targets Breast Cancer, needed a strategic overhaul to maximise the opportunities presented by a new digitally savvy, younger customer audience.

The members of the corporate team reviewed their options, looking at the existing organisational structure:

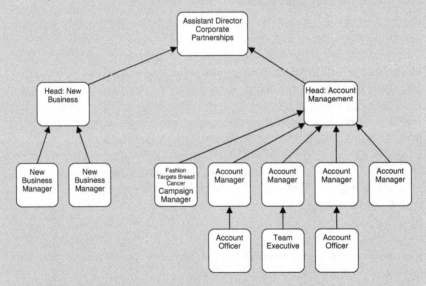

They developed a business case that made the following recommendations:

To move to a new business focus: the new business team would focus exclusively on new business and, once established, hand over all accounts to the partnerships team. Additionally, a case was made to increase the head count of new business managers from two to three, with the third being a senior manager to reflect the need to focus on sectors that require specialist knowledge, such as the pharmaceutical sector.

To create three specialised sub-teams within the account-management team: one team would focus on strategic partnerships, one on commercial partnerships and one on employee engagement. Each of the sub-teams would be led by an account manager and initially supported by an account officer, with a view to expanding the sub-teams as the new business team won and handed over new partnerships across the various specialisms.

To recruit a partnership executive: this person would support both the new business and the account-management teams.

To recruit a corporate development specialist: this new role would focus exclusively on developing the corporate engagement tools (for example volunteering opportunities and new fundraising ideas and tools) necessary to win and deliver new types of partnerships.

To change the reporting lines of the Fashion Targets Breast Cancer campaign manager: this role was changed to report directly to the assistant director of corporate partnerships and engagement in order to ensure stronger strategic support was in place for the planned campaign revamp.

The proposed and agreed team structure looked like this:

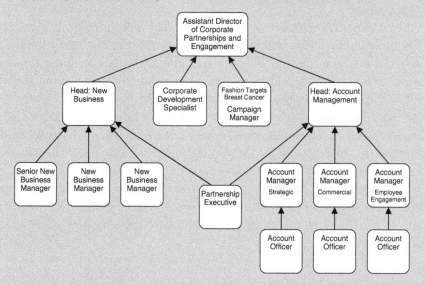

The changes were all approved and the team embarked enthusiastically on a new journey. Accounts were redistributed according to sub-team specialisms, which resulted in a much stronger focus and higher levels of expertise.

A new corporate engagement package is in development. The new business team has won its first staff engagement multi-year partnership (with EDF Energy) and two new strategic partnerships. A new Fashion Targets Breast Cancer campaign has been launched, and early results indicate significant increases in product sell-through rates and strong digital engagement.

Increasing resources to manage a specific partnership

For some partnerships, it may be necessary to recruit a specific account manager on a fixed-term contract. To maximise the opportunities of a Charity of the Year partnership, for example, your charity may need to increase its resources in the short term.

Before applying for major partnerships, it is worthwhile discussing internally how such a partnership would be resourced and developing a rough budget so that the senior management and trustees have an understanding of the potential expenditure if you are successful. You may need to recruit additional resources before any income is received. The partnership, therefore, could potentially run at a deficit for a period or cross two financial years, which could cause issues for return on investment or financial accounts.

It is beneficial to talk to the charities that were previously partnered with the company. This will help you to find out how the partnership was resourced on both a national and a regional level, and to understand the various roles and responsibilities, any pressure points for managing the relationship and what the other charities would have done differently in hindsight. The objectives of the partnership may be different year on year, but this kind of consultation is a good starting point. Talking to the company to understand its needs and expectations from fundraising, communications and volunteering perspectives is essential.

A partnership team structure and resource plan should be developed to suit your organisation and calculate the associated budget. It is useful to build in flexibility in the budget to respond to opportunities as they arise during the year.

Recruitment and getting the best people

Fundraising is the lifeblood of most charities; however, recruiting and retaining good fundraisers is often a challenge. Good corporate fundraisers will always be in high demand, so what are the best recruitment tactics to adopt?

Skills needed for a good corporate fundraiser

The ability to communicate well and to build strong relationships are vital skills for a corporate fundraiser. With fundraising, personal relationships are critical: a company contact may work with the charity account manager on a day-to-day basis for a year or longer. Good verbal and written communication are needed in both external and internal contexts, as corporate teams work very closely with other departments to deliver successful partnerships.

Commercial awareness and an understanding of how companies operate are vital. Good judgement and the ability to spot opportunities and potential challenges are also important qualities, alongside a logical, problem-solving approach.

Team members specialising in new business will have slightly different skills from account managers, such as negotiating and influencing skills. Experience in sales may be beneficial. However, it is worth noting that account managers also need new business skills so as to spot opportunities and expand existing relationships to other parts of the business.

Some of these skills can be developed over time or through training, and some are inherent and will need to be tested during the interview process.

Ensuring the application process delivers the goods

With any role, the more specific the job description, the more likely it is to attract, find and keep the right candidate. A relevant job title that details the correct level of responsibility is important to encourage potential candidates to investigate further – for example, 'New Business Team Leader, Account Executive'. Be really clear about which skills are essential and which are desirable.

It is important to be clear on whether candidates from the corporate sector will be considered for the role. Often, skills are transferable; however, this is dependent on the specific role and experience needed. Allow the candidates to decide whether they will accept a drop in salary as opposed to making the decision yourself that it is not worthwhile interviewing them.

Searching for good fundraisers should be conducted in the same way as attracting new corporate partners. The application materials will give potential candidates a feel for the organisation, so it is essential that they are appealing and clear to encourage good fundraisers to apply. The recruitment process itself should also be professionally handled.

It is becoming increasingly common to spreading the net wide during the recruitment process – for example, through posting adverts on free charity websites, advertising through the Institute of Fundraising's Corporate Fundraising Special Interest Group (see www.institute-of-fundraising.org.uk/groups), and using personal networks (including LinkedIn), all of which can be valuable tools for finding suitable candidates. It is of course important to attract candidates who are seeking a new position but also those who are not actively looking but might move for the right organisation or role. Recruitment agencies can have a role, and headhunters may be used if the role is senior or particularly specialised.

To help with the decision process and gain their support, it can be beneficial to include a colleague on the interview panel who is from another team and who will work closely with the new employee. If the candidate is to be the sole account manager of a particular corporate partner, it could be appropriate to involve them in the decision process. This could be in the second round of interviews – perhaps in a separate discussion or over coffee. However, do not put any candidates in front of your corporate partner unless you are prepared to appoint them.

It is essential to use the interview process to ensure that you have the information you require to make an informed decision. Here are some suggestions to help with this process:

• **Probing questions:** in addition to using prepared interview questions, probe any areas of ambiguity on the application form, such as time without work and short periods in jobs. In addition, understand what the candidate's specific role was in gaining new partnerships in their current or past positions.

• **Role-plays:** to test the key skills required as a corporate fundraiser, use a ten-minute role-play at the start of an interview to test how candidates would build relationships with corporate contacts either at a mock initial new business meeting or sitting next to a potential partner at an event. This exercise will reflect how a corporate partner might feel with the potential new team member.

• **Presentations:** being able to deliver compelling presentations is a key skill for a corporate fundraiser, so ask the candidate to either prepare a presentation or deliver one they have given recently.

• **Judgement through scenarios:** good judgement is vital for corporate fundraising, so give the candidates some scenarios that team members have found themselves in to see how each candidate would deal with the situation and so you can understand their thought process. For example, ask how they would deal with a situation where a corporate partner is demanding more than the organisation can deliver or where there is an internal issue with another department, or ask whom they would involve or consult with regard to a specific ethical dilemma. Candidates can prepare for the usual questions in an interview, but their responses to scenarios or role-plays or their performance in presentations can provide useful insights into their true skills.

If the pool of candidates does not meet your expectations, it is usually better, if in doubt, not to appoint. It is more advisable to advertise again: it will avoid the risk of damaged relationships and can save time and money in the long run.

Retaining good corporate fundraisers

Fundraising is a small enough sector for talented corporate fundraisers to get noticed quickly or want to move on to the next level after 18 months to 2 years. Therefore, in order to retain good fundraisers, it is important to have a retention strategy, including professional development support, formal training and less formal opportunities such as mentoring.

Given that every person is different, identify the factors that motivate and demotivate individual team members through regular staff meetings and appraisals. Increases in salary are not always feasible in the sector; however, there are many more ways to retain a good corporate fundraiser at whichever level they are.

Firstly, although it may sound obvious, ensure that the team member knows that they are valued. Often, this is only communicated when someone is about to leave. Secondly, ensure the team member is aware of the options regarding career progression within the organisation. Can a short-term position be created until an opportunity becomes available? If opportunities are not available within the team to move up a level, look for ways to stretch the employee within their existing role by setting challenging objectives or giving additional responsibility, such as managing a larger partnership, becoming the lead for a project within the team or planning a section of the team away day.

Some good corporate fundraisers are keen to stay in front-facing roles rather than move into management positions. If this is the case, do you have a structure which allows them to grow and develop within the team? Having a structure such as this will be beneficial for the team and the organisation.

Options such as flexible working hours, working from home or other benefits can be motivating for staff. They are also becoming increasingly important given that more organisations are offering them.

It is a challenge to retain good fundraisers. Developing a formal policy or talent management programme with human resources, if your organisation does not already have one, will help to increase your chances of holding on to these valuable people.

Conclusion

The nature of corporate fundraising brings with it specific challenges in relation to structuring the corporate fundraising function and recruiting, developing and retaining the best staff. Good corporate fundraisers are in high demand and therefore the turnover of staff can be high, yet the very success of corporate partnerships is based on the development of relationships and good account management. These two situations can easily be seen as mutually exclusive. However, this chapter has shown how effective structuring, recruitment and personnel policies can enable your corporate fundraising strategy to succeed.

CHAPTER THIRTEEN

Legal and regulatory issues

Chris Knight

Introduction and context

The chapters in this book have each illustrated the importance of understanding the nature of the relationship between charities and businesses. This is certainly the case for legal aspects, where misunderstanding can expose the parties to risk or unlawful activity. Forewarned is forearmed, and both charities and corporates want to get it right.

Some charities operate throughout the UK, but the laws and regulations of the four countries differ slightly. For specific law and regulation, the emphasis of this chapter is on England and Wales, although some reference will be made to Scotland and Northern Ireland (whose regulators, as we shall see, produce helpful guidance as a starting point). Some aspects, such as risk management, apply generally.

Corporate fundraising usually results in one of two arrangements: donations or collaborations. The charity gains in both scenarios. However, for the business, nothing significant is sought when making donations, whereas collaborations offer mutual reward. The law has something to say about both arrangements but the distinction is critical.

There are also two reasons the law features in corporate fundraising: compliance and risk management. The law often says something must be done, or not done, in a particular way: this is compliance. Equally often, the application of the law and reference to lawyers is a risk management exercise in which the parties want to be clear about who is doing what and when, and what happens if something goes wrong. So charities and their fundraising teams need to do things right, for compliance, and know what they are getting into, to manage risk.

This chapter will look at the law through the lens of a case study involving the fictitious charity Purple Days, or just Purple for short. Purple is a growing national charity that provides care and support services to elderly people and that campaigns for improvements in provision and treatment of health and social care. It also acts as an umbrella body for individuals and organisations involved in care for elderly people. Like most charities these days, it faces funding challenges and has lots of ideas about how it might overcome them.

What are donations, trading and fundraising?

Definitions and understandings for charity law purposes

Donations are gifts where nothing significant is received in return. These can be gifts of cash, goods, services, property (land and buildings), other physical assets (such as a vehicle), intangible assets (such as shares), or staff and volunteer time.

Often, when a business makes donations to a charity, these will be tax deductible. The operation of tax is different depending on what is given, but that is the general principle.

For the wider endeavours of corporates in making donations, the term **corporate responsibility** (or corporate social responsibility) is often used.

Trading is not a well-defined term in law. However, for the present purposes we can take it to mean a (usually) regular activity which makes money. For charities, there are two types of trading:

1. primary-purpose or charity trading, which fulfils the charity's objects;

2. non-primary-purpose or non-charitable trading, which does not itself directly fulfil the charity's objects even if it raises money which is then spent on its objects.

There is no such distinction for non-charities. This is because, while charities must only do charitable activities, non-charities are free to do any kind of lawful trading.

The distinction is important for two reasons. First, charities should concentrate on primary-purpose trading as doing otherwise may undermine their ability to fulfil their charitable purposes, because a charity's activities must be directed towards fulfilling those purposes. Second, a charity is not taxed on primary-purpose trading but, beyond a certain threshold, it will be taxed on non-primary-purpose trading.

Fundraising in charity law terms means an activity which raises money for a charity but which does not directly fulfil the charity's objects. Some fundraising is also characterised as non-primary-purpose trading. The main difference between non-primary-purpose trading and fundraising is that non-primary-purpose trading always involves an exchange of money for something else (such as a service), whereas fundraising can include both an exchange and requests for donations and other activities.

Professional fundraisers are defined as people or businesses which carry on a fundraising business where the funds are raised for charitable, benevolent or philanthropic purposes. This does not include a charity or its trading subsidiary or staff. Professional fundraisers engaging with charities must be subject to a contract covering prescribed essentials and must state, at the point of asking for money, how the fundraiser's fees are calculated and which charity the fundraising is for.

Commercial participation concerns a person or business which engages in a promotional venture with the intention that, as part of that activity, money will be given to a charity. This does not include professional fundraisers, which have their own rules (see above). As with professional fundraisers, a commercial participation arrangement must be subject to a contract covering prescribed essentials. The commercial participator must also give a statement to the public regarding the amount given and the charity which is to benefit, given at the point where the statement is made regarding the charitable donations.

> Our charity, Purple, charges money for certain care services for elderly people: this is primary-purpose trading because it directly furthers the charity's aims. It operates a few cafes open to the general public: this is non-primary-purpose trading, as it has nothing directly to do with furthering the charity's aims. It also organises an annual 10km run to raise funds: this is fundraising because the event does not fulfil the charity's objects even if the money raised is put towards those objects.

Implications

Gift Aid

Many corporate donations will attract Gift Aid, but not for the charity's benefit. Whereas a gift from an individual tax payer should lead to the charity being able to claim Gift Aid to enhance the gift, corporate Gift Aid benefits the business through tax reduction: the benefit to charities is that this should act as an encouragement to businesses to give. So a gift of cash from a company will not be enhanced for the charity by Gift Aid, but the company can deduct the amount of the gift from its taxable profits and thus reduce its tax liability. Similar arrangements apply to gifts of land, shares and goods. Donations of staff via secondment or volunteering are also tax deductible for the business.

Tainted donations

These are donations which are 'tainted' in the sense of the donor having an ulterior motive. HMRC's tainted donations rules are designed to prevent tax avoidance hiding behind sham gifts. As always, however, such rules catch the good and the bad. So a donation will be tainted if:

1. the donation and some other arrangement between the donor and the charity are connected; and

2. the main purpose of the donation is financial advantage arising from the charity for the donor or someone connected to the donor; and

3. the donor is not the charity's subsidiary or social housing provider.

Item 3 is to allow for legitimate arrangements between charities and their subsidiaries. An example may help to illustrate: suppose a stationery business owner offers to make a donation to a charity but says he will only do so if the charity buys its stationery from his business; the donation is tainted by his business motive. Overall, the rules prevent a donor avoiding tax where they are effectively saying 'I'll make a donation if you enter into this arrangement which benefits me': you scratch my back and I'll scratch yours. The donor of a tainted donation will have to pay tax as if it were not a donation. Penalties also apply, probably for the donor and possibly also the charity.

See also 'Cash gift' on page 172 as regards money laundering dangers.

Charities, trading and tax

As we saw when we looked at the definition of trading, there is an important distinction between trading activities which further a charity's objects and those which do not. One important consequence is that the exemption from income tax and corporation tax which charities enjoy will be lost in relation to non-primary-purpose trading income. This is subject to a 'small-trading exemption', a threshold below which HMRC will ignore the trading for tax purposes: at the time of writing, this is £50,000 non-primary-purpose annual turnover for charities with a gross annual income over £200,000, 25% of turnover for smaller charities, and £5,000 for those with an annual income under £20,000.

The relevance for corporate fundraising arises when certain fundraising activities are treated as trading.

> Say our charity, Purple, gives a very prominent profile, effectively amounting to advertising, for a company in exchange for a 'donation'; this is likely to be trading. Entering into such an arrangement would thus lead to tax consequences for Purple. If the charity itself undertook the arrangement, the donation, which is in reality a fee, would be taxable (subject to the small trading limits referred to above). If the arrangement were undertaken by the charity's trading company, the tax could be avoided (see also 'Trading subsidiary companies' on page 181).

Fundraising charities

Fundraising itself is not a charitable purpose, so it is odd that the following two scenarios are often encountered.

Many larger businesses have their own charities to support corporate responsibility and charitable giving, with names such as A. B. Smith & Co. Charitable Foundation. Such charities must operate independently from the business and the trustees must be free to choose what to do to fulfil the charity's aims, rather than being a mere conduit for the business's fundraising and corporate responsibility strategy.

There are also charities established with the primary aim of fundraising for another charity. Often the other charity will be overseas and the UK charity will have been established to harness domestic fundraising potential and raise profile. The Charity Commission scrutinises such charities closely these days: again, being a mere conduit is not appropriate. Fundraising in itself is not a charitable aim, and doing everything for only one recipient organisation does not demonstrate sufficient independence.

Professional fundraising

The law identifies professional fundraising as an activity to be regulated and treated with particular caution. Essentially, this is to protect charities and the general public from poor or unscrupulous practice.

As briefly mentioned above, a professional fundraiser is a person or organisation which carries on a fundraising business. The definition is quite wide but does not include charities themselves, their trading companies or their employees. Three main consequences arise when a charity engages a professional fundraiser.

First, the professional fundraiser must make a statement at the point of solicitation, i.e. when asking for funds, about which charity will receive the funds, the proportion of funds for each charity if more than one is involved, and the way the fundraiser's payment is calculated.

Second, a written agreement (contract) must be put in place covering prescribed basic provisions (detailed later in this chapter).

Third, the charity must be very careful, as with any contract, to ensure the terms of the contract (which will often be the professional fundraiser's standard terms) are for the charity reasonable, commercial and without inappropriate risk.

See 'Professional fundraising' on page 180 for further detail on professional fundraising arrangements.

Governance and risk management

Everything a charity does needs to be viewed through the lens of governance, and that includes corporate fundraising. Trustees govern the charity, which is to say they oversee, control, steer and have responsibility for it. Given that risk management is almost synonymous with governance, this brief section will summarise the key aspects of governance.

> Our charity, Purple, is very keen on building its profile, and one proposal it is considering is making better use of the data it holds on its service users and supporters. Surely this is fertile ground for fundraising? Significant

developments like this should always be considered by the trustees. Compliance, risk and reputation issues can thus be governed.

Trustees' duties

The legal basis for the duties of trustees is found in the Trustee Act 2000, the Companies Act 2006 (regarding charitable companies) and the Charities Acts 2011 and 2016. The following list summarises the core duties of trustees, as outlined in the Charity Commission's guidance *The Essential Trustee*:[1]

1. Ensure your charity is carrying out its purposes for the public benefit.

2. Comply with your charity's governing document (rules, constitution, articles, etc.).

3. Act in your charity's best interests (which includes managing conflicts of interest and duty).

4. Manage your charity's resources responsibly (which includes risk management).

5. Ensure the charity is accountable (i.e. accounting, and reporting and transparency to members, supporters and the public).

The Charity Commission also lists 'act with reasonable care and skill', although this is not a duty but a standard: it is the legal standard to which trustees are held accountable and which applies to all of the duties. It is alternatively known as the 'duty of care'.

The position as regards trustees' duties is broadly similar in Scotland and Northern Ireland.

Also of key importance is the Charity Commission's guidance on fundraising.[2] Among other things, this includes six principles, which are really a reflection of trustees' duties in the fundraising context:

1. planning effectively;

2. supervising your fundraisers;

3. protecting your charity's reputation, money and other assets;

4. identifying and ensuring compliance with relevant laws or regulations;

5. identifying and following any recognised fundraising standards;

6. being open and accountable.

The regulatory position on fundraising in Scotland and Northern Ireland is changing quite rapidly (at the time of writing). A useful starting point for an up-to-date position relevant to those jurisdictions would be the websites and published guidance of the regulators, the Office of the Scottish Charity Regulator and the Charity Commission for Northern Ireland.

Delegation

In all but the most straightforward charities, there will be people involved other than the trustees. This means proper governance becomes the art of delegation. Committees, staff and external advisers all have their place. However, it remains the trustees' responsibility to govern and ensure everyone is doing what they are supposed to do.

To clarify delegation within a charity, it is best to have in place terms of reference for any committee, clear job descriptions for staff, terms of engagement for any external advisers and (if matters are complex) a scheme of delegation (or similar) to bring all of this together.

It is well known that tasks can be delegated but responsibility cannot. However, this is trickier to practise than to preach; the distinction can be difficult to see. Trustees must always know what is going on with sufficient detail and regularity to exercise control.

> Purple has five trustees: two are the charity's founders and the other three were recruited from among supporters. The chair is also the chief executive and married to one of the campaign workers. Trustee meetings are quarterly and quite short. Most of the business is dealt with by the chair overseeing staff directly day to day, without involving the trustees.

> This is not a sound set-up: there is too much responsibility vested in one person and the trustees have little visibility of the charity's business. The trustees are not fulfilling their duties, and risks abound. This poor governance could adversely affect any area of the charity's business, including fundraising.

Policies

If governance has complexity then it needs clear thinking and communication. This means appropriate policies must be put in place. In fundraising, these may include risk, delegation, financial controls, PR, events, volunteers, data management and supporter relations.

A basic template for a policy should include the area of work the policy covers, how this work relates to the charity's aims, a non-exhaustive list of responsibilities and who bears those, the level of delegated authority as to decision-making and finance, who reports to whom, communication method and frequency, and who has responsibility for the area covered by the policy, both among trustees and as delegated (to a committee or staff team for example).

Risk management

All charities should undertake risk management, and this should be a continual feature of governance rather than just an occasional exercise. Everyone with decision-making responsibility should be alert to risk and know how to respond.

Each charity should create a system which works for its circumstances. However, a framework any charity can use and develop is this:

1. **Identify:** establish what your charity's main risks are; these may be generic or specific. It can help to think in terms of themes, such as legal, operational, financial, external, environmental and so on.

2. **Assess:** decide how acute the risk is. One way of doing this is to score each risk (say from 1 to 5) for likelihood of occurrence and impact. Combining the likelihood and impact scores then automatically creates a scale of priorities.

3. **Act:** decide what to do to avoid, mitigate or manage the risk. Make sure you assign someone to be responsible and apply a timescale.

4. **Monitor:** make sure the action is undertaken and see how effective it is.

5. **Review:** consider how the risk has been managed. Some risks will become a lower priority or be removed from the register, and some will be added.

Due diligence

Due diligence means making checks so you know everything relevant about what it is you plan to do. It is a kind of risk management and therefore a function of governance.

In fundraising, this can mean the charity undertaking due diligence regarding a potential corporate partner or a proposed project, and it can also mean a potential partner undertaking due diligence on the charity.

You should ensure corporate partners are well governed, solvent, uncontroversial and not out of line with the charity's aims. Mostly these checks can be conducted at your desktop, but you may need to ask to see some materials, such as the company's corporate responsibility policy or accounts.

Due diligence regarding a project means ensuring it is viable, not unreasonably risky and will deliver what you hope it will. This will involve financial and operational projections, a project plan and perhaps external advice on insurance, legal issues, market-testing and so on.

If a corporate partner wants to undertake due diligence on your charity, then within reason let them: it demonstrates good thinking. You will need to be aware of the confidentiality of the charity's data and comply with data protection principles and laws (see page 183 for further detail on these principles) if this involves third parties' data. You may need to consider putting in place a non-disclosure agreement with the proposed corporate partner.

> Purple has been approached by a business which wants to make a donation of £50,000 in exchange for some profile, including its name on the annual report, a table and a named award at the annual black tie dinner, mutual links on the company's and the charity's websites, and the chance to market to Purple's members and service users. The business is quite well known for its speedy growth, aggressive marketing and high staff turnover. It wants to soften its image by associating itself with Purple.
>
> Purple should do some basic due diligence to establish the business's motives and an agreed way of working. The danger of exploitation of the charity's profile and data should be managed. Due diligence may lead to a decision not to partner with this business. There are trading and tax issues to be aware of, as noted in 'Charities, trading and tax' on page 164, and the arrangement is a commercial participation, as explained on pages 163 and 174.

For more information on due diligence, see chapter 5.

Different types of corporate partner

Part of risk management and governance in corporate fundraising is understanding your partners. They come in various shapes and sizes but the most common business structures are as follows:

• **Company:** there are several kinds of company, including a company limited by guarantee and a community interest company, but you are most likely to engage with a company limited by shares. This has two levels of governance: shareholders, who each own a part of the company, and directors, who govern it from day to day. You may deal with a director, a member of staff or an agent of some kind. Essential details and documents are found online in materials provided by Companies House (www.gov.uk/government/organisations/companies-house).

• **Partnership:** this has one level of governance, the partners, who each own a part of the partnership. A modern form of partnership you may encounter is a **limited liability partnership**. You may deal with a partner, a member of staff or an agent. Limited liability partnerships are also listed at Companies House, though traditional partnerships are not.

• **Entrepreneur or sole trader:** in legal terms, these are simply individuals who are in business with a trading name but no separate legal structure. There is no public register. You may deal with the individual themselves, a member of staff if they have any, or an agent.

Those within charities fundraising with corporates will need to be clear which legal entity they are dealing with. The type of legal entity can have consequences for the charity – for example, in terms of the way different types of entity (or an individual) enter into a contract, the type of due diligence you will be able to do, and the tax treatment of gifts and other arrangements.

Regulation

The regulation of charity fundraising has a chequered history. Laws, regulators and initiatives have come and gone. Over the years there have been scandals involving fundraising, governance, data management and sham charities.

This has led in the last few years to more effective changes, such that we now have a new regulator and a renewed desire to improve charity compliance and accountability, and to restore public trust.

Fundraising regulators

The primary regulatory body is the Fundraising Regulator (www.fundraisingregulator.org.uk). This replaced the Fundraising Standards Board and now regulates charity fundraising in England and Wales. It liaises closely with the Charity Commission and the Information Commissioner's Office. One of its key roles is to have responsibility for the Code of Fundraising Practice, which is available on its website.

Scotland has its own fundraising regulation and Northern Ireland is developing some.

There is also the Institute of Fundraising (www.institute-of-fundraising.org.uk), which is a professional membership body for UK fundraisers. It has a very helpful resources section on its website.

Charity regulators

The Charity Commission regulates charities in England and Wales. The Commission has a large amount of guidance on its website, including on fundraising, trading and governance (see page 166).

The Office of the Scottish Charity Regulator and the Charity Commission for Northern Ireland likewise regulate charities in those jurisdictions.

Regulation of data management

The Information Commissioner's Office (www.ico.org.uk) regulates data management in the UK. Its website has a number of guides as well as news and updates by sector, including for charities.

This is a fast-developing area of regulation, and fundraisers must keep up to date. For example, at the time of writing, the General Data Protection Regulation is awaited (in May 2018), which will further tighten the rules. (For more information see 'Data management' on page 183.)

Regulation of tax

HMRC regulates tax, which, as already noted, features in charity fundraising. There are specific sections of HMRC's website devoted to detailed guidance for charities and tax, including www.gov.uk/charities-and-tax/overview and www.gov.uk/government/publications/charities-detailed-guidance-notes.

Corporate responsibility and business collaborations compared

Corporate responsibility is the means by which businesses act responsibly in relation to their environment and act generously towards their communities. In its pure form, a business seeks nothing in return for this. However, in the real world, this will usually be a means of showing to staff, customers and the public that the business is sound, ethical and worth dealing with.

Business collaborations go further, in that the business engages with a particular charity (or non-profit or social enterprise) for the two entities' mutual benefit. Such engagements can range from a charity's corporate membership scheme (which gives networking benefits) to a wide promotion of the business within the charity and the promotion of the charity within the business.

The term **business collaboration** is not defined in statute or regulation: it is merely a convenient description used in this chapter and includes anything which has legal, tax or regulatory implications for either party, including **commercial participation** arrangements. Note also, the term **partnership** is also often used in these contexts to mean a collaboration, including between a corporate and a charity. However, such arrangements are almost never partnerships in the legal sense (see above section on corporate structures) but contractual relationships.

Corporate responsibility and business collaborations form a web of similar-looking situations: an act of corporate responsibility can easily be viewed as an act of business collaboration and can certainly morph into one over time. There are also many hybrid arrangements, as outlined on page 177.

Our charity, Purple, has been operating a corporate membership scheme which amounts to little more than a donation in exchange for a thank you in its annual report and on its website. In this form, the scheme amounts to corporate responsibility.

The charity now intends to offer bronze, silver and gold memberships in return for a scale of benefits rising at gold level to the chance to nominate someone for a trusteeship, networking events and a named award at the charity's annual dinner. This would be a business collaboration constituting non-primary-purpose trading by the charity. Unless the income from this scheme in addition to the charity's other non-primary-purpose trading falls below the small-trading exemption, Purple should run it through a trading subsidiary.

Corporate responsibility

Corporate responsibility comes in many forms. As this chapter has outlined, it can involve elements of mutual benefit, but we will look at those later. For now, we will look at situations where giving, not receiving, is the main aim: pure philanthropy.

Cash gift

This is a gift of cash, whether electronic, cheque or physical cash.

Sensible due diligence should be undertaken. If a corporate approaches a charity to make a one-off gift of a modest size, then little or no due diligence is necessary. However, if the gift is large or the circumstances unusual, some thought should be given. 'Large' is relative: a small local charity will have a different perspective from a larger national charity. Check the identity and ownership (if you're dealing with a business rather than an individual) of the donor and the source of the funds. You need to remain aware that money from criminal activity (including tax avoidance, fraud and other financial crimes) will be caught by the Money Laundering Regulations, and a charity falling foul of those will itself commit a criminal offence.

Also be aware of the difference between unrestricted and restricted funds. If a charity asks for money for a particular purpose, or if a business gives money and asks for it to be used for a particular purpose, that money will be restricted such that the charity can *only* spend it on that purpose. Financial and accounting controls will then need to adhere to this restriction. If appropriate, try to build some flexibility into your invitations to donate so that, if necessary, the charity can spend the money on its wider purposes.

Companies' own charities

Companies' own charities were mentioned on page 164. This is a developed and structured way for a company to undertake charitable endeavours. However, as already mentioned, the charity *must* be independent from the business which established it. It must not aim to promote the business, there should ideally be a majority of trustees who are independent of the business, and charitable purposes must be its focus rather than fundraising events.

These points of compliance relate to the charity concerned. However, it is as well for fundraisers to be aware they may sometimes be dealing with both a business and its linked charity.

Matched giving

A business will sometimes pledge to give money equivalent to that raised or donated by someone else, such as an employee or the charity itself. For example, it may pledge to double whatever the charity raises for a particular campaign, up to a set cap, or to match the fundraising efforts of its staff. The fundraising of an individual member of staff is a matter for that individual, but their employer's gift by way of matched giving will be a donation of that business and subject to the corporate Gift Aid scheme (see page 163).

Gifts in kind

A business sometimes gives not cash but rather time (through staff volunteering or secondments), goods and materials, or services. Goods and materials often relate to the business itself, so a car company might give a car to be raffled by the charity, and a DIY business might donate decorating materials.

A secondment should be subject to a written secondment agreement between the business, the charity and the staff member. A volunteering arrangement may be low key, but if it is significant and/or ongoing a written agreement may be necessary. Some arrangements intended as gifts in kind can also amount to commercial participation.

> Purple is entering into an arrangement with a well-known high-street retailer which will provide large numbers of volunteers; the association with the charity fits well with the retailer's market and strategy. The retailer will pay for training and materials. It will be a high-profile partnership.
>
> This is likely to be a giving arrangement, an act of corporate responsibility. The association may well be a good fit for the retailer and promote it to an extent, but the emphasis is principally on benefiting the charity.

If, however, the emphasis were on the retailer's business, perhaps by the retailer clearly pushing its own brands and messages while providing benefit to the charity in doing so, this would amount to a commercial participation arrangement and require a contract and other compliance appropriate for that.

As an aside, in either case, the volunteers should sign a straightforward agreement covering behaviour, safety and expectations.

Support for employees

Quite apart from the efforts and generosity of a business and its management, staff often want to support charities. This may be by volunteering, fundraising, profile-raising or being a trustee.

Businesses can support such endeavours by allowing paid leave for volunteering or trusteeship, promoting employees' efforts via the business's website and so forth. Much of that support is cost-neutral for the business and can be a very good way of charities partnering with corporates.

Commercial participation

Definition

As noted on page 163, commercial participation concerns a person or business which engages in a promotional venture and as part of that venture states that money will be given to a charity.

Requirements

These arrangements are defined and largely still governed by the Charities Act 1992. Subsequent opportunities to reform or update this regime were not taken until the Charities (Protection and Social Investment) Act 2016, which since November 2016 has provided tighter rules. The contract between the commercial participator and the charity must include:

1. the names and addresses of the parties;

2. the date and duration of the agreement, and how it can be terminated;

3. provisions for transfer of funds to the charity as quickly as possible;

4. a requirement for the commercial participator to make a statement to the public as to the charity (or charities) which will benefit financially and how much will be given, expressed either per item or service sold or in terms of the absolute sum, as appropriate;

5. if more than one charity is benefiting, then the proportions to be received by each;

6. a statement of the fundraising standards which apply (currently the Code of Fundraising Practice);

7. provisions for the protection of the public from unreasonable fundraising approaches;

8. how the charity will monitor the commercial participator's compliance with items 6 and 7.

Having a contract of this kind will not be unexpected for a substantial charity or business, but what about a smaller charity or business: is a lesser version of compliance, or even complete exemption, permitted? Unfortunately the legislation does not allow for that. However, the requirements above are not that onerous and do not necessarily lead to a long contract (a couple of pages may be sufficient), and there are template contracts available.

For charities whose accounts must be audited, the 2016 Act also introduced a requirement for certain fundraising information to be included in the annual trustees' report. This must include outlines of the charity's approach to fundraising, work with professional fundraisers and commercial participators, monitoring of fundraising, complaints received, and measures for protection of the public from unreasonable approaches.

Participation statements

Examples of statements for item 4 above are:

> For every 5kg bag of our pet food you buy, we will donate £1 to the XYZ Animal Trust.

> 25p from the sale of this box of Christmas cards will be given and split equally among the following charities: ABC Children's Charity, Homelessness UK and the Well Age Foundation.

> For all purchases made using this Fictco card, 1% of the purchase price will be given to the XYZ Charity, registered charity 12345678.

If appropriate, of course, a short explanation of the charity's work can follow, for example:

> 10% of the sale proceeds from Miaow Munch will be given to the Stanton on Hale Trust, which provides support for families in financial difficulty in Stanton on Hale.

And let's see one for our charity, Purple. A local shop has produced a shopping bag to sell, with all proceeds from the bag sales going to Purple. At the point of sale, i.e. at the shop's checkout, a statement should be included saying something like:

> All proceeds from the sale of these bags will be given to Purple Days, which provides care and support for elderly people.

Liability and responsibility for compliance

It is unlawful to fail to comply with these provisions. In some cases liability lies with the charity, and in other cases it lies with the commercial participator. However, it will often be those within the charity rather than the business who will know about the above regime, so the lead may well need to be taken by the charity.

All charities have responsibility for ensuring they are compliant with fundraising regulation. The reputational damage of getting it wrong affects the charity sector as a whole.

Trading subsidiary involvement

It may be necessary for the charity's trading subsidiary to be involved in the contract or the charity may need to set up such a company if it does not have one. (Subsidiaries are dealt with in detail in 'Trading subsidiary companies' on page 181.) This is because the use of the charity's name and associated intellectual property in many cases amounts to commercial trading. Unless such trading is small scale (see 'Charities, trading and tax' on page 164 regarding the small-trading exemption), then the charity itself should not undertake it. So the charity needs to be involved as the owner of the intellectual property and the subsidiary needs to be involved as a licensee of that intellectual property. The subsidiary will then become the entity that leads the arrangement with the commercial participator.

The Institute of Fundraising, among other bodies, has templates for contracts, both two-way (no subsidiary involved) and three-way (subsidiary involved).

> The fundraising team at Purple has been asked by the CEO to consider a partnership with a well-known clothing retailer. The retailer's popularity with elderly people and the charity's reputation in the sector are both considered strengths. For every item purchased from the retailer's newly promoted brand in its first year, 10% will be donated to Purple, and the charity's name will feature prominently.

> This will need a contract complying with the commercial participation requirements of the Charities Acts. Because the charity's intellectual property will be a significant feature (and perhaps for other reasons, such as the

activity being non-charitable trading), the charity's trading subsidiary will need to be a party to that contract. All promotional materials (labels, stands, posters, website, adverts, etc.) will need to include a participation statement.

Hybrid situations

Often, situations are neither clearly corporate responsibility nor clearly commercial participation but some sort of hybrid.

Charity support schemes

These can include, for example, a business's Charity of the Year (COTY) scheme, dedicated charity days, schemes involving micro-donations made from individuals' salaries (such as the Pennies from Heaven scheme), payroll giving, charity advocates within the business, make-a-will schemes (law firms provide a free will and the individual makes a donation to a charity) and many other situations. A business will often focus on a particular charity and promote it, or allow it to be promoted within its business.

Whether such things amount to corporate responsibility or commercial participation will depend on the details of each scheme, and the distinctions can be quite subtle. A business may have a baking fundraising day for a charity where the only promotion for the company is a small story on its website – this is likely to be corporate responsibility. However, if the company wants to promote itself (or a brand, project, new office opening, etc.) and decides that its promotional efforts will be accompanied by a donation to a charity, that will be commercial participation. An example would be a new office launch reception where the company states it is donating money to a charity.

A COTY scheme is a good illustration of an arrangement which can be either corporate responsibility or commercial participation. The test is to be found in the definition of commercial participation (see page 163). If the scheme is a year-long version of what otherwise tend to be one-off events (bike rides, bake sales, quiz nights, etc.), this is likely to remain a corporate responsibility endeavour. The key is whether the business is primarily promoting the charity or else promoting itself and in doing so (and as an ancillary benefit) also aiming to promote the charity. This latter would be commercial participation. Remember, the term 'promotional venture' is widely understood, so, if the activities of the business deliberately and primarily promote that business as well as the charity, that will be a commercial participation.

A giving or corporate responsibility arrangement will usually be served well enough by an exchange of a letter of intent and, if relevant, a mutual licensing agreement for the use of each other's names and logos. A commercial participation arrangement would need the required contract (see page 174).

Corporate membership schemes

Some charities operate a scheme for businesses and individuals to become 'corporate members' for a set price in return for certain benefits. This generally means membership of the scheme and not the charity's legal structure (for example, a company member in the case of a charitable company). The benefits for the member may include an acknowledgement on the charity's website or the annual report, access to special events, or preferential treatment of some kind. The charity of course receives the membership fee but sometimes also other benefits, such as access to the business's contacts or preferential rates when doing business with it.

Although often characterised as donations, such schemes usually amount to non-charitable trading: the charity is selling a service in exchange for a fee. Thus, unless the income from this and other non-charitable trading falls within the small-trading exemption limit (see page 164), it should be undertaken by the charity's trading subsidiary.

Branding

Brand includes an organisation's name, logo, unique designs (if any), adopted colours, strapline or other unique wording, and reputation. There are two aspects to this: the corporate's brand and the charity's brand.

If the corporate partner's brand is not prominent in a collaboration with a charity, the arrangement may be pure corporate responsibility or a gift. For example, a gift may be acknowledged in the charity's annual report or on its website with a 'thank you to our partners'.

However, if the corporate's brand features prominently, there is a clear benefit to the business. Such an arrangement is commercial: the charity is providing a promotional opportunity for the business. The charity should ensure this is appropriate and, if so, make an appropriate charge. It is likely such an arrangement should be undertaken by its trading subsidiary. If the arrangement is one where the business promotes itself and, while doing so, says it is helping the charity, that will be a commercial participation arrangement (see page 174).

If the charity's brand is a key part of a business collaboration, the charity's trading subsidiary should be involved and an appropriate charge made to the corporate partner. The charity is making available its brand for the benefit of the business: this is non-charitable trading. Some arrangements involve the charity licensing its brand for use by the business. This should be subject to a written contract setting out the permitted uses and other essentials.

A charity should undertake a careful analysis of any proposed brand-sharing arrangements to ensure they are appropriate, that any risks are acceptable and that compliance is ensured.

Sponsorship

Money from a business to support a charity can easily constitute non-primary-purpose trading rather than pure donation. Very often the word 'sponsorship' is used loosely, and it can indicate a wide variety of arrangements.

If, for example, a charity's annual report is paid for by a donation from a business, which is acknowledged by a thank you, this is a simple donation but might be referred to as sponsorship by those involved.

However, if, for example, a charity's annual fundraising dinner is supported by gold, silver and bronze corporate packages that grant to participating businesses a scale of benefits (such as their brand featured in various places, named awards, a table at the dinner, the opportunity to make a speech, etc.), this is a commercial arrangement amounting to non-primary-purpose trading. Again, the charity is making available a service (promotional opportunity) in exchange for a fee.

Events

These can include dinners, sports and challenge events, fairs and sales, supporter and beneficiary days, quiz nights – in fact, any gathering at all for the purpose of promoting the charity or fundraising for it.

In the corporate fundraising context, a key question is: who is running the event? If it is conceived and run by the business, the charity's role may be simply to receive any money raised. A charity will often be invited to supply promotional material, suggest fundraising methods, or attend to take photos or speak to those at the event. Such events will still often amount primarily to a donation from the business, with benefit to the business being a subsidiary part. An example is a sporting challenge run by a business mostly for staff engagement and corporate responsibility reasons, where a particular charity is chosen for a fundraising focus.

If the charity organises the event and the business becomes involved, then the situation may be different. There are still many situations amounting primarily to a donation. For example, in the case of a large fundraising and promotional event for the charity where businesses are invited to put forward and pay for a team to participate, unless promotion of those businesses is significant, this is likely to amount only to a donation by those businesses. If, however, the promotional aspect is significant for the businesses, the event will be commercial, requiring a contract and possible use of a trading subsidiary. Brand and sponsorship issues may also feature (see pages 178–179).

Running a charity event can be complex, and if a charity does not have sufficient expertise it should seek professional advice. Other points to consider, as well as the above, are VAT (events are often but not always exempt), risk management, reputation and insurance.

Let's have another look at the plans of our charity, Purple:

An employee of a business is a keen advocate of the charity and has been spearheading fundraising efforts and volunteering for some time. These have been pure gifts from the business and the individual concerned. However, she now wants the business to focus on the charity more intensely for a period of a year. Plans include a Three Peaks Challenge, which she and her colleagues will organise, and significant sponsorship of the charity's community fun day, which the charity will organise.

The Three Peaks Challenge can feature contributions from the charity, for example in the form of promoting it and the business on the charity's website. So long as the main focus remains the charity and any mention of the business is ancillary, this will be corporate responsibility and a pure gift. The business can promote the challenge on its own website also, on the same basis. If, however, the business were to promote itself or one of its products or services and in doing so it promised money would go to the charity, this would be a commercial participation.

Whether the fun day involves a commercial arrangement depends on what is significant – the sponsorship amount or the promotion of the business. If it is just the amount of money, that is likely to be a gift. If it is the promotion of the business, that will be a commercial arrangement. Often the two go together: if a business is contributing a lot, it will usually expect a promotional opportunity in return.

Professional fundraising

This is not necessarily fully within the day-to-day remit of charities fundraising with corporates, but it is linked and a useful area to know about.

Definition

As noted on page 162, a professional fundraiser is a person or business which carries on a fundraising business where the funds are raised for charitable, benevolent or philanthropic purposes. Professional fundraising businesses are third parties – i.e. completely separate from the charity, and a contract partner just like any other organisation with which a charity contracts. They are not, in general, agents of the charity, which is a closer relationship where the agent can act on the charity's behalf.

Requirements

These are very similar to those for commercial participation. They are governed by the Charities Act 1992 and the Charities (Protection and Social Investment) Act 2016. There must be a contract in place which must include:

1. the names and addresses of the parties;

2. the date and duration of the agreement, and how it can be terminated;

3. provisions for transfer of funds to the charity as quickly as possible;

4. a requirement for the professional fundraiser to make a statement to the public as to the charity (or charities) which will benefit financially – and, if more than one charity is benefiting, the proportions to be received by each;

5. a requirement for the professional fundraiser to make a statement to the public as to how much he/she/it is receiving, how it is calculated and the actual amount or a reasonable estimate of this;

6. a statement of the fundraising standards which apply (currently the Code of Fundraising Practice);

7. provisions for the protection of the public from unreasonable fundraising approaches;

8. how the charity will monitor the professional fundraiser's compliance with items 6 and 7.

Businesses often have their own template contracts or terms and conditions. These can be poorly drafted and heavily weighted in the business's favour. The charity should review these very carefully and demand any changes necessary to comply with the law and manage risks reasonably. This requires legal and commercial assessment.

Trading subsidiary companies

As noted on page 176, many fundraising activities are inappropriate for a charity to do itself and so must be done via a trading subsidiary. This section looks briefly at how such companies should be operated by charities.

Reasons

There are three main situations requiring a subsidiary.

First, risk management. There may be activities which present an acceptable risk but where the trustees and senior management still prefer to ring-fence (that is, contain the activity and risk) in order to protect the charity as far as possible. This can be achieved by placing the activity in a separate company. The liabilities of that company should then be contained within that company and not threaten the charity. Note, this ring-fencing can be undermined such that the charity becomes exposed to risk. If the charity provides a guarantee or indemnity for the subsidiary, it will be bound by the terms of that. Also, there can be circumstances where a parent assumes, by its close connection and governance, liability for the activities of a subsidiary. The message is this: if you create a separate company, keep it separate!

Second, non-charitable trading. This is the typical reason charities create subsidiaries. Charity shops, fundraising challenges and business collaborations of many types are usually operated via subsidiaries.

Third, strategy. If an activity or project is substantial enough, it may merit being undertaken through a subsidiary. The activity may be so substantial that it would dominate the mainstream charitable activities if it were dealt with by the charity. Also, if the activity requires particular expertise, then that can be addressed with a specialist board whose make-up is very different from the charity's.

Requirements

Operating a subsidiary must be done correctly. Although it will be a non-charitable company, it will be owned by a charity so the arrangements must conform to principles of charity law, regulation and governance:

1. It should be a corporate entity, such as a company and not unincorporated (such as a trust), so as to help manage risk.

2. It can be a company limited by shares, a company limited by guarantee, a community interest company or perhaps a community benefit society (though this latter is a rare choice).

3. Usually it will be wholly owned by the charity. However, a joint-venture subsidiary can be useful for collaborative projects involving two or more charities.

4. The charity's investment must be cautious. The charity can own a nominal share of the company but should not invest substantial share capital. Any loan capital must be arranged on arm's length commercial terms.

5. The board of the subsidiary can have charity representatives, such as trustees or senior staff. This is desirable for connectivity. However, there must be independence: the subsidiary must have enough independent directors to form a quorum so it can manage conflicts of

loyalty. This can be difficult to achieve in practice as it requires suffi-cient independent directors to be attracted to the business.

6. Any resources the charity makes available to the subsidiary should be subject to commercial terms. This might include premises-sharing, staff time and back-office support.

7. There should be a written agreement between the charity and the subsidiary, commonly called a 'collaboration agreement' or 'inter-company agreement'. This should cover objectives, governance, finance, sharing of staff and resources (including premises), dispute resolution and anything specific to the situation.

8. The subsidiary's distributable profits can be transferred to the charity, thus avoiding tax liability for the amount that is transferred. Care and accounting advice are needed to ensure the subsidiary does not transfer too much and breach company law.

The charity–subsidiary model is very common but the independence required is rather a fiction. The subsidiary and charity must be indepen-dent, yet the subsidiary in truth is rarely independent enough to survive without the charity and its very existence is to serve the charity. The regu-lators are aware of this paradox, yet the independence rules above must still be observed.

Data management

A feature of modern life is data: it flows through everything we do and this applies very much to charity fundraising activities. How data is mana-ged is the subject of detailed law and regulation, which is constantly changing.

Requirements

The principal piece of legislation on data management is the Data Protec-tion Act 1998. However the position is developing in that the General Data Protection Regulation 2016 will come into force in May 2018. This is an EU-driven development of the regime set out in the Data Protection Act and will replace it. Brexit is unlikely to affect its validity.

For public bodies there is also the Freedom of Information Act 2000 and the Environmental Information Regulations 2004, both of which provide a right of access to information held by public bodies. Some chari-ties (such as universities) are also subject to these laws owing to the type of work they do or if they work alongside public bodies.

The Data Protection Act imposes responsibilities on *data controllers* (those with responsibility for data: either the charity itself or sometimes the trustees) and *data processors* (those actually dealing with it, often professional fundraisers within charities). The main principles are:

1. Personal data must be processed fairly and lawfully.

2. Personal data must only be obtained and processed for a lawful purpose.

3. Personal data must be adequate, relevant and not excessive for the purpose.

4. Personal data must be accurate and if necessary kept up to date.

5. Personal data must not be kept longer than necessary for its purpose.

6. Personal data must be processed in accordance with the rights of the persons to whom it relates.

7. Appropriate technical and organisational measures shall be taken against unauthorised use, processing, loss or damage of data.

8. Personal data must not be transferred outside the European Economic Area unless the country has adequate data protection laws.

The General Data Protection Regulation, like the Data Protection Act, applies to the collection and use of individuals' data. The General Data Protection Regulation talks a lot about 'direct marketing', which for charities is the same as fundraising. There is no general exemption in the General Data Protection Regulation for charities.

The main principles in the General Data Protection Regulation are that personal data must be:

1. processed lawfully, fairly and transparently;

2. collected and processed for specified, legitimate purposes;

3. adequate, relevant and limited to what is necessary for the purpose it is collected;

4. accurate and if necessary kept up to date;

5. kept in a form which permits identification of data subjects (the individuals) for no longer than necessary;

6. processed in a manner which ensures appropriate security of the data, including protection against unauthorised or unlawful processing, loss or damage.

These are obviously similar to the Data Protection Act principles. Data processing must be lawful, which means the individual must have consented or the processing is necessary for some other reason such as public interest, compliance with a legal obligation or the legitimate interests of the charity. This has led to a debate as to whether all communications must be subject to individuals expressly 'opting in' to consent: but while this is one condition it is not the only one.

Also be aware that electronic communications have further laws, covering text and email for example.

Data management requires a very effective administration system. Trustees, and fundraisers as part of their role, must ensure data is managed effectively and the complex ways in which data is collected and processed are compliant. There can be significant fines for default.

And finally

You didn't think you'd read a chapter on law without an exclusion clause, did you? You were right. It is hoped you will find the outline of guidance above helpful. However, note that the content of this chapter reflects the law as at the time of writing and not every aspect of fundraising law and regulation is covered. Also, every situation is different and this guidance cannot cover all possibilities. To be sure of your legal footing when conducting your own corporate fundraising, you should get your own legal advice.

Notes

1   *The Essential Trustee: What you need to know, what you need to do (CC3)* [PDF], www.gov.uk/government/publications/the-essential-trustee-what-you-need-to-know-cc3, Charity Commission, 2012.
2   *Charity Fundraising: A guide to trustee duties (CC20)* [PDF], www.gov.uk/government/publications/charities-and-fundraising-cc20, Charity Commission, 2016.

CHAPTER FOURTEEN

Haven House Children's Hospice: how we grew our corporate fundraising income

Natalie Chevin and Sarah Pye

This case study follows the journey Haven House Children's Hospice took from its roots as a newly formed organisation with a relatively rudimentary corporate fundraising function to the sophisticated fundraising organisation it is today. Moving from a reactive approach to fundraising to getting firmly on to the front foot wasn't always easy. This case study discusses some of the difficult strategic choices – partnership and investment decisions – Haven House made along the way.

Background

The hospice was first conceived as the brainchild of Sue Irwin, a registered nurse and health visitor who, with friends and colleagues, had a vision for a charity that could provide care to life-limited children and their families at no cost to them.

The money to set up the hospice was raised in the mid to late 1990s entirely through a volunteer-led fundraising appeal. Perhaps inevitably, however, progress was slow. The current hospice building, formerly a family home built over 100 years ago, was acquired on a long lease from the local authority in 2000. Once the hospice opened formally in 2003, its annual running costs made permanent fundraising staff a requirement. By 2008, a fundraising function was in place, but it was not until 2011 that this started to take the shape that exists today. Soon after, corporate fundraising became part of the strategic plan, with an emphasis on the involvement of local companies. By 2017, the hospice had a team of six staff specialising in high-value partnerships across major donors, trusts, companies and special events. This made it easier to work with a wider range of (often larger) companies while the separate community engagement team maintained relationships with local companies. This combination resulted in partnerships with over 30 companies at any one time.

Strategy

As for many charities, our move into corporate fundraising began initially in reaction to companies expressing an interest in supporting us. Once specialist staff were appointed, however, a new, more strategic approach developed. The key features of the strategy were as follows:

• We became proactive rather than reactive in connecting with companies. This involved more structured research into companies and targeted approaches to them. This included using connections through their staff or management, and inviting companies to send teams of volunteers to work in our gardens or our shops as part of those companies' corporate responsibility policies. By working with these volunteers, we built relationships and gave those individuals the chance to see what we do at first hand.

• We widened our target audience to include larger companies.

• We reached companies across a wider geographical area (including the City of London), recognising that many staff of those companies may live in the vicinity of the hospice.

• We broadened out into new sectors to mirror successes in the financial services sector. Historically, our successes in the City tended to be within the banking and finance sectors, whereas we wanted to extend our reach into broader areas.

• We created a full-time post to support new business activity (see 'New business' on page 189).

• We worked with local businesses as part of our overall community engagement strategy. Instead of being reactive, with short-term and one-off results, the aim was to engage companies and maintain support over the longer term, whether through the company or its employees (or ideally both).

Through being a member of CHaL (Children's Hospices across London), a consortium of London children's hospices that were selected as the partner for BlackRock (an asset management firm), we recognised the potential that existed for working with other charities when applying for Charity of the Year (COTY) partnerships. One premise of CHaL is that the larger, London-based companies, with staff and customers across the capital, will potentially be more attracted to supporting a pan-London cause than individual hospices which only cover a region within London. This was borne out with BlackRock: the company adopted CHaL for one year and raised over £800,000 predominantly through staff-led fundraising events, a record for BlackRock.

In 2015/16, we estimated that corporate fundraising accounted for approximately £625,000 compared with approximately £200,000 five years earlier in 2010/11.

Staffing structure

In our strategic review, which took place in 2014/15, we looked at the range of skills needed to work effectively with companies of differing natures and sizes. We considered whether Haven House's existing account-management skills were complementary to those needed to develop new business. We decided that the functions of new business and account management should be combined in each corporate fundraiser's role. We anticipated that this would have the benefit of making relationship-building part of everyone's remit from the start and that this would help to avoid a sales-led approach to corporate relations.

The additional appointment of a full-time member of staff to support new business was done in recognition that a blended approach would be the most effective option. The aim of the role was to provide support with research and pipeline development while leaving overall new business approaches and subsequent account management with the corporate fundraisers.

Recruitment of staff

Haven House is easily accessible via the Tube on the Central Line and in between the North Circular A406, the M25 and the M11 so has good links to road networks. The locality is suburban and not as central as that of some charities. Despite this potential attraction, in terms of recruitment, we find the perception of a children's hospice being a sad place to work and, generally, connotations around the word 'hospice' make recruitment slightly challenging. To combat this, a large part of our work within our communities and with the local media is focused on improving perceptions and correcting those misunderstandings. This involves the wide use of case studies of children and families, and also of staff and volunteers, to ensure the reality of our work gets wider attention and so that the hugely satisfying benefits of working at Haven House are more broadly understood.

Experience has shown that following a classic recruitment process is not always the most effective option for recruiting corporate fundraisers, who are in high demand in the sector and are often based in city locations. A proactive approach has therefore been taken involving being present at appropriate sector events to raise the profile of the charity. We also attend events with networking opportunities so as to engage with potential employees who may have geographical links with the charity. We additionally use an initially informal approach (whether candidates are approached directly by us or via a recruitment agency), meeting with prospective employees over coffee at the hospice so that a tour can take place at the same time. The tour is key to prospective employees understanding that a children's hospice is not a daunting or sad place, as some believe, and that there is much more to a children's hospice than simply end-of-life care.

The experience of the tour has also been shown to help staff from recruitment agencies to become better equipped to promote Haven House to their candidates. In 2017, for example, the Head of Major Gifts held an open day for these agencies which allowed their staff to gain a better understanding of Haven House and its location.

After the informal discussions, often involving the outgoing member of staff, interviews are held. The more traditional interview process is then used to specifically test the candidates' skills in corporate fundraising, account management and developing new relationships.

New business

Our corporate fundraisers follow the recognised new business approach of developing leads and making contact with potential partners in order to develop a relationship which, at some future point, will hopefully result in a mutually beneficial partnership.

As a hospice, we are fortunate that general awareness of our work leads to some unsolicited leads, but there is a growing emphasis on solicited leads in order to target specific companies that match the agreed profile in the strategic approach. Examples of how new leads have been generated include:

• Members of the local community (including Haven House volunteers) who work in central London nominated Haven House for support from their company.

• A local branch of a national company put our charity forward for broader adoption.

• A parent's employer nominated Haven House for support.

• Special events have been developed specifically to attract corporate supporters and sponsors, including a gala ball, a business breakfast and a golf day, all held in City or West End venues.

• We work in partnership with complementary charities, and in this way doors are opened through a joint/consortium approach. This includes our work via CHaL. In addition, in 2016–2017, following solicited staff nominations and a staff vote in which we competed against two other large, national charities, we won the Citi COTY partnership in collaboration with Richard House Children's Hospice, our neighbouring children's hospice in Beckton, East London.

Pitching to prospects

Our corporate fundraising team has clear criteria for the choice of companies with which we will enter into any form of pitching process. Our priority is to pitch for partnerships where we have a strong fit with the company, rather than taking the lottery approach of pitching for as many partnerships as possible just in case we win. Where a company specifically requests a pitch, we will always do so as we feel this is an indication of at least a reasonable match. We are confident that we can win staff votes, which is evidenced by a specific occasion when we won the staff vote over two well-respected national charities.

Our success at winning partnerships, we believe, is linked to our commitment to listening to the needs of the company and reflecting those back in the pitch. In particular, we ensure the values and culture of the company have been recognised and we use in-depth research to discover what we call 'what the company likes to shout about'. In addition, being able to offer a range of volunteering opportunities for staff has been an important factor in our ability to demonstrate added value to companies.

Range of corporate fundraising mechanisms

We have expanded the range of fundraising mechanisms involved in our partnerships. COTY-type partnerships have been managed effectively at both local and national levels, including successful partnerships with the Financial Ombudsman Service and the Bank of England. Flagship events – such as a ball, a golf day, business breakfasts and our annual corporate quiz night – are key income-generating tools in addition to being used to develop new business.

Despite the wide range of our national partnerships, we have chosen not to enter into commercial participator partnerships (where, for example, a donation is made based on sales of a product) as we have found that, for us as a local charity, the net return such partnerships offer is too low. However, in the last few years we have had a focus on securing sponsorship for our events to ensure the hospice gains the maximum amount from funds raised during the event. The team recognises that, as sponsorship requires the meeting of a company's specific marketing objectives, there needs to be a culture of innovation with, where necessary, the development of events or activities to meet those objectives. For example, while we were in partnership with Mizuho, it was noted that the company was one of the founding signatories of the Women in Finance charter.[1] With this in mind, we identified the opportunity to create an event designed to attract a female audience and invited Mizuho to become a sponsor of our new Women in Business lunch.

Payroll giving at Haven House is managed as part of the corporate fundraising portfolio and we have recruited some donors through this method through ongoing partnerships with their employers. However, we do not feel we have the resources to invest in this form of giving to a significant level. As an alternative, we have found the Pennies from Heaven concept works effectively.[2] This scheme enables employees to round their net monthly salary down to the nearest pound and the amount (between 1p and 99p) is donated to a charity. The Financial Ombudsman Service has been our longest-standing supporter using Pennies from Heaven and in 2017 the organisation was awarded a Silver Pennies from Heaven Award.

Like many hospices, Haven House is approached regularly by companies wishing to offer volunteers, and we are in the fortunate position of having genuine opportunities to offer. The grounds of the hospice, for example, are maintained predominantly through volunteer support. Our annual summer fair benefits from such support, with over 100 volunteers on the day carrying out a range of roles including running stalls, managing car-parking and general support. Our retail operation encourages teams of corporate volunteers to take part in challenge days where teams from the same company volunteer in a Haven House shop on consecutive days or weeks to see which team boosts the shop's takings by the most over the set period of time.

Although we recognise the interest some companies have in offering pro bono expertise (such as business consultancy), we have found it challenging to match the skills offered with those genuinely required by the charity.

Best practice

Haven House is committed to embedding best practice in our fundraising operations, including corporate fundraising. All fundraising job descriptions include a responsibility to keep abreast of the Fundraising Regulator's Code of Fundraising Practice. Some managers have more specific responsibilities regarding codes in their job descriptions. The team has mandatory training on data protection, and twice-yearly organisational away days are used to bring together all staff from across the charity. This ensures all staff are fully aware of others' roles and contributions, and it provides an opportunity to address identified training needs with respect to best practice. Fundraising department team meetings are held every five to six weeks and fundraising regulation is a standing agenda item.

Account management

As part of our commitment to each corporate partner, we nominate a named account manager from the corporate team who is the lead contact for the duration of the partnership. This role ranges from the strategic (for example, ensuring the objectives of each partnership are clear and that there is an agreed delivery plan) to hands on, according to the needs of each client. During the BlackRock and CHaL partnership, our CHaL account manager (who was a Haven House member of staff seconded to CHaL for that period) was based at the BlackRock offices for up to three days per week. It is more usual, however, for accounts to be managed through scheduled meetings, conference calls and ad hoc contact, with intense contact needed when, for example, a major event is being organised.

Due diligence and ethical policy

Our Haven House team researches each new company before any initial application is made to ensure there is a natural fit between the company and the charity. Similarly, many of the corporate application forms we complete request information regarding the charity's governance processes, indicating that the due diligence process is mutual.

Summary of critical factors for growth

We have identified a range of factors which have influenced our growth in corporate partnerships:

• **Volunteering.** Our ability to offer a range of volunteering opportunities in our shops, grounds and events facilitates both individual and group involvement.

• **Tours.** Seeing is believing: hospice tours engage staff and show first hand how donations are used. Meeting nurses, children, families and key staff is a powerful and influential experience.

• **Impact.** Around 75% of the charity's income is generated through fundraising and so the impact of corporate support is clear. We evidence this through the provision of project reports with a very clear focus on impact and outcomes.

• **Focused account management.** Our corporate team recognises the need to support the aspirations of the staff in our partner companies. In this, the regular involvement and engagement of Haven House staff from outside fundraising, particularly care staff, is critical. Care staff, where possible, will always lead hospice tours and will even be part of pitch teams where appropriate – as indeed will family members of children supported by the hospice who can speak from personal experience, thus widening involvement beyond just the corporate's project lead and our fundraising account manager.

Notes

1   'HM Treasury's Women in Finance Charter' [web page], Mizuho Bank, 2013, www.mizuhobank.com/uk/careers/wif/index.html, accessed 20 August 2017.
2   For details about this scheme see www.penniesfromheaven.co.uk.

CHAPTER FIFTEEN

Ricoh UK Ltd: how and why we partner with charities

James Deacon

What determines why or how corporate–charity partnerships develop? In this chapter, we share our insights at Ricoh UK: our values and ethos and how our corporate culture governs Ricoh UK's community engagement policy and choices when forming charity partnerships.

Background

Originally established in Japan in 1936 by Kiyoshi Ichimura, the Ricoh Group is a global technology company specialising in office-imaging equipment, production print solutions, document management systems and IT services. The majority of our revenue comes from products, solutions and services that improve the interaction between people and information. The Ricoh Group also produces digital cameras and specialised industrial products. We are known for the quality of our technology and for the standard of our customer service and sustainability initiatives.

Ricoh's UK sales and service organisation, Ricoh UK Ltd, was established in 1979 and employs 2,350 people, with annual sales of £490 million (financial year ending 31 March 2017). The company has expanded considerably since 2000 through organic growth plus strategic acquisitions and mergers with Lanier (2005), NRG UK (2007), Infotec (2010), IKON Office Solutions (2010) and Ridgian (2017).

Values and corporate responsibility

The Ricoh Group was founded on Ichimura's philosophy of 'the spirit of three loves: love your neighbour, love your country, love your work'. This outlook still remains in place today, broadened into a set of five core values, The Ricoh Way:

- customer centricity;
- ethics and integrity;
- innovation;
- teamwork;
- winning spirit.

These values underpin our company culture, driving a continuous corporate commitment to responsible business, sustainability and corporate social responsibility. We differentiate corporate responsibility (ethical business conduct in general) from corporate social responsibility (societal engagement, or community investment). We have a formalised charter regarding the delivery of corporate social responsibility, with three core themes:

- environmental conservation;

- raising the next generation;

- community development.

To Ricoh, globally, corporate responsibility is cultural. It is about how we work and is integral to our ethos. It translates simply and informally as 'doing the right thing' in all aspects of business operation, including the composition and ethical sourcing of raw materials, the class-leading energy efficiency of the company's factories and products, transparent pricing and contracts, responsible employment practices, minimisation of environmental impact and active investment in societal support.

Developing an approach to community investment

Ricoh UK's initial involvement in community investment was as one of the first companies (in 1984) to become a member of Business in the Community (BITC), which is part of HRH the Prince of Wales's Responsible Business Network. In 1996, through our membership of BITC, HRH the Prince of Wales invited Ricoh UK's then managing director to be one of the trustees to establish In Kind Direct – a brokerage service for surplus goods and services donated by businesses which are offered to registered charities at heavily discounted prices. Ricoh UK donates surplus used, good-condition, multi-function devices (such as printers, copiers, scanners and faxes) to charities via In Kind Direct.

During the 1990s and up to 2007, our corporate social responsibility contribution was largely through non-formalised corporate philanthropy, with ongoing donations of used stock via In Kind Direct and occasional corporate donations of cash to a limited range of charities nominated by board members. Donations were monitored and recorded, with data submitted annually to BITC in order to achieve annual inclusion in its Percent Standard,[1] which recognised those organisations that annually donated more than 1% of their pre-tax profits to good causes.

In 2007, Ricoh UK implemented a corporate social responsibility policy, formalising a structured approach to corporate donations (cash and goods/services in kind) as well as towards supporting and enabling employees to volunteer during working hours. All Ricoh UK employees have two days of 'special leave' – i.e. time off for volunteering activities, above and beyond their contractual annual leave entitlement. This leave time can be taken in increments appropriate to the activity being undertaken, whether that is hours, a quarter-day, a half-day and so on.

Ricoh UK supports two core charities: BBC Children in Need and The Prince's Trust. These charities were selected for three core reasons:

• their alignment with two of Ricoh's global corporate social responsibility themes: 'raising the next generation' and 'community development';

• the ability of these charities to directly engage employees in a wide variety of activities;

• the willingness of these charities to provide Ricoh UK with detailed information about the impact of the company's support.

BBC Children in Need

BBC Children in Need has been supported by Ricoh UK since 2005, initially through informal employee-led fundraising in the immediate lead-up to – and during – the annual appeal day. Employees would self-organise fundraising through raffles, book sales, cake sales, dress-down days and general 'money into the bucket' donations.

Since then, we have expanded our scale of contribution to BBC Children in Need. Since 2010, Ricoh UK staff have volunteered at our UK national call centre to help answer donation calls during the annual BBC Children in Need Appeal show telethon in November. Staff taking donations at the call centre help to process many tens of thousands of pounds every year for the charity.

As well as transacting public donations for BBC Children in Need, Ricoh UK contributes its own funds to BBC Children in Need. These funds are raised through various employee-led and company-supported events, with our employees typically raising in excess of £10,000 on an annual basis and, in 2016, raising closer to £25,000. The majority of the funds raised by Ricoh UK in 2016 were from a large team abseil challenge down the 32-storey Broadgate Tower in London, where we have a large office and employee base.

Other significant fundraising events for the charity have included an annual coast-to-coast cycle ride since 2013, with anywhere between 15 and 30 participants including the chief executive officer. Each event raises between £5,000 and £10,000, with the company funding the logistics and accommodation and riders funding their own subsistence.

The Prince's Trust

Expanding upon many years' involvement with HRH the Prince of Wales's Responsible Business Network, in 2013 Ricoh UK embarked on a charitable partnership with The Prince's Trust. The Prince's Trust helps young people aged 11 to 30 who are unemployed or struggling at school to transform their lives. Many of the young people the charity helps are in, or leaving, care, facing issues such as homelessness or mental health problems, or have been in trouble with the law. Through interaction with the various programmes provided by The Prince's Trust and its patrons, more than three in four young people achieve a positive outcome, moving into jobs, education and training.

We selected The Prince's Trust for partnership based on several key aspects:

- its alignment with Ricoh's global corporate social responsibility themes of 'raising the next generation' and 'community development';

- the charity's proven high success rate (more than 75%) in helping young people to achieve successful outcomes;

- its alignment with other HRH the Prince of Wales's Responsible Business Network programmes (BITC, In Kind Direct) that Ricoh UK was already engaged with;

- opportunities offered by the charity for employees to engage in skill-based volunteering, directly interacting with the beneficiaries, such as mentoring young people, facilitating employability skills workshops and hosting work placements for young people;

- the charity's wide range of well-structured, time-proven types of fundraising and skill-based volunteering that allow partners to support the cause effectively;

- opportunities offered by the charity for Ricoh UK to have board-level involvement in leadership teams specific to the industry sector, helping to shape the strategic direction of The Prince's Trust as well as to share sector best practices.

Employee volunteering

A key factor in the success of The Prince's Trust partnership for Ricoh UK – in terms of employee uptake of volunteering to support The Prince's Trust and the total impact – was our incorporation of various types of volunteering and mentoring into our four-tier Leadership Development Framework. This framework uses volunteering to help Ricoh UK's leaders at all levels (supervisors, managers and directors) to learn, develop and/or reinforce key leadership skills.

Our Leadership Development Framework has four levels:

1. **explore:** entry-level tier for future supervisors and team leaders who are not yet managing a team;

2. **enable:** first-line managers and new-starter managers;

3. **inspire:** middle management;

4. **aspire:** senior managers and future board members.

Each cohort is around 12 delegates per course, and each level consists of 6 modules across a 6- to 12-month period. One module for each level is an activity or project associated with The Prince's Trust:

• **Explore.** This involves a short-to-medium-term fundraising project, either Zero to Hero (one to two months in planning with one day of actual fundraising, aiming to raise at least £3,000) or Million Makers (three to six months in planning with either several fundraising events or one large event, aiming to raise at least £30,000). The cohort must compile a business plan, submit this to a *Dragons' Den*-style panel composed of members of the Aspire cohort to which they apply for seed-funding for their project, and then work as a team to project manage their planned event through to completion. Explore delegates learn essential business skills such as decision-making, virtual meetings, budget management, communications and marketing, motivating others, managing conflict, project-planning and time management. One of Ricoh UK's Explore teams that led a Million Makers project raised a net total of £47,000 for The Prince's Trust by organising and promoting a black-tie gala dinner evening.

• **Enable and Inspire.** Delegates from these cohorts plan and deliver a one-day Employability Skills workshop for young people on The Prince's Trust Team programme. Typically three or four Enable/Inspire delegates deliver the workshop to 15 to 20 young people, covering aspects such as CV writing, mock interviews, and how to dress and present oneself for an interview. Ricoh UK delegates give very strong positive ratings to the personal impact that their involvement in such programmes has had upon both themselves and their immediate teams, with many stating that they feel proud to have been able to help disadvantaged young people and to have seen the change and impact that their interaction has had upon the hopes and future chances of young people.

• **Aspire.** These delegates are from our senior leadership team. They act as *Dragons' Den*-style advisers to help shape the Explore cohorts' initial business plans for fundraising projects, and they also act as mentors to support the Explore delegates throughout their Zero to Hero or Million

Makers fundraising project. This ensures that the fundraising projects operate effectively, avoiding 'novice' mistakes or bad decisions, and helps to accelerate the cohort's leadership development and maximises the amount of money raised.

FIGURE 15.1 THE PRINCE'S TRUST AND RICOH UK'S LEADERSHIP FRAMEWORK

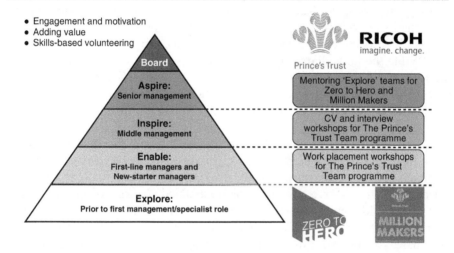

Apart from the involvement of employees in Ricoh UK's Leadership Development Framework, a significant number of other employees also support The Prince's Trust through facilitating around 15 work placements per year for young people on the charity's employability programme. During the 2016 financial year, we directly employed four young people who had first come into contact with the company via work placements with The Prince's Trust.

Other charities and good causes

Ricoh UK gives employees assistance in self-organising support for a large variety of local and national charities. These are of employees' own choosing, though we ensure the choice aligns with Ricoh's three global core corporate social responsibility themes. Examples of employee volunteering include local litter-picking, coppicing (a form of woodland management), tree-planting, building birdnest boxes, changing schools' infrastructure (such as playground makeovers and classroom redecoration), and recataloguing and cleaning a local museum's artefacts.

Additionally, numerous employees have participated in BITC's Right to Read initiative, acting as reading volunteers within primary schools, typically for one hour per week, helping Year 1 (age 5 to 6) pupils with reading and the phonics system.

A short but potentially high-impact project involved a group of almost 50 Ricoh UK volunteers from our Northampton headquarters who, across a single working week, restored an overgrown and neglected community garden in Leicester Street, Northampton, for elderly residents, turning it into a clean, tidy, welcoming floral garden and vegetable allotment for the residents to once again enjoy. This was Ricoh UK's first multi-agency project, leading the coordination of resources and inputs from the local housing association and landlord, a nearby homeless centre, a groundworks contractor and the local garden centre.

While the immediate impact was relatively small – essentially taking a bramble patch back to bare earth and replanting and returfing it so it became a garden again – we inadvertently brought two agencies together: the Northampton Hope Centre and Northamptonshire Partnership Homes.

The Northampton Hope Centre regularly has a surplus of the food stock donations from which it feeds its homeless clientele. It was seeking a means to reallocate the surplus – ideally to those on benefits – at a greatly discounted rate – for example, a pre-assembled 'basket' of goods worth £20 being sold for £5. Northamptonshire Partnership Homes has a high proportion of tenants receiving benefits, forming a large potential customer base for the surplus food stock donations. The outcome of this combination was the development of a new 'social supermarket' concept for Northampton. The Northampton Hope Centre has now been able to develop this concept to the point that it has submitted a funding application to the Big Lottery Fund for help with the launch, promotional efforts and appeals for food donations, with the potential to help hundreds, maybe thousands, of low-income households.

Employees also fundraise for a huge variety of charities and good causes, notably for children's charities, health charities and school funding appeals.

Fair access to employment: supporting ex-offenders

Ex-offenders can have a wide range of criminal convictions, with sentences ranging from a court fine to time in prison. Over 1 million offenders were convicted in UK courts in the year ending September 2016,[2] with the UK prison population standing at more than 86,000.[3] Whatever the offence, employment is crucial to allow people to move on from their past and contribute to society. If ex-offenders are employed for at least one day in the first 100 days after release from prison, an ex-offender is 50% less likely to reoffend.[4]

In 2014, Ricoh UK became a signatory of BITC's Ban the Box campaign, which aims to help provide fairer access to employment for ex-

offenders. Ban the Box calls for employers to review their recruitment policies and practices to offer a fair opportunity for ex-offenders to compete
for their roles. This can be achieved by removing the tick-box that asks
about prior convictions from initial job application forms and instead
asking about criminal convictions later in the recruitment process. This
should be underpinned by a clear policy on the employment of ex-offenders and training and support for staff to enable them to make appropriate
case-by-case assessments of candidates' suitability.

Beyond this, we have also facilitated work placements for prisoners
under Release on Temporary Licence, and we have facilitated employability workshops led by volunteer employees (covering, for example, CV
writing, interview skills, how to present oneself at interview, and how and
when to disclose unspent criminal convictions) to groups of serving
inmates within prisons. In March 2017, we opened the Ricoh Digital
Training Academy within HMP Onley, which provides an in-prison print
room and training academy facility in which prisoners gain qualifications
in maths, English and printer maintenance and operation. This gives them
opportunities to seek employment as print-room operators or field service
technicians upon release.

External impact of Ricoh UK's Community Investment programme

During the 2016 financial year, Ricoh UK contributed a total community
investment of £420,226, which comprised:

- £30,299 in gifts in kind (products and services via In Kind Direct);

- £27,504 in gifts in kind (Managed Print Service donated to The Prince's
Trust);

- £31,242 in corporate donations;

- £102,514 in employee donations via payroll giving;

- £88,990 in donations from employee fundraising events;

- £63,879 in donations from the UK public transacted by Ricoh UK's call
centre for BBC Children in Need;

- £4,413 as the cost of hosting events for volunteering and fundraising;

- £71,385 as the cost of employee volunteer leave used during working
hours.

A total of 3,824 hours towards volunteering and fundraising were
contributed by 471 unique Ricoh UK employee volunteers during working
hours.

Through the goods and services donated via In Kind Direct, in conjunction with employees' donations of time, skill and fundraising, as well as corporate donations directly from Ricoh UK, in the 2016 financial year, we supported 76 beneficiary organisations across the UK.

In the same financial year, a total of 53 young people on The Prince's Trust Team programme were directly supported through interaction with Ricoh UK's volunteers, and four of these young people have subsequently been employed full time by Ricoh UK. The trust seeks to maintain periodic contact with the young people who have completed the 12-week Prince's Trust Team employability programme to better understand their long-term outcomes. Contact is usually by SMS-based text survey. In the case of the cohorts' completers working with the Princes' Trust Team based in Northampton, at six months after completing the programme, 53% of respondents were in employment and a further 28% were re-engaged in further education, higher education or training. This represents an 81% success rate, something that we have been especially proud to be a part of with The Prince's Trust.

At Ricoh UK we have also steadily raised our brand profile and reputation as a responsible business, particularly since mid-2015 with the appointment of a new and dedicated community investment manager. Since then, there has been a step-change in the scale and frequency of employee volunteering and fundraising, in conjunction with increased internal and external communication about such activities. This scale of delivery has sustained our year-on-year progression within BITC's annual Corporate Responsibility Index, in which we achieved a 99% score and a five-star rating in March 2017 – one of only three participant organisations to achieve this score and rating within the 2016 financial year.

In association with these credentials and the additional external communications in the sector about responsible business, we are increasingly frequently contacted by other leading responsible businesses wanting to benchmark and exchange best practices, and inviting us to sector round tables and networking events. All of these provide commercial opportunities and increase our social impact.

Internal impact of Ricoh UK's Community Investment programme

One of our key drivers for implementing Ricoh UK's Community Investment programme was the anticipated positive impact upon employees, both in terms of employees' perception of the company as a responsible business and by increasing employee engagement through employees' personal participation in some of the various volunteering and fundraising initiatives.

Since the inception of our Community Investment programme in 2007, one of the key statements included within our annual employee-engagement survey has been 'Ricoh takes corporate social responsibility seriously'. This statement typically scores in excess of an 85% agreement rating by employees and is usually the highest – or occasionally one of the top two highest – positively rated statements across the survey.

Through our employee-engagement survey, we have been able to conclusively demonstrate that volunteering is a key driver of employee engagement. We have done this by including the following question within the survey: 'During the past 12 months have you taken part in any volunteering or fundraising organised by Ricoh?' The yes/no response to this question enables us to differentiate the rates of engagement between employees who have or haven't volunteered or fundraised. The levels of engagement are consistently higher among employees who have volunteered or fundraised.

FIGURE 15.2 RICOH UK: EMPLOYEE ENGAGEMENT AND VOLUNTEERING

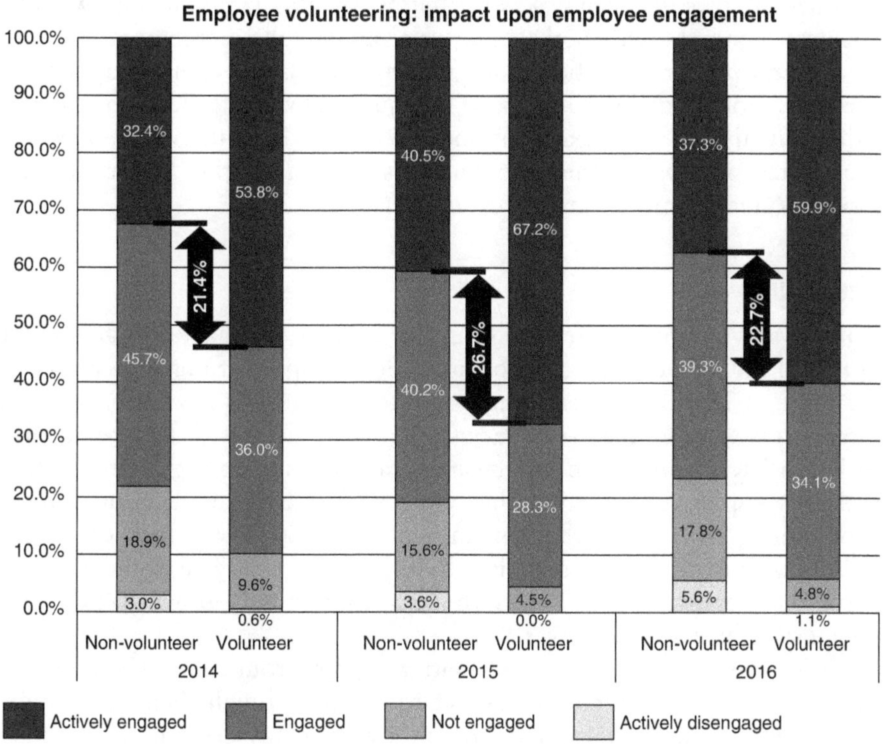

Employee volunteering: impact upon employee engagement

Employee engagement is an important indicator to the Ricoh Group because, from external benchmarking, it has been shown that 'actively engaged' employees are at least one and a half times (and as much as three times) more productive than those who are merely 'satisfied'. Also, actively engaged employees tend to be the most loyal, with lower rates of absence and of staff turnover, both of which further improve the financial performance of the company. Finally, actively engaged employees usually have very high levels of company advocacy, another important benefit to the Ricoh Group when recruiting the best talent – often through employee referrals and through strong employer brand endorsement by employees among their friends and families.

Anecdotal evidence from newly hired employees is that a key factor in them applying for a role within Ricoh UK is the desire to work for a responsible business, and their decision to apply for a role is often confirmed after researching the company's online profile specifically relating to corporate social responsibility. A key benefit of this for our company is that new hires are often self-selected to be aligned with the Ricoh Group's own core values to 'do the right thing'. This further reinforces the company's working culture and drives continued increase of uptake in employee volunteering and fundraising activities.

Our proven responsible business abilities and programmes have key commercial benefits, being a contributing success factor in our winning business contracts with both commercial and public sector organisations. Buyers and procurement bodies are placing increased weighting upon their suppliers' (or tenderers') ability to not just deliver excellent commercial value but also provide excellent social value at the same time. This has accelerated notably within the public sector since the Public Services (Social Value) Act came into force in January 2013.

The future

With a view to immediate and future next steps, we have recognised the potential for further expansion of the scale of impact of our own responsible business agenda by cascading it out to Ricoh UK's key suppliers. Our intention is to encourage voluntary (rather than mandated) uptake of some of Ricoh UK's own responsible business initiatives and programmes within these key suppliers. To deploy this, we have formed a supplier-engagement programme, with a launch event in September 2017 to which the senior leaders of our top 45–50 suppliers have been invited. The event will give them the opportunity to spend the day finding out about Ricoh UK's responsible business initiatives.

The day will include subject-matter experts from Ricoh UK outlining the benefits that suppliers can expect to accrue through their own implementation of similar initiatives. Ricoh UK is ready to help with initial implementation of these initiatives by its suppliers if support is requested. Subsequent supplier-engagement events will operate in a round-table format, with a specific responsible business theme put forward for discussion, benchmarking and the sharing of best practice among the suppliers and Ricoh UK practitioners.

We have already successfully explained corporate responsibility internally to our employees as 'doing the right thing', and our supplier-engagement programme intends to use this same phrase as its ongoing tagline. The phrase will be associated with all supplier-engagement communications and associated branding, as the simplest way to articulate responsible business to the Ricoh UK supplier base. Subsequently, this will be reinforced to select groups of key Ricoh UK suppliers through their attendance at immersive 'seeing is believing' events, where they will be able to learn and experience first hand the power and positive impact of various Ricoh UK responsible business initiatives, such as employee volunteering, recruitment of ex-offenders and being a living wage employer.

Tips for charities approaching companies

In our experience of choosing charities to partner with, we would recommend, from the other side of the fence, that your charity considers the following questions when seeking to create a successful partnership with a corporate organisation:

• What values does the company have? Does it have any core corporate responsibility themes or existing charitable partnerships listed on its website? If so, how do your charity's values and aims align with these values, themes and existing partnerships?

• How can you demonstrate tangibly to the company your success rates and which outcomes you've successfully achieved towards your mission?

• What types of opportunity, including well-structured, time-proven types of fundraising and skill-based volunteering, can you offer the company that will increase their levels of engagement with, and loyalty to, their workplace (as well as engagement with your charity)? For example, activities that will help employees to develop leadership skills or improve personally.

• Can you see any ways in which your charity's projects could be incorporated into the corporate's existing training frameworks to help develop employees or improve other aspects of employee engagement, such as lowering staff turnover and rates of employee absence?

• In what other creative ways can you communicate how working with your charity could help in other aspects of the company's success? For example, an improvement to the corporate's overall reputation which can give it an edge over other less responsible companies, thereby bringing commercial benefits.

• How will you show your charity's ability and willingness to provide detailed information on the impact of the company's support?

The answers to these questions will help reveal whether your charity is a good match for the company in question, and vice versa. They will also help you determine if your charity can offer a high enough level of benefits to the corporate that would reflect the high level of value that you will undoubtedly want for your own organisation.

Notes

1   The Percent Standard has since been replaced by the CommunityMark.
2   *Criminal Justice Statistics quarterly, England and Wales, October 2015 to September 2016 (provisional)* [PDF], Ministry of Justice, 2017, p. 1, www.gov.uk/government/uploads/system/uploads/attachment_data/file/592058/criminal-justice-statistics-quarterly-update-september-2016.pdf, accessed 14 September 2017.
3   'Population and Capacity Briefing for Friday 8th September 2017' [Excel spreadsheet], Ministry of Justice, National Offender Management Service, HM Prison Service, and Her Majesty's Prison and Probation Service, 2017, www.gov.uk/government/statistics/prison-population-figures-2017, accessed 8 September 2017.
4   *Analysis on the Impact of Employment on Re-offending* [PDF], Ministry of Justice, 2013, p. 26, www.gov.uk/government/uploads/system/uploads/attachment_data/file/162375/impact-employment-reoffending.pdf, accessed 8 September 2017.

Index